Canadian History Through the Press Series

VOL. XII.—No. 12.   MONTREAL, SATURDAY, SEPTEMBER 18, 1875.   { SINGLE COPIES, TEN CENTS. / $4 PER YEAR IN ADVANCE.

DRAMATIS PERSONÆ.

We publish on this page the portraits of the three personages who are most directly involved in the unfortunate drama which has just been creating so great a stir throughout the country.

JOSEPH GUIBORD was a printer of long standing in Montreal. He was a man of irreproachable morals, of the steadiest habits, of rigid honesty, and altogether a model workman. His only fault in ecclesiastical eyes was that he belonged to the *Institut Canadien*. This institution was in his day, and is still, under the ban of the Church, and those who die in its membership are liable to be refused sepulture in consecrated earth. Guibord was aware of this penalty, and it affected his spirit at times, but having been suddenly cut off by apoplexy, he had no opportunity, even if so disposed, to make the necessary retraction. What happened is well known. His remains were refused burial from the date of his demise, in 1869, until within a few days ago, and even then, the mob drove them away from the gates of the Roman Catholic Cemetery.

Reverend Mr. ROUSSELOT is Curé or Rector of the Church of Notre-Dame, Montreal, and in that capacity is the official custodian of the Cote des Neiges Cemetery. He represented the Bishop throughout all the phases of this lamentable controversy. He may be regarded as the defendant in the trial of the *Institut Canadien* against the *Fabrique* of Notre-Dame. Mr. Rousselot, is a Frenchman by birth, but has long been a resident of Montreal, where he is deservedly esteemed for his many good qualities and the talents which have raised him to his present responsible position, one of the highest in the gift of his superiors.

Mr. JOSEPH DOUTRE, Q. C., has been a notable champion of advanced Liberalism in Lower Canada for many years. He is a lawyer of standing and good practice in this city. He espoused the cause of Guibord from the beginning, pleaded it in the three trials which have taken place, and won it before Privy Council. It is he who is charged with the burial of the remains, and though foiled in the first attempt, is determined to persevere until he succeeds.

Besides these three interesting portraits, we present in this issue two other views of the Guibord affair—the removal of the body from the vault in Mount Royal Cemetery, and the arrival of the hearse at the Cote des Neiges Cemetery, where the mob closed the gates and refused admission. These were the two prominent incidents which occurred on Thursday, the 2nd inst., and since then nothing of importance has happened. The mob was very violent in both language and gesture, and had there been any resistance to its will, there is no doubt that blood would have been shed. The police arrived upon the scene of tumult when it was too late, a circumstance which is usual with our civic authorities. It is expected that when the second attempt at interment is made, all proper preparations will be secured. In whatever way this business is viewed, it can only be pronounced as most deplorable, exciting passions and awakening prejudices which the best men of the country have been trying for so many years to allay.

JOSEPH GUIBORD.

From a Photograph by Grenier

REV. MR. ROUSSELOT.   JOS. DOUTRE, Q. C.

From a Photograph by Desmarais.   From a Photograph by Grenier.

THE GUIBORD UNPLEASANTNESS.

The Guibord Affair

The Guibord Affair

Lovell C. Clark

Canadian History Through the Press Series

General Editors:
David P. Gagan, Anthony W. Rasporich

Holt, Rinehart and Winston of Canada, Limited
Toronto : Montreal

Editor's Preface

Newspapers are widely accepted by historians as useful vehicles of contemporary opinion. In a nation such as Canada, which is historically dependent upon Great Britain and the United States for the books and periodicals which are the principal disseminators of informed opinion, the local daily or weekly newspaper has been almost the sole native medium of information and attitudes. Moreover, the proliferation of Canadian newspapers since the early decades of the nineteenth century has created for students of Canadian history a vast reservoir of opinion reflecting the political, social, cultural, linguistic, religious, and sectional diversity of our country. The *Canadian History Through the Press* series is an attempt to tap this reservoir by reproducing a cross section of journalistic opinion on major issues, events, and problems of the Canadian past.

Using the press as a vehicle for the study of history has already been done with some success in the French series, *Kiosk*, which examines public issues and popular culture in volumes ranging from the Dreyfus affair to French cinema. *Canadian History Through the Press* is not quite so ambitious a venture, but it does aim to introduce the student to events which were compelling subjects of discussion for Canadians through the medium in which public discussion most frequently took place. At its best, the Canadian press is a rich source of historical controversy, providing the historian with a sense of the excitement and contentiousness of contemporary issues. Newspaper editors like William Lyon Mackenzie, George Brown, Henri Bourassa, and George McCullagh were themselves often at the centre of the political stage or were, like J. W. Dafoe of the Winnipeg *Free Press*, Joseph Atkinson of the Toronto *Star*, and Gérard Pelletier of *La Presse*, pundits whose voices were carefully heeded by national and local politicians. This is merely one example of the power of the press; but whatever subject – Confederation, the Quiet Revolution, social reform, foreign policy, or pollution – the press has operated (in Marshall McLuhan's words) as a "corporate or collective image [that] demands deep participation."

As editors of *Canadian History Through the Press* we are committed to the idea that students should be introduced to the study of Canadian history through contemporary documents from the very outset. The newspaper is a familiar, and therefore comfortable medium for the novice historian. We have chosen to use it exclusively, fully aware of the limitations of the press as an historical source. When a prominent Canadian politician observed recently that his colleagues spent much of their time "quoting yesterday's newspaper," he was acknowledging the power of the press not merely to reflect, but also to dictate opinion. Also Will Rogers' caricature of the man who "only knew what he read in the paper" is an equally cogent reminder that newspapers should not be used exclusively as a weathercock of opinion. The student, then, must and inevitably will come to grips with both the limitations and the advantages of newspapers as sources of history. In this respect, our series is also aimed at introducing the student to one of the historian's most crucial problems, that of discriminating between conflicting accounts and interpretations of historical events.

The volumes currently planned for the *Canadian History Through the Press* series embrace topics ranging from the War of 1812 to the Quiet Revolution of the nineteen-sixties, from economic history to religious issues. While it is not immediately possible, we hope that in time the series will embrace an even wider spectrum of subjects permitting us to sample not merely the thrust, but also the quality, of Canadian life.

David P. Gagan,
Anthony W. Rasporich,
January, 1971.

Lovell C. Clark is Professor of History at the University of Manitoba.

David P. Gagan, general editor of the *Canadian History Through the Press Series*, is Assistant Professor of History at McMaster University, Hamilton, Ontario.

Anthony W. Rasporich, general editor of the *Canadian History Through the Press Series*, is Associate Professor of History at the University of Calgary, Alberta.

Contents

Preface   *xv*

Introduction   *1*

Guide to Documents   *23*

Guide to Journals   *121*

Selected Bibliography   *124*

Author's Preface

The newspaper extracts presented here convey only a small part of the controversy evoked by the Guibord Affair. The episode attracted widespread attention in the press not only of Canada, but also of the United States and Britain. The selection is drawn mainly from the leading French and English journals of Montreal, where the Affair occurred. The only outside material comes from two Toronto newspapers, one Liberal and one Conservative. Except for a few reprints, the press elsewhere is not represented. Thus the sample is rather limited, partly for reasons of availability and convenience of presentation. However, a selection drawn from a wider geographical area, would not have resulted in substantially different or more varied arguments on either side of this contentious question. The reader may rest assured that the principal points of view are contained herein, and that no source has been intentionally omitted which might throw additional light upon the topic.

The excerpts begin in September, 1869, on the eve of Joseph Guibord's death. They do not deal with the preceding fifteen or twenty years of friction between the Institut Canadien and Bishop Bourget, although many of the extracts purport to give the history of that period. The *Introduction* tries to compensate by focussing upon these earlier years in considerable detail. The history of the Institut Canadien, however, and especially its relations with the clergy, is a subject which it is hoped the student will investigate more fully for himself.

The excerpts are concerned mainly with the Guibord Affair and make only incidental reference to other topics. Only the last item, Wilfrid Laurier's address of 1877, stands somewhat isolated from the others, but a little reflection quickly places it in context as a reply to the joint Pastoral Letter of the Bishops of 1875, and as a defense of (British) liberalism against the attacks of ultramontanes.

As for the Guibord Affair itself, the student may profitably undertake to assess the case for each of the contending sides, and then go on to consider the larger issues evoked by the Affair – the relations of Church and State, and the legitimate boundary (if any) between religion and politics. He may also enquire into related questions to which this study has been able to make only brief allusion, *viz.*, the role of the ultramontane clergy in French Canadian society of the mid-nineteenth century, and the consequences for that society of the ultramontane emphasis upon unity of faith and language, and uniformity of morals, customs, and institutions.

The *Introduction* attempts to view the subject of ultramontanism in the larger context of the Roman Catholic world during the troubled reign of Pope Pius IX. It suggests that it was because Bishop Bourget's attention was fixed upon the turbulent European scene, and upon the plight of his beloved Pontiff, that he sought to insulate his people from what he considered to be the subversive and dangerous ideas responsible for such conditions. It was for the same reason that he saw the Institut Canadien as a threat to French Canadian society. Upon this view the ultramontanism in Quebec during the nineteenth century was almost a personal as well as a passing phenomenon.

The student's own investigations may lead him to consider that this view unduly minimizes the importance and duration of ultramontanist influence, and he will find many historians who will agree with him. Indeed, he may come to the quite different conclusion that ultramontanism has had a long and pervasive influence upon French Canadian society. This is the kind of informed debate, however, which helps to make the study of history so worthwhile. If this little volume provokes such debate it will have more than served its purpose.

I cannot conclude these remarks without acknowledging my indebtedness to the staff of the Public Archives of Canada, Ottawa, for their unfailing help and courtesy, and to Nancy Susan Robertson, whose unpublished Master's thesis on the Institut Canadien was invaluable.

Lovell Clark,
University of Manitoba.

The Guibord Affair

Introduction

The Guibord Affair was a celebrated court case over the location of a grave. When Joseph Guibord died under ban of the sacraments of the Church, the authorities of Côte des Neiges Cemetery in Montreal refused to bury his remains in consecrated ground. His widow thereupon took legal action to compel them to do so. The prolonged court proceedings, lasting from 1869 to 1874, provoked zealous controversy among partisans of both sides, and ended with a verdict in favour of the widow's plea. Popular passions had been aroused to such an extent that a first attempt to carry out the court decision was defeated by a riotous mob, which regarded the proposed interment as profanation of a Roman Catholic cemetery. Eventually, six years after his death, the burial of Joseph Guibord was effected under police and military protection.

The parties to this unseemly dispute were nominally the widow, *née* Henrietta Brown, and the cemetery administration, known as the Fabrique de Montréal. In reality, the two antagonists were the Institut Canadien de Montréal, of which Guibord had been a member, and Monseigneur Ignace Bourget, Bishop of Montreal. The furore over Guibord's grave was the culmination of a bitter, twenty year quarrel between the Institut and the Bishop. Ostensibly the question at issue was the presence of prohibited books in the library of the Institut, and the refusal of the latter to submit to the Bishop's wishes in the matter, but fundamentally the quarrel went much deeper.

The clash between the Institut and the Bishop was the reflection of a larger struggle in the Roman Catholic world which reached a climax in the third quarter of the nineteenth century. An earlier struggle within the Church, of much longer duration, had been known as one of Gallicans *versus* ultramontanes, terms which have particular reference to French history. It was a struggle between those Roman Catholics who favoured a French national or state Church, as opposed to those who looked beyond the mountains to Rome as the locus of authority within the Church. The nineteenth century struggle, which concerned not France alone but the Roman Catholic world generally, is commonly referred to as one of liberals *versus* ultramontanes. Although the terminology is misleading, since there were Roman Catholics who were both liberal and ultramontane in their views, it is acceptable if it is understood to mean simply an antithesis between liberal and conservative elements within the Church. The issue was no longer one of the centre of authority within the Church; there was general agreement that it must be Rome. There was no unanimity, however, on what the character of this Rome-centered Church should be.

The nature of the debate may be clarified if examined within the context of the remarkably long reign of Pope Pius IX, 1846 to 1878, a period which coincided largely with the active career of both the Institut and of Bishop Bourget. These were troubled years of violent revolutionary and nationalist upheavals, and of disturbing new ideas. In this situation some ultramontane Roman Catholics sought to persuade the Church to accommodate itself to modern liberal ideas. Notable among these was Count Charles de Montalembert (1810-1870), a politician and historian, whose opposition to absolutism in all its forms is conveyed by his advocacy of "a free Church in a free state." His insistence that the Church should encourage civil and religious liberty was echoed among the French clergy by Bishop Felix Dupanloup (1802-1878) and others.

On the other hand there was an older strand of ultramontanism, stemming from Joseph de Maistre (1753-1821), which utterly rejected liberalism and espoused an authoritarian regime as the surest safeguard of the Church. An extreme exponent of this conservative wing was Louis Veuillot (1813-1883), who has been described as one of those who are always more royalist than the king, more Catholic than the bishops. He was the enemy of all conciliation and accommodation with modern ideas, and a merciless opponent of those whom he regarded as Catholic liberals. Even Pius IX is said to have rebuked him for his bitter zeal. Veuillot, who was editor of *L'Univers,* is considered to have been one of the most influential journalists of the nineteenth century.

For some time Pius IX did not side with either of these opposing camps. At the outset of his reign he even introduced some liberal innovations into the government of the then considerable Papal States. Eventually, however, the horrors of the revolutionary outbreaks in Europe from 1848 to 1850, during which he himself was forced to flee Rome, the gradual erosion of his temporal domains by the Italian nationalists, and the emergence of disquieting concepts, particularly in science and politics, all led him to condemn the ideas espoused by Montalembert and other Catholic liberals. No doubt he concluded that if the Papacy was to be an anchor of stability in a revolutionary world, that anchor must be imbedded in conservatism.

A number of encyclicals document Pius' conservative reaction, especially *Quanta Cura* (1864) with its appended Syllabus listing eighty errors of the time. Among these were: pantheism, naturalism, absolute rationalism, moderate rationalism, indifferentism, latitudinarianism, socialism, communism, secret societies, various errors concerning the relations of Church and State, and errors having reference to modern liberalism. The 80th error was the view that: "The Roman Pontiff can, and ought to, reconcile himself, and come to terms with progress, liberalism and modern civilization."[1] The Syllabus appears to reflect a genuine confusion between liberal Catholicism, which was perhaps justifiably censurable as constituting lax adherence to the faith, and Catholic liberalism, which was a perfectly legitimate political option. On the other hand it may be that Pius intended to condemn liberalism in all its forms, and this was the interpretation usually placed upon the Syllabus. Henceforth, liberals generally considered that the Pope had proclaimed himself their enemy, and Catholic liberals were very much on the defensive. In the concluding years of Pius' pontificate they were defeated.

Meanwhile, Pius was preparing for the first ecumenical council to be held in three centuries. Long before it convened in Rome on December 8, 1869, it had become apparent that papal infallibility would be the dominant issue. Although there were few prelates who did not subscribe to the doctrine itself, there were many, including Bishop Dupanloup, who were opposed to defining it because they considered that to do so would further estrange the Protestants, and would arouse the hostility of both Catholic and non-Catholic governments. Like other Catholic liberals, Montalembert also felt that the definition of papal infallibility would be inopportune, although he said he would abide by it. In a letter published shortly before his death in March, 1870, he denounced the absolutist character of contemporary ultramontanism, and re-affirmed his conviction that the Church would prove capable of adapting to the conditions of modern society without impairing the immutability of its dogma or its morality.

In spite of the misgivings of Dupanloup and Montalembert, and of many other Catholic liberals, the First Vatican Council voted, on July 18,

1870, to proclaim the Dogma of Papal Infallibility. Two months later, the troops of Victor Emmanuel II occupied Rome and put an end to the last of the Papal States. Thus the spiritual authority of the Papacy was being exalted almost at the very time its temporal domain was being obliterated. The latter event had been made possible by another disaster that autumn, equally traumatic for French Canada. On September 4, 1870, Emperor Napoleon III and the main French army had surrendered to the Prussians at Sedan. The humiliation of the motherland during the winter and spring was about to begin.

Such, in part, were the troubled years of Pius IX, and it is against this European background that the clash between the Institut Canadien and Bishop Bourget becomes understandable. Ignace Bourget's tenure of office (1840-1876) paralleled that of Pius whom he venerated, and whose conservative views he faithfully reflected. As Bishop he displayed tremendous zeal and energy. He organized retreats and religious conferences, and instituted or revived religious confraternities and devotional exercises. During his time as Bishop, perhaps a dozen religious orders were brought from France to engage in missionary, educational, and social work, not only in the large diocese of Montreal, but elsewhere in North America. These included the Oblates, the Jesuits, the Clerks of St. Viator, the Sisters of Sacré Coeur, the Sisters of the Good Shepherd, and the Fathers, Brothers, and Sisters of the Holy Cross. He established other religious communities charged with special tasks in teaching, nursing, temperance, charitable, and other work. He founded colleges, hospitals, schools, and institutions of every kind. Nor was this all. He made important changes in the organization of his diocese which were eventually copied elsewhere in Quebec, was largely instrumental in persuading the Primate to convene periodically a provincial Council of the Bishops, and, finally, enforced changes upon his clergy which brought the liturgy into conformity with that of Rome.

Bourget looked out for his flock in other ways, and here, Rome, where he journeyed eight times during his years as Bishop, was his model as always. The conservative and authoritarian brand of ultramontanism which Rome exhibited in these years was duplicated in Bourget and his followers, with one important difference. Whereas ultramontanism elsewhere was international (or supranational), in Quebec it was strongly tinged with nationalism, even racialism. The French Canadians were a tiny minority in a sea of English Protestants. The need for protective vigilance over the flock was thus not only much greater, but also manifold, embracing race and culture as well as faith. Unity of faith and language, and uniformity of morals, customs, and institutions, became all-important to Bourget and his ultramontane colleagues. In their view heterodoxy was a menace to nationality as well as to faith; an additional danger to those of rationalism and liberalism designated by Rome. One of Bourget's ardent disciples, Abbé (later Bishop) LaFlêche, gave eloquent expression to this need for unity and conformity in his *Quelques considerations sur les rapports de la société civile avec la religion et la famille* (1866).[2]

The other party to the quarrel was the Institut Canadien. This had been founded in Montreal in 1844 by young French Canadian intellectuals as a centre for mutual improvement and discussion. They built up a library of books and journals from France and elsewhere. The members read papers on a variety of topics – literary, economic, philosophic, scientific, and the like – held debates and public lectures, and exchanged ideas. The Institut thus fulfilled an important need, particularly at a time when there was no French-speaking university in Montreal, and when the English population of the city outnumbered the French. Originally the constitution had limited membership to French Canadians but this was changed in 1850, with the result that of 675 members in 1855, 84 were of another nationality.[3] The Institut survived a fire which completely destroyed its library in 1850, became incorporated in 1853, and in the course of the next few years acquired substantial premises of its own on Notre Dame Street. Similar institutes were founded in other cities and towns throughout Quebec and eventually there were reputed to be as many as sixty, but only those of Montreal, Quebec, and Ottawa existed for any length of time. In 1857 the membership of the Montreal Institut was apparently over 700, and this seems to have been the peak figure.

The founders of the Institut were mainly young liberals who had received many of their ideas from Europe, especially in the heady climate of opinion following the revolutionary upheavals of 1848. It must be remembered, however, that they also had a Canadian radical tradition to look back to in the rebellions of 1837-38. The great Tribune, Louis Joseph Papineau, was an honorary patron of the Institut, and undoubtedly had the political allegiance of many of its members. A number of Papineaus, including Amédée, the eldest son, served as president of the Institut at various times. Among other leading members were Antoine Aimé Dorion, J. B. E. Dorion, Dr. Louis-Antoine Dessaulles,

Joseph Doutre, Rodolphe Laflamme, and C. A. Geoffrion – all members of the Parti Rouge which Papineau founded after his return from exile in France. Among the journals which voiced their views were *L'Avenir*, a radical liberal paper founded in 1848, and the more moderate *Le Pays* which replaced it in 1852. The ten-man editorial board of *L'Avenir* was drawn entirely from members of the Institut. At a meeting of the Institut in 1854, congratulations were extended to fourteen members who had been elected to Parliament,[4] and it appears that eleven of these were Rouges.[5] The connection between the Institut and the radical Rouge Party was thus extremely close.

It was this identification with radicalism which was responsible, perhaps more than anything else, for the feud which developed between the Institut and Bishop Bourget. During the Canadian political struggles of 1848, many members of the Institut joined *L'Avenir* in supporting Papineau's republican Rouges against Lafontaine's Reformers, and during the tumultuous events attendant upon the Rebellion Losses Bill of 1849 they espoused annexation to the United States. This advocacy of a policy which would seem to lead inevitably to the extinction of French Canadian nationality, is explicable only if one assumes that its youthful exponents saw the American Union not as a 'melting-pot,' but as a 'states rights' confederacy of which Quebec would be a virtually sovereign member. To the Roman Catholic clergy, on the other hand, republicanism and annexationism were both anathema. The Church enjoyed a very special position in British North America. It had, for example, a legal right to collect the tithe in Quebec, something which certainly would not be accorded to it under the constitution of the neighbouring republic, where, moreover, anti-Catholicism was prevalent.

As though these differences were not enough, external as well as internal developments augmented them. The revolutions in Europe during 1848-50, and the reaction which followed their failure, provoked still more radical rhetoric in *L'Avenir* and in lectures at the Institut. The flight of Pius IX from Rome during the upheavals brought a pastoral letter from Bishop Bourget urging prayers for the Pope's safety. But *L'Avenir* urged support for the Italian revolutionaries. A gulf was steadily being dug between the two camps. In a pastoral letter of May 11, 1850, announcing the founding of *The True Witness And Catholic Chronicle* (which the hierarchy had agreed to support), Bishop Bourget made reference to "impious journals, or enemies of your faith,"* it being quite clear to the faithful that *L'Avenir* was among these.[6] Clerical antagonism only served to push the young radicals to further extremes. Attacking the Church's legal right to the tithe as even more immoral than seigneurial tenure, they now proceeded to proclaim ever more loudly the need for separation of Church and State. The demise of *L'Avenir* early in 1852, and its replacement by the more moderate *Le Pays,* did not halt this escalation of radical liberalism. Indeed, it appears to have become concentrated in the Institut.[7] The defection from the Institut in 1852 of a small group of moderates who objected to the extremism had no appreciable effect either.[8]

The developments of the 1850s intensified the intransigence on both sides. Charles Daoust, editor-in-chief of *Le Pays* and a Member of the Legislative Assembly, continued to urge the separation of Church and State, while Joseph Papin, another member of the Institut and also an M.L.A., attacked the support of denominational schools with public funds. Similar sentiments found expression in the Institut, notably from two French Canadian Protestants, Henri Lafleur and Narcisse Cyr. They had joined the Institut after returning from studies in Geneva, and Cyr in 1851 had founded *Le Semeur Canadien,* an intensely proselytizing Protestant publication which rested on the Institut's shelves along with *Les mélanges religieux* and other ultra-Catholic journals. The many séances of this period (47 during 1854, for example) featured a number of radical speakers, some from France and others from among the local radicals. Dessaulles, a nephew of Papineau, was one of the most popular. In a series of lectures during 1851 which advocated annexation, Dessaulles spoke of Pius IX and the Emperors of Russia and Austria as the only important representatives of despotism in the civilized world. Again, in 1856, in a lecture on Galileo, he depicted the Church as the enemy of progress, liberty, independence of mind, and all free expression of thought.[9] This verbal violence could hardly fail to convince Bishop Bourget that he was confronted by the same kind of anti-clerical revolutionaries who were proving to be such a sore trial to the beleaguered Ponti whom he revered.

At the provincial Council of Bishops in 1854, Bourget secured a disciplinary ruling regarding literary institutes which harboured books against faith or morals, gave lectures contrary to religion, or contained immoral or irreligious journals. The priest was to deny the sacraments to members of such institutes unless there was some hope that by remaining members they might be able to reform the situation. The offend-

7

ing institution had to be named explicitly by the Bishop before disciplinary action followed.[10] Bourget issued no condemnation and so only the threat was there. It was this no doubt which prompted some members of the Institut in the spring of 1855 to move a motion for the exclusion of *Le Semeur Canadien* and another Protestant journal, *The Witness*, from the reading room. The motion was defeated. *Le Pays* explained much later that as a liberal society based on the principle of tolerance the Institut had no choice but to defeat the motion.[11] No repercussions followed from this, perhaps because Bishop Bourget was absent in Europe from late 1854 until the summer of 1856. His prolonged stay in Europe at this time appears to have reinforced his conviction that liberalism was the enemy of religion and the cause of revolution. On his return he purported to see in the Institut Canadien a subversive organization similar to those which were fomenting uprisings in the Italian states and elsewhere. He undoubtedly exaggerated both the character and the importance of this radical element in French Canada. Nevertheless, his apprehensions found expression in three pastoral letters issued early in 1858.

The first letter of March 10 revealed Bourget's fears. It referred to the troubles of 1837 and 1838 (when he had been very close to the scene as assistant to Mgr. Lartigue, Bishop of Montreal), and what might happen if a revolution on a larger scale should occur. The turmoil in Europe was mentioned and the hope expressed that people would not bring comparable hardship upon themselves by espousing the ideas which drifted into Canada from Europe. Seven cardinal rules were prescribed for averting revolution. The Institut Canadien was not named, but three of the rules were obviously directed at it. These required the members of a literary institute to take strict care not to permit the introduction of books contrary to faith and morals. If there were such books in the institute, the members should use all their influence to have them removed, failing in this, they should then resign, protesting energetically and publicly so as to warn others.[12]

This first pastoral brought swift results. At a meeting of April 13, 1858, the moderate elements in the Institut, determined to conform to the wishes of the Bishop, presented a motion that a committee should be appointed to draw up a list of the books which in its opinion should be withdrawn from the library. A debate ensued, during which an amendment was moved by Pierre Blanchet stating that the Institut had always been (and was alone) competent to judge the morality of its library, and that it was quite capable of administering it without the intervention of outside influence.[13] The amendment added that the Institut had always been solicitous in ensuring that the library was composed of books proper to nourish the heart and develop the intelligence, and that the library had never contained books of an obscene or immoral nature. The crux of the argument was over the definition to be given to the words 'obscene' and 'immoral.' The dissenters were clearly prepared to take the view that any book which was on the Index fell into this category, while the others, in true liberal fashion, were willing to let each individual decide this for himself. Dessaulles pointed out that the Library of Parliament contained many books on the Index and yet Catholics were not subject to penalties for frequenting it. Many years later he claimed that the real issue was that the radical group was opposed to ecclesiastical control.[14] Blanchet's amendment was carried by a vote of 111 to 88. Thereupon the dissenters circulated a letter of resignation which was signed by 138 and presented on April 22. Among the signatories were: Napoléon Bourassa, Hector Fabre, Louis A. Jetté, and Louis Labrèche-Viger.[15] The secessionists shortly afterwards formed the Institut Canadien-Français, a name which indicated the return to a national basis for membership.

These events brought a second pastoral letter from Bishop Bourget on April 30.[16] After praising the courage of the dissenters, he stigmatized as an error the contention of the Institut that it was alone competent to judge the morality of its library. This was contrary to a decree of the Council of Trent (1545-63) which declared that it was for the bishop or his deputy to make such a judgment. A second error of the majority was its claim that the library of the Institut did not contain, and had never contained, obscene or immoral books. This claim was refuted by the testimony of the secessionists, whose letter the Bishop quoted in part, and even more so by the fact that a great many of the books were on the Index. The Bishop then described the two tribunals in Rome which examine books and the rules which they follow. He warned that those who read or keep forbidden books incur the sentence of excommunication, as well as rendering themselves culpable of mortal sin. He appealed to the members of the Institut to submit to the laws of the Church, and made it clear that if they persisted in their present course they would incur terrible penalties. It should be noted that in this second pastoral Bourget was assuming that the decrees of the two tribunals, the Congregation of the Holy Office and the Congregation of the Index, were valid in Quebec. In 1856, when he had urged a declaration to this effect by the provincial hierarchy, Mgr. Baillargeon, his superior, had rejected the proposal as inopportune and dangerous.[17]

Bishop Bourget's first pastoral had been relatively mild in tone, and even the second one had constituted a warning which said that there was yet time to return to the fold. The third pastoral of May 31, however, was a thunderbolt which if not instantly fatal was ultimately so. It was an unqualified condemnation of the Institut, of the political party with which its members were associated, and of their leading journal, *Le Pays*. The disciplinary penalty envisaged by the provincial Council of Bishops in 1854, namely, deprivation of the sacraments, now applied. The encyclical of Gregory XVI, *Mirari vos* (1832), was cited in order to refute the revolutionary doctrines of the sovereignty of the people and of the separation of Church and State. The editor of *Le Pays*, who was an M.L.A., was quoted (but not named) voicing such doctrines. Condemnation was passed on irreligious, heretical, and immoral journals, and upon the most dangerous of all, liberal journals. *Mirari vos* was used to demonstrate the proposition that "it is not permissible for any one to be free in his religious and political opinions."* In sum, Bourget's third pastoral was a thoroughgoing assertion of theocracy, with the Pope and the hierarchy being made the arbiters not merely on religious questions but on all others as well.[18]

The membership of the Institut slowly but inexorably declined in the years which followed. By 1861 it had fallen to 450, and by 1867 it was about 300.[19] By 1875 it was apparently 175, of which nearly one-half was English.[20] Yet for a time during the 1860s the Institut continued to flourish in all other respects in spite of Bourget's condemnation. The library and other facilities, and the activities, continued to expand. There was renewed controversy between the ultramontanes and the radical liberals over events in Europe, particularly the progress of Italian unification and the defeat of the Papal forces at Castelfidardo in September, 1860. Many Roman Catholics believed that the Pope's temporal power was an essential safeguard for his spiritual authority. *Le Pays*, on the other hand, exulted in the triumph of the liberal cause and of the principle of nationality. Prince Napoleon, cousin of the Emperor, had eloquently defended in the French Senate the policy of non-intervention which had made these achievements possible. When he came to Montreal in September, 1861, his reception by the Institut was as cordial as that by the clergy was coldly correct.[21] The Institut greeted him with a laudatory address, which the Prince later repaid with a valuable gift of books and art treasures.

As for *Le Pays,* of which Dessaulles was now the editor-in-chief, Bishop Bourget became so incensed with its position on the Italian question, and especially with its apparent pleasure over the discomfiture of the Pope, that he prepared to embark upon public polemics with it. He wrote seven letters in which, among other things, he accused *Le Pays* of erroneous principles, misrepresentation of facts, and impudent lies; of being anti-Christian, anti-Catholic, anti-social, and a calumniator of the Papal government; and of being immoral and dangerous. He ordered *Le Pays* to publish his letters. In a masterly reply on March 4, 1862, the directors (Wilfrid Dorion & Co.) declined to do so, and Bourget, evidently thinking better of it, decided to drop the matter.[22] A public clash did occur at the end of the year, however, as a result of a lecture which Dessaulles gave at the Institut,[23] which caused the Bishop to fulminate from the pulpit against the frightful monster of rationalism which had again raised its hideous head in the Institut.[24]

These successive confrontations were clearly harmful to the Institut In October, 1863, a committee was struck to enquire into ways of overcoming the difficulties which had arisen between Bishop Bourget and the Institut. The peace-making mission comprised Dr. J. E. Coderre, Joseph Doutre, Dessaulles, and Wilfrid Laurier, the latter being a young law student of twenty-two. The committee had an interview with the Bishop but was unable to reach an agreement with him because, according to Dessaulles, "even on the question of local journals, those published in Montreal for example, the demands went beyond those which are tolerated everywhere else. . . ."*[25] The interview indicated that the Bishop was in no mood for compromise, and this was confirmed by an alarmist pastoral of December 23, 1863, in which he inveighed against "those who have attacked the Faith by their impious writings and their blasphemous discourses,"* and who by their "irreligious sophistries which cause revolutions, overthrow empires and countries."*[26]

In spite of this rebuff it was decided that a further attempt should be made to reach agreement with the Bishop, and so the President of the Institut, together with one of the members of the committee, had a second interview with him, evidently in May, 1864. On this occasion they left a catalogue of the library with him so that he might indicate the works to which he objected, and which they suggested could be placed under lock and key, being made available to Catholic members of the Institut only upon authorization by the President or the committee of management. Six months passed without any response from Bishop Bourget. Finally, on the eve of the Bishop's departure for Rome, one of the committee called upon him in order to retrieve the catalogue and to discover what were the offending books, if any. "His Lordship replied that he had in fact found such books but that he had not felt obliged to indicate them because it seemed to him that could not lead to any practical result."*[27] This was the end of the Institut's attempts to reach an understanding with the Bishop of Montreal. It was clear that he would accept nothing less than complete submission to his authority, and it was equally clear that the Institut could not concede this without repudiating entirely its liberal creed. Bishop Bourget was confronted with an intransigence and inflexibility that matched his own.

In this impasse a number of the Catholic members of the Institut decided to appeal to Rome. The decision could hardly have been more ill-timed, for Rome had gone completely over to reaction. Pius IX's Syllabus of Errors, which had been issued in December, 1864, was opposed to everything for which the Institut stood. Bishop Bourget had hailed the Syllabus in a circular to his clergy on January 1, 1865, as a timely refutation of the false principles which had already infiltrated our happy and peaceful country through the bad journals and discourses of the liberals.[28] An appeal to a conservative, even reactionary, Pope by a group of avowed liberals who were protesting their condemnation by a staunch ultramontane Bishop, was doomed to failure. Nevertheless, a petition dated October 16, 1865, was signed by seventeen members of the Institut and transmitted to Rome, which officially acknowledged receipt of it under date of July 20, 1866.[29] The petitioners, who were acting in their own name and not of the Institut, complained that the Bishop had condemned them without giving them a chance to present their case; that they had been subjected to ecclesiastical censure as though they constituted a secret society, which was not the case; and although Catholic members of the Institut had invited the Bishop to indicate the prohibited books, he had declined to do so.[30] Such was the substance of the appeal, and there matters remained for almost four years.

In the intervening period the Institut gave every outward evidence that it was flourishing. It acquired a new and impressive building containing a hall with 700 stuffed seats, offices, library space, a reading-room, and additional rooms which could be rented. It continued to add to its library. In 1866 its assets appear to have exceeded $30,000.[31] In 1867 the Institut entered into an agreement with Victoria University, the Methodist institution in Cobourg, whereby the Institut gave law courses in Montreal and the University conferred the degree of LL.B. This proved very successful and in 1869 there were 43 students enrolled. In 1868 the library contained 7,474 volumes and the reading room 75 journals in both French and English.[32] Yet, in spite of all these indications of progress, nothing could disguise the fact that the Institut's meetings were not as frequent nor as well attended, and that the membership was dwindling away.

The condemnation of 1858 had explicitly required the denial of the sacraments to those who persisted in remaining members of the Institut, and although this sanction appears to have been variously enforced, depending upon the priest, it was evidently invoked sufficiently often to deter Catholic membership. The members had hoped that the condemnation would be suspended pending the outcome of the appeal, and Dessaulles argued vehemently that it was not morally binding until the complainants had been heard, but few of the clergy (and certainly not Bishop Bourget) seemed to agree. Significantly enough, the Annuaires of the late 1860s no longer report the aggregate membership, but only the number of new members, probably in many cases non-Catholic. Most disheartening sign of all, from the Institut's point of view, was that the young people were reluctant to join. Annual reports deplored the failure of the youth to take advantage of what the Institut had to offer. Distinguished radicals virtually begged the younger generation to enlist, but with little success. It was evident that the stigma of condemnation was beginning to tell, and it brought with it ostracism as well. The Institut found itself excluded as a group from the Saint Jean-Baptiste parade.

In the closing years of the decade, the events which all along had been intensifying the clash between liberalism and ultramontanism reached crisis proportions. While the last remnants of the Papal States were being menaced by the forces of Garibaldi and Victor Emmanuel, Bishop Bourget was busily organizing Canada's first military expeditionary force. In February, 1868, the first group of some 500 French Canadian Zouaves set out to defend the territories of the embattled Pope. That summer the formal summons was issued for the first Church Council in over three centuries, for which Pius had been preparing for years, and which was to carry the Papacy to the furthest extreme of conservative reaction. In the months that preceded the Council, and even after it had convened in December, 1869, the tiny band of Catholic liberals led by Dupanloup and Montalembert continued to speak up, but they were soon drowned out in the conservative tide which resulted in the proclamation of Papal Infallibility in July, 1870. Two months later came Sedan and the occupation of Rome. It was against this background of events that the Institut received its death sentence. It survived long enough, however, to fight one final spectacular battle with Bishop Bourget.

The story can be followed in the newspaper excerpts below, but it may be useful to outline here the main developments. In the summer of 1869 Bishop Bourget forwarded from Rome two decrees,[33] one condemning the Institut Canadien, and the other condemning the *Annuaire* for 1868. Catholics, and particularly young people, were to be drawn away from the Institut so long as it was known that pernicious doctrines were taught there. The decree commended the rival Institut Canadien-Français and the *Courrier de St. Hyacinthe,* and urged that they be supported. The *Annuaire* for 1868, which contained a lengthy address on tolerance by Dessaulles, and shorter addresses by Horace Greeley and C. A. Geoffrion, was placed on the Index of prohibited publications without reasons being given. The Papal decrees made no mention of the appeal made by the seventeen members of the Institut in 1865, and indeed Gonzalve Doutre later claimed that judgment on the merits of the appeal had not been given.[34] Nor had the decree stated that the members of the Institut were to be deprived of the sacraments; on the contrary, they suggested the less drastic course of encouraging an alternative society. Nevertheless, Bourget's circular letter treated the decrees as though they were in response to the appeal of 1865, and proceeded to deny sacraments to those who remained members of the Institut 'so long as it teaches pernicious doctrines,' or who read or kept the *Annuaire* for 1868.

It was the *coup de grâce* and A. A. Dorion and others now urged that the Institut be dissolved. The recalcitrant members rejected this advice and sought to ward off the death blow by adopting the two resolutions of September 23, 1869.[35] This tactic brought from the Administrator of the Diocese a clear and explicit demand for unconditional surrender; an unqualified repudiation of the liberal creed which had animated the Institut during the twenty-five years of its existence.[36] Bishop Bourget's reaction to the resolutions of September 23 was conveyed in a letter from Rome, dated October 30, 1869. The Bishop denounced the resolutions as only an act of hypocrisy which feigned submission to the Holy See. He added that "this act of submission forms part of a report of the Committee, unanimously approved by the Institut, in which a resolution is proclaimed, until then kept secret, which establishes *the principle of religious toleration, which has been the principal ground of the condemnation of the Institut."*[37] It should be noted that this 'principal ground' of condemnation was entirely new, and had not appeared in Bourget's pastoral letters of 1858, nor, so far as known, in any of the documents which had been forwarded to Rome by the petitioners of 1865. Moreover, there arises a mystery of how it could be a principal ground if it were kept secret, and why, supposing it had become known to the Bishop, he had made no mention of it. It will be recalled that the ostensible cause of the quarrel all along had been the prohibited books in the library of the Institut.

Bishop Bourget's letter reached Vicar General A. F. Truteau, Administrator of the Diocese, on November 17, 1869. On the following day Joseph Guibord died and his burial became the subject of prolonged litigation. Guibord, born in 1809, was a printer and a member of the Institut, of which he had been vice-president one year, and had also been one of the seventeen signatories of the appeal to the Pope in 1865. He had not been a practising Catholic in recent years and had not received the last rites of the Church prior to his sudden death. The Administrator declared that as Guibord had been a member of the Institut at the time of his death, and subject to canonical penalties, he was to be refused ecclesiastical burial. The Curé of Notre Dame, Father Victor Rousselot, thereupon refused burial in the consecrated part of the Côte des Neiges Cemetery where the Guibords owned a plot, but offered it in the part reserved for unbaptized infants and those dying out of the faith. Friends of the deceased, notably Rodolphe Laflamme and Joseph Doutre, prominent lawyer members of the Institut and former presidents of it, now applied to the courts on behalf of the widow, Henrietta Brown, for a writ of mandamus requiring the Fabrique de Montréal to grant burial in the consecrated part of the Cemetery. Appearing for the defendants were Louis A. Jetté and Francis Cassidy, both former members of the Institut, of which Cassidy had been president in 1850-51, and F. X. A. Trudel, who won the nickname of 'Grand Vicar' for his extreme ultramontane views. Trudel later became a senator, and editor and proprietor of *L'Etendard*, a far right-wing journal.

Among the many grounds advanced in support of the plaintiff, it was alleged that the decrees of the Congregation of the Index had never been recognized as part of the canon law of France or New France, that consequently Bishop Bourget had exceeded his authority, and that, by virtue of the Gallican laws, the Church was subject, as it had been in the days of New France, to the surveillance and control of the civil authorities. On the other side, it was argued on behalf of the defendants that treaties, constitutional enactments, and the law of the land had ever recognized that the Roman Catholic Church in Canada possessed the free exercise of its religious rites, independently of all control by the civil authorities; that the Fabrique had offered civil burial, which was all that it was bound to do; and that for the refusal to grant ecclesiastical burial the defendants were responsible to the religious authority only, and not to the civil authorities, who were incapable of judging of the motives on which such refusal may have been founded. The case posed the very issues of ultramontanism and liberalism, of Church and State, which had been in the forefront of the developments of the time. Quite naturally it provoked furious debate *pro* and *con*.

The court proceedings may be recounted briefly. On May 2, 1870, Judge Charles Mondelet delivered judgment in favour of the plaintiff. On September 10, 1870, Justices Berthelot, Mackay, and Torrance, of the Court of Reviews, reversed this decision. On December 2, 1870, Joseph Doutre, who was now apparently handling the case alone, appealed to the Court of Queen's Bench. On this occasion he created a legal sensation by presenting a petition of recusation against Justices Caron, Duval, Drummond, and Monk on the ground that being Roman Catholics they could not decide impartially in such a case. This petition was rejected (by Justice Badgely, the non-Catholic, as well as by the others) and in separate decisions handed down on September 7, 1871, the five justices upheld the decision of the Court of Review in favour of the Fabrique. Doutre asked leave to appeal to the Judicial Committee of the Privy Council in England and this was granted in June, 1873. The widow had died on April 2, 1873, and had been interred in the plot owned by her late husband in the consecrated portion of the Cemetery. The Institut had been made her heir and decided to proceed with the appeal.

Judgment was rendered on November 21, 1874, five years to the day after Guibord had been refused ecclesiastical burial. The judgments of the Court of Review and the Court of Queen's Bench were reversed and that of Judge Mondelet upheld. The Fabrique was ordered to inter Guibord's remains in that part of the Cemetery where Roman Catholics who receive ecclesiastical burial are usually interred, and was also required to pay all the considerable legal costs. The story of Joseph Doutre's determination to see the judgment carried out, and the furore which was aroused on all sides, can be followed from the newspaper extracts. A first attempt on September 2, 1875, was prevented by an angry mob. At length, on November 16, with the aid of almost the entire Montreal police force and a large part of the local militia, Joseph Guibord's remains were deposited in the plot which had at first been denied to them. The Institut had scored a triumph over its implacable opponent. Or had it? Bishop Bourget declared the ground in which Guibord was interred to be a profane place, forever separated from the consecrated portion of the Cemetery.

What remains to be said is more in the nature of an epilogue. Some sources have suggested that the members of the Institut Canadien hoped the Guibord case would give the society a new lease of life.[38] This seems doubtful. The demise of the Institut had been assured with the decrees that came from Rome in the summer of 1869, and the visits there of Gonzalve Doutre and L.-A. Dessaulles during the winter of 1869-70 failed to effect a commutation of the death sentence. It is more likely that the die-hard radicals, rather than hoping for a revival of the Institut as a result of the litigation, had been driven into an intransigence which matched that of Bishop Bourget. They would go down in a blaze of glory with liberal colours flying. The court case certainly provoked sensational and widespread interest, but it also sapped the energies of the Institut. There are very few meetings reported in the pages of *Le Pays* during 1870 and 1871, and by the end of the latter year *Le Pays* itself had disappeared, partly no doubt as a result of the renewed displeasure which Bishop Bourget had voiced regarding that journal in a pastoral letter of October 3, 1871.

A.A. Dorion, the distinguished Rouge leader, had resigned from the Institut shortly after the death of Guibord, as had also C. A. Geoffrion. Laflamme openly avowed his membership at the time of his election to Parliament in 1872, but, significantly enough, on the eve of his re-election in 1874, he too resigned. Dessaulles carried on a violent polemical battle with the publication of his pamphlet, "La Grande Guerre Ecclésiastique", in the summer of 1873, which earned him the severe condemnation of Bishop Bourget, who also administered a rebuke to

La Minerve for unaccountably publishing excerpts from it.[39] But before long Dessaulles gave up the struggle and went to France where he ended his days. In 1877 another former youthful member of the Institut was making his peace with the Church in an address to the Club Canadien in Quebec City.[40] If Wilfrid Laurier did not go to Canossa to the extent of repudiating liberalism altogether, he did nevertheless disown its continental European antecedents. Far more than Laflamme, to whom a Federal cabinet post beckoned, more even than Dorion, who was to end his days as a Chief Justice with a knighthood, Laurier had a career before him. There was no future for a French Canadian who differed greatly with the ecclesiastical authorities, at least not so long as these were of the stamp of Bishop Bourget.

And what of the Institut Canadien? How and when did it end its days? Not with a bang, as the excitement over the Guibord case might lead one to suppose, but with a whimper, indeed so quiet a whimper that no one seems to know when the Institut finally expired. It was still in existence at the time of Joseph Doutre's death in 1886, for there is a newspaper report of a resolution of mourning by the Institut.[41] The building on Notre Dame Street had evidently been sold prior to this time, no doubt in order to extinguish the debts. By 1889 its very credit-able library was in the possession of the Fraser Institute, a predominantly English organization, and today the bulk of the collection reposes in the Fraser-Hickson Library on Kensington Avenue. As for the Institut, it may have lingered on to the close of the century, but this is speculation.

If the Institut met defeat, so before long did Bishop Bourget and his ultramontane colleagues. For a time their theocratic pretensions seemed to be carrying the day. A group of their supporters was emboldened to draw up the Catholic Programme of 1871, placing religion in the fore-front of the interests which it was the duty of political parties to safe-guard, designating the Conservative Party as the only one offering acceptable guarantees to religion, and counselling Roman Catholics to support only those Conservative candidates who most nearly conformed to the principles in the Programme. While *Le Nouveau Monde* and such extreme right-wing journals as *L'Ordre* enthusiastically supported the Programme, it is significant that *La Minerve*, the official organ of Sir George Cartier and the Conservative Party in Quebec, was decidedly hostile. An open letter by Archbishop Taschereau, the Primate of Quebec, was hailed by both *La Minerve* and *Le Pays* as a repudiation of the Programme, as indeed it seemed to be. At all events, it does not appear that the 'Programmatistes' had any marked success.

In 1875 the ultramontane Catholics succeeded in persuading the provincial Council of Bishops to issue a joint pastoral letter,[42] which repeated the confusions of the Syllabus of Errors between liberal Catholicism and Catholic liberalism. It is not likely that a majority of the hierarchy fully approved of this pastoral, and undoubtedly there were many who were opposed, but the ultramontane tide was running strongly in these years. Although the pastoral did not mention any political party, some of the lesser clergy placed their own interpretation upon it and took wholeheartedly to political activity on behalf of the Conservative Party. The result was that the Liberals were reluctantly obliged to take several by-election results to court and have them annulled on the ground of undue clerical influence. They also complained to Rome about the activities of the ultramontanes.

Most important of all the developments, and one which endured until the 1960s, was the abolition in 1875 of the Quebec Ministry of Education, which meant the virtual elimination of laymen from the control of education and their replacement by clergymen. Yet apart from this more lasting triumph of ultramontanism, the tide soon began to ebb. Like their radical opponents in the Institut, the ultramontanes were always a minority influence in French Canadian society, even among the clergy. Sir John A. Macdonald had sought to reassure Alexander T. Galt, who was alarmed at ultramontane activities, by observing that Bourget and 'Pio Nono' were old men, and that with their passing a return to normal might be expected. Such indeed turned out to be the case. The mediatory mission in 1877 of Mgr. Conroy, an apostolic delegate, in response to Liberal protests, and the advent of a liberal Pope in Leo XIII, along with other developments, eventually brought an end to ultramontane pretensions. Mgr. Bourget, who retired as Bishop in 1876, and Bishop LaFlèche of Three Rivers, who died in 1898, were almost the last of their kind. Like their spiritual mentor, Pius IX, they had set themselves in opposition to the irresistible developments of their age. In the long run Montalembert was proved right and not his ultramontane opponents, whose intransigent and retrograde philosophy has long since been abandoned by the Roman Catholic Church.

Notes to Introduction

1. Anne Fremantle, *The Papal Encyclicals* (New York: Mentor Books, 1956), p. 152.

2. See the excerpts in translation in Ramsay Cook, ed., *French-Canadian Nationalism: An Anthology* (Toronto: Macmillan, 1969), pp. 92-106.

3. Le Père Théophile Hudon, S.J., *L'Institut Canadien de Montréal et l'Affaire Guibord: Une page d'histoire* (Montréal: Librairie Beauchemin, 1938), p. 20.

4. John Dougall, *History of the Guibord Case: Ultramontanism versus Law and Human Rights* (Montreal: "Witness" Printing House, 1875), p. 5.

5. Philippe Sylvain, "Libéralisme et ultramontanisme au Canada français: affrontement idéologique et doctrinal (1840-1865)," in W. L. Morton, ed., *The Shield of Achilles* (Toronto, McClelland and Stewart, 1968), p. 127.

6. *Ibid.,* p. 122. (In this and other instances the asterisk indicates a translation by the editor of the passage cited.)

7. *Ibid.,* p. 125.

8. For an account of this defection, which is often confused with the one of 1858, see Léon Pouliot, S.J., "L'Institut Canadien de Montréal et l'Institut National," *Revue d'Histoire de l'Amérique Française* (Mars, 1961), 481-486.

9. Sylvain, *op. cit.,* p. 130.

10. *Mandements, lettres pastorales, circulaires et autres, documents, publié dans le diocèse de Montréal,* tome II (Montréal, J. Plinquet, 1887), p. 466.

11. *Le Pays,* 27 décembre, 1867.

12. *Mandements . . . ,* III, pp. 367-8.

13. *Le Pays,* 15 avril, 1858.

14. Sylvain, *op. cit.,* p. 222.

15. The letter was published in *Le Pays,* 24 avril, 1858.

16. *Mandements . . . ,* VI, pp. 24-38. (A footnote explains that this pastoral letter was accidentally omitted from its chronological place, which would have been in Vol. III.)

17. Sylvain, *op. cit.,* p. 223.

18. See Sylvain's masterly analysis, pp. 224-227.

19. Dougall, *op. cit.,* p. 8.

20. *Ibid.,* p. 10.

21. Sylvain, *op. cit.,* p. 232.

22. *Ibid.,* pp. 236-244, for extracts from a summary of Bourget's letters, and the whole of the *Le Pays* reply.

23. *Le Pays,* 27 décembre, 1862.

24. Sylvain, *op. cit.,* p. 249.

25. L'Institut Canadien, *Annuaire pour 1866,* p. 23.

26. *Mandements . . . ,* IV, p. 22.

27. *Annuaire pour 1866,* p. 23.

28. *Mandements . . . ,* IV, pp. 39-40. Quoted in Sylvain, *op. cit.,* p. 251.

29. *Annuaire pour 1866,* p 24. Among the signatories: L.-A. Dessaulles, R. Laflamme, J. Doutre, J. E. Coderre, W. Laurier.

30. *Ibid.*

31. *Ibid.*, p. 25.

32. *Annuaire pour 1868*, p. 4.

33. See below, *Le Nouveau Monde*, 2 septembre, 1869.

34. *Le Pays*, 14 à 18 juin, 1870.

35. See below, *Le Pays*, 23 septembre, 1869.

36. *Ibid.*, 27 septembre, 1869.

37. See below, the Privy Council judgment in *The Montreal Herald*, 8 December, 1874. (Italics added.)

38. See, for example, Hudon, *op. cit.*, pp. 77, 85.

39. *La Minerve*, 3 à 7 juin, 1873.

40. See below, epilogue.

41. *Le Monde*, 5 février, 1886.

42. See below, *The True Witness And Catholic Chronicle*, 15 October, 1875.

REMOVAL OF THE BODY FROM THE VAULT IN MOUNT ROYAL CEMETERY.

ARRIVAL OF THE HEARSE AT THE COTE DES NEIGES CEMETERY : THE MOB CLOSE THE GATES AND REFUSE ADMISSION.

THE GUIBORD UNPLEASANTNESS.

Guide to Documents

1. Rome Condemns the *Institut*. *Le Nouveau Monde*, Montreal, September 2, 1869.

2. The *Institut* Debates its Course. *Le Nouveau Monde*, Montreal, September 9, 1869.

3. Official Response of the *Institut* to the Condemnation. *Le Pays*, Montreal, September 23, 1869.

4. The Church's Ultimatum. *Le Pays*, Montreal, September 27, 1869.

5. The Insidious Goal of the *Institut*. *Le Nouveau Monde*, Montreal, September 27, 1869.

6. Death and Attempted Burial of Guibord. *The Montreal Herald*, November 23, 1869.

7. *Le Nouveau Monde* Applauds the Church's Stand. Montreal, November 27, 1869.

8. Divine *v.* Civil Law. *The True Witness and Catholic Chronicle*, Montreal, December 3, 1869.

9. The Court Case: free thinkers persecute the Church. *L'Ordre*, Montreal, January 25, 1870.

10. The Court Case: biased reporting by Catholic journals. *Le Pays*, Montreal, March 28, 1870.

11. The Court Case: M. Doutre and the Jesuit martyrs. *L'Ordre*, Montreal, March 29, 1870.

12. The Court Case: a popular interpretation. *Le Pays*, Montreal, March 29, 1870.

13. The Court Case: religious freedom *v.* Gallicanism. *The True Witness and Catholic Chronicle*, Montreal, April 15, 1870.

14. Judge Mondelet's Decision: a victory for civil liberty. *Le Pays*, Montreal, May 3, 1870.

15. Mondelet Abolishes Traditional Liberties of Roman Catholics. *La Minerve*, Montreal, May 3, 1870.

16. Mondelet's Tyranny. *L'Ordre*, Montreal, May 3, 1870.

17. A Decision for Freedom and Progress. *The Daily Witness*, Montreal, May 4, 1870.

18. *L'Ordre* Defends its Attack on Mondelet. Montreal, May 10, 1870.

19. Mondelet's Decision Unconstitutional. *L'Ordre*, Montreal, May 11, 1870.

20. The Duty of True Catholics. *The True Witness and Catholic Chronicle*, Montreal, May 13, 1870.

21. Is Spiritual Care a Civil Right? *The True Witness and Catholic Chronicle*, Montreal, May 20, 1870.

22. The Superior Court Reverses the Decision. *L'Ordre*, Montreal, September 10, 1870.

23. Filthy Books in the *Institut*'s Library. *Le Nouveau Monde*, Montreal, September 22, 1870.

24. A Member of *l'Institut* Attacks *Le Nouveau Monde*. *Le Pays*, Montreal, October 27, 1870.

25. The Appeal: can a Catholic judge be impartial? *The Montreal Herald*, December 3, 1870.

26. The Case for a Strong Union of Montreal Literary Societies. *Le Pays*, Montreal, April 22, 1871.

27. The Superior Court's Verdict Upheld, but *l'Institut* given leave to appeal to the Judicial Committee of the Privy Council. *The Gazette*, Montreal, September 8, 1871.

28. Progress of the Dispute So Far. *The Montreal Herald*, September 9, 1871.

29. The Judicial Committee of the Privy Council Upholds *l'Institut. Le Bien Public,* Montreal, November 22, 1874.

30. A Pox On Both Their Houses. *The Globe,* Toronto, November 23, 1874.

31. An Infringement on the Rights of the Church. *La Minerve,* Montreal, November 23, 1874.

32. The Established Church of Lower Canada. *The Daily Witness,* Montreal, November 27, 1874.

33. Transcript of the Privy Council's Judgment. *The Montreal Herald,* December 8, 1874.

34. The Guibord Case and the Privy Council. *Le Nouveau Monde,* Montreal, December 16-21, 1874.

35. *Le Nouveau Monde's* Extreme Ultramontanism. *The Daily Witness,* Montreal, December 22, 1874.

36. The Eagle and the Arrow. *The True Witness and Catholic Chronicle,* Montreal, December 25, 1874.

37. A Riot at the Cemetery. *The Gazette,* Montreal, September 3, 1875.

38. *La Minerve's* Provocations. *The Daily Witness,* Montreal, September 3, 1875.

39. The Queen's Law or Mob Rule. *The Montreal Herald,* September 3, 1875.

40. A Plea for Civil Obedience. *The Gazette,* Montreal, September 3, 1875.

41. The Character of the Late Joseph Guibord, *The Daily Witness,* Montreal, September 4, 1875.

42. The Good Thief. *La Minerve,* Montreal, September 6, 1875.

43. Religious Fanaticism Could Provoke Repression. *Le Bien Public,* Montreal, September 6, 1875.

44. A Plea for Moderation on Both Sides. *L'Evénement,* Montreal, September 3, 1875. [in *The Globe,* Toronto, September 7, 1875].

45. M. Doutre's Madness. *Le Nouveau Monde,* Montreal, September 7, 1875.

46. How the Church may be Avenged. *Le Nouveau Monde,* Montreal, September 8, 1875.

47. A Catholic Writes to the Editor of *The Montreal Herald.* September 8, 1875.

48. Spiritual and Temporal Powers. *The Globe,* Toronto, September 8, 1875.

49. Bishop Bourget to the Editor of *The Gazette.* Montreal, September 9, 1875.

50. M. Doutre is the Disciple of a Maniac. *Le Nouveau Monde,* Montreal, September 10, 1875.

51. Archbishop Lynch of Toronto to *The Globe.* Toronto, September 10, 1875.

52. The Civic Authorities and the Rioters. *The True Witness and Catholic Chronicle,* Montreal, September 10, 1875.

53. Archbishop Lynch Defends the Church. *The Globe,* Toronto, September 11, 1875.

54. *The Globe* Comments. Toronto, September 11, 1875.

55. The Guibord Case and Catholic Political Liberty. *The Daily Witness,* Montreal, September 13, 1875.

56. The Protestant Press and the Guibord Affair. *La Minerve,* Montreal, September 13, 1875.

57. Archbishop Lynch on Censorship. *The Globe,* Toronto, September 14, 1875.

58. *The Globe* Replies. Toronto, September, 14, 1875.

59. Joseph Doutre Replies to Archbishop Lynch. *The Globe,* Toronto, September 15, 1875.

60. M. Doutre in Ontario. *Le Nouveau Monde*, Montreal, September 20, 1875.

61. The Errors of the Protestant Press. *La Minerve*, Montreal, September 23, 1875.

62. Presbyterians Support the Catholic Position. *La Minerve*, Montreal, September 25, 1875.

63. Toronto Protestants More Vicious than Montreal Catholics. *La Minerve*, Montreal, September 28, 1875.

64. The Questionable Loyalty of *l'Institut*'s Leaders. *Le Nouveau Monde*, Montreal, September 29, 1875.

65. The Patriotic Work of *l'Institut Canadien*. *The Daily Witness*, Montreal, October 1, 1875.

66. Law and Order. *The Globe*, Toronto, October 6, 1875.

67. A British View. *The Times*, London, September 21, 1875 [in *The Globe*, Toronto, October 7, 1875].

68. Lawbreakers at Montreal and Toronto. *The Globe*, Toronto, October 8, 1875.

69. A Pastoral Letter from the Bishops of Quebec. *The True Witness and Catholic Chronicle*, Montreal, October 15, 1875.

70. Guibord Buried At Last. *The Gazette*, Montreal, November 17, 1875.

71. Burial of Guibord. *The Mail*, Toronto, November 17, 1875.

72. Burial of Guibord. *The Globe*, Toronto, November 17, 1875.

73. The Triumph of Persecution. *La Minerve*, Montreal, November 18, 1875.

74. Bishop Bourget's Remarkable Rhetoric. *The Globe*, Toronto, November 24, 1875.

75. Epilogue: Laurier Defends Liberalism.

A Note on the Documents

Unless otherwise noted, the documents reproduced below conform, in spelling, grammatical usage and punctuation, to the originals. Since *Canadian History Through the Press* is, in a limited sense, a history of Canadian journalism, it has seemed advisable to preserve contemporary usage however questionable it might appear to be, in order to illustrate the changing quality of Canadian journalistic writing.

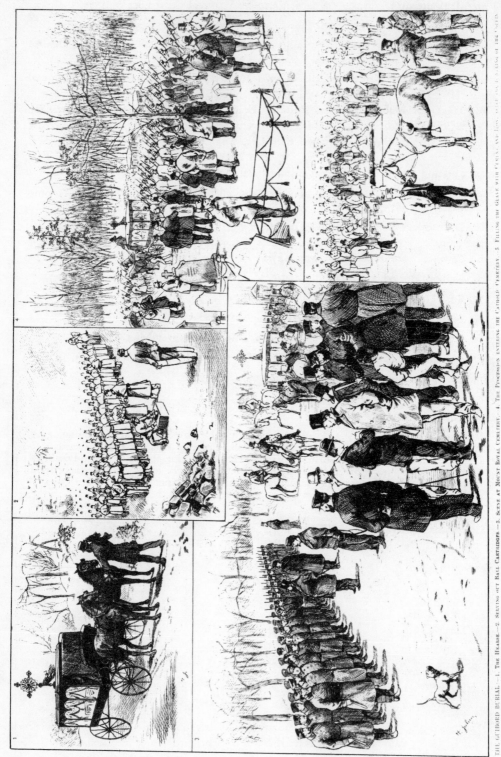

THE GUIBORD BURIAL.—1. THE HEARSE.—2. SERVING OUT BALL CARTRIDGES.—3. SCENE AT MOUNT ROYAL CEMETERY.—4. THE PROCESSION ENTERING THE CATHOLIC CEMETERY.—5. FILLING THE GRAVE WITH CEMENT AND IRON, STOP ON LEANING OF THE GRAVE.

1 ROME CONDEMNS THE INSTITUT

Le Nouveau Monde, Montreal
September 2, 1869 [translation]

An announcement to be read during the sermon in all the churches of the Diocese of Montreal where public mass is held, on the Sunday to be set by the Diocesan Administrator, by order of His Excellency, the Bishop of Montreal, in his circular letter dated the sixteenth of July, 1869.

"You have not forgotten, Our very dear brethren, the pastoral letters that we addressed to you on the 30th of April, 1858, to make you understand the obligation that your religion imposes on you not to read those books forbidden by the Church, not to subscribe to those newspapers professing evil principles, and not to participate in discussions which would be impious or irreligious.

"At this time, as you no doubt remember, we had the sad duty of pointing the *Institut Canadien* out to you as dangerous to your faith and of notifying you that you could not, in all conscience, have anything to do with it.

"Some of the members of this *Institut*, thinking that we treated them with exaggerated severity, appealed to the Holy See about four years ago to complain to it of Our behaviour and asked that they be treated as other children of the Church who can, when they so wish, partake of the sacraments.

"The Sacred Congregation charged by Our Holy Father the Pope with examining this vital question has just submitted its reply, and We hasten to transmit it to you.

"The following is a faithful translation of the Latin text that was presented to Us:

'Most illustrious and Holy Lord,

The Most Eminent and Most Reverend, the Inquisitors General, in a general meeting of the Holy Roman and Universal Inquisition, held on Wednesday, the seventh day of the present month, having examined the long-standing difficulties regarding the *Institut Canadien*, and having fully and carefully examined everything, wished that your Excellency be notified that the doctrines contained in a certain yearbook, in which the records of the said *Institut* are registered, should be totally rejected, and that these doctrines expounded by this same *Institut* should be cast out. The most Eminent and Reverend fathers, noting, moreover, their strong fears that with such evil doctrines, the instruction and education of Christian youth would be imperilled, have said that you must be praised for your zeal and vigilance, and they have ordained that Your Excellency should personally be exhorted to confer with the Clergy of your Diocese, so that Catholics, especially the young, be drawn away from the *Institut* so long as it is well known that pernicious doctrines are taught there . . .'

"These are the instructions of the Holy See which were sent to Us by His Excellency, Monsignor Simeoni, Secretary of the Sacred Office for the Propagation of the Faith, this 14th of July.

"We must at this same time, Our very dear brethren, bring another very important fact to your attention. It is that the Year-book of the *Institut Canadien* for 1868, celebrating the 24th anniversary of the *Institut Canadien* on the 17th of December, 1868, and condemned by a Decree from the Holy Office dated 7th July this year, was placed, on the twelfth of this same month on the list of prohibited books, by the Sacred Congregation of the Index. Our Holy Father the Pope has approved of this decree the 16th of the current month and has ordained that it be duly promulgated. . . .

"Thus, Our very dear brethren, two things are specifically and strictly forbidden; firstly, to take part in the activities of the *Institut Canadien,* as long as it teaches pernicious doctrines, and, secondly, to publish, keep, save or read the Yearbook of the said *Institut* for 1868. These two commandments of the Church are of a serious nature and consequently it will be a mortal sin to violate them knowingly. Consequently, he who persists in wishing to belong to the said *Institut,* or who in reading, or even merely in keeping the abovementioned Yearbook without the permission of the Church, deprives himself of the sacraments, even the sacrament of the dead, for to be worthy of approaching it one must detest sin that kills the soul and be of a disposition never to commit it again.

"These are the important regulations that the Holy See itself outlines for you, with the sole interest of the eternal salvation of your souls . . ."

A. F. Truteau V.G.
Administrator

2 THE INSTITUT DEBATES ITS COURSE

*Le Nouveau Monde, Montreal
September 9, 1869* [translation]

Following the notice inserted in *Le Pays* the members of the *Institut Canadien* got together Thursday evening to consider the decision of the Sacred Congregation of the Inquisition condemning the doctrines of the *Institut* as well as its Yearbook for 1868. The gathering was a very large one and included all the principal members. . . .

. . . Here is what we have learned from reliable persons.

After the president, M. N. Aubin, chief reporter for *Le Pays*, explained the object of the meeting, M. Joseph Doutre got up and moved that the *Institut* accepts as official, in the Yearbook of 1868, only the report of the president; and since the condemnation of the Index had no bearing on that, the *Institut* would ignore it. He supported his proposal in a long speech in which he repeated for the hundredth time the vital words of persecution, intolerance, modern ideas, etc.

The Honourable M. A. A. Dorion (we were misinformed yesterday in saying that he was not a member of the *Institut*) moved that a committee be appointed to consider whether it would not be appropriate to dissolve the *Institut Canadien* after its affairs had been liquidated.

The honourable mover of this motion made it most reasonably clear that it was too late for the *Institut* to reject a part of the Yearbook and accept the remainder. "We all applauded the speeches that are found therein, and it would be an act of cowardice to repudiate them today. The repudiation, to have meant anything, should have been made in 1868."

"The *Institut Canadien* was founded as an educational service to the young; now anyone can claim that it has strayed from that objective. Thus, the *Institut* does not follow its aims. Besides, the accusation that has just been laid against it will merely increase this straying."

Opinions remained divided between these two motions and the discussion which followed was very heated and continued until midnight. Then the Honourable M. Dessaulles proposed an adjournment till the following Thursday and it was passed.

The individual who gives us this information believes that the majority shares the opinion of M. Dorion.

3 OFFICIAL RESPONSE OF THE INSTITUT TO THE CONDEMNATION

*Le Pays, Montreal
September 23, 1869* [translation]

Last evening, at a large gathering of this *Institut*, the following report was unanimously adopted:

To the President and to the members of the *Institut Canadien*.

Sirs: The special committee nominated at the September 9th meeting, 1869, to consider the general situation of the *Institut Canadien*, has the honour of submitting its report:

The members of your committee, having for the most part been present at the meeting at which this committee was formed, understood that the general terms of their commission were to allow them the freedom to consider all aspects of those difficulties which prevent the *Institut* from attaining that degree of usefulness to which all the members aspire. These difficulties have become more serious, recently, as a result of a decree originating from the authority of Rome and dated July 7, 1869, condemning the doctrines contained in the *Institut Canadien*'s Yearbook of 1868, doctrines which are specified in this decree as being the doctrines of the *Institut*, and exhorting the clergy to rally together and lead the youth away from the *Institut*, as long as it teaches pernicious doctrines. Your committee understood that it was towards a resolution of the difficulties created for the Catholic members by the decree that their efforts should primarily lead, and if in the eventuality that they were considered insoluble, according to these members, its duty would be so to declare and subsequently advise what else could be done.

Your committee is happy to say, that after having fully examined the situation, it came to the conclusion that the *Institut* as a body and the Catholic members could adopt steps appropriate in reconciling the Catholic members with their own religious authorities, without necessitating the modification of the organic constitution that rules us, and without diminishing the services that the *Institut* can render in the literary and scientific development of this country.

Those members of the *Institut* who do not belong to the Catholic religion cannot be indifferent to the necessities inherent in the position of their Catholic colleagues, because these necessities can determine the presence or absence of Catholics in this *Institut*. In a country such as ours, those whom religion divides have common duties and interests which ought often to bring them together. Beyond the religious field, literature and science offer large vistas for the communication of ideas and for useful research, and it would be most unfortunate if by a lack of appreciation of the particular demands of a religion in at least its legitimate limits, some of the members of the *Institut* would find their union with members belonging to another religion impossible.

With a view to easing these difficulties, the *Institut* has already, at a large meeting held March 7, 1864, adopted the following resolution: "That the constitution of the *Institut Canadien*, in not asking that any member account for his religious faith, does not imply the denial of any religious truth or authority, and entirely allows to rest in their consciences the individual responsibilities and duties of the members in their dealings with an established form of worship; that in order to place the religious freedom permitted by this *Institut* above all types of conflict and screened from all difficulty it is essential that dealings or discussions regarding any question which could wound the religious susceptibilities of any member of this *Institut* be avoided with care."

As this resolution did not receive any outside publicity nor was it adhered to with sufficient fidelity according to the view of some, the opinion that the *Institut* devoted itself to the teaching of any doctrine whatever became prevalent in some areas. Whether this opinion is rightly or wrongly founded, it would be futile to combat in any way other than explicit action and the rigorous and constant execution of the word and spirit of the resolution of March, 1864.

This is the conclusion reached by your committee in suggesting to the members, whatever creed they follow, that they solemnly and as one body affirm,

"That the *Institut Canadien*, formed as it was with a purely literary and scientific objective, has no type of doctrinaire teaching and carefully excludes all teaching of pernicious doctrines among its own membership."

In the category of pernicious doctrines your committee includes all written or oral expression of opinion which would violate the terms of the resolution of March 1864. *L'Institut* has never been accused of tolerating among its members the expression of ideas contrary to morality and the doctrines which people believed were taught there were not even pernicious in the opinion of those who attributed them to the *Institut* except in the eyes of a particular cult. Thus stated, this manifesto is merely a reaffirmation of that policy which the *Institut* has already declared.

The committee, composed largely of Catholics, thought it a duty to address the followers of this religion through the vehicle of its Catholic members in order to suggest to them that the situation demanded of them a particular position in order to conciliate their membership in the *Institut* with the demands of their religion.

The decree that has been referred to, if it is recognized as binding by them, would then produce the alienation of Catholic youth from the institution and the subsequent deprivation of an important segment of our population of the benefits of this association.

Consequently, the Catholic section of this committee suggests that a resolution be adopted in the following terms:

"That the Catholic members of the *Institut Canadien* having learned of the condemnation of the *Institut Canadien*'s Yearbook for 1868 by decree of the Roman authority declare themselves subject, purely and simply, to this decree."

Your committee has reason to believe that, with this double step taken by both the body and the Catholics of the *Institut*, the difficulties that have existed for many years and alienated citizens, distinguished by their ability and their knowledge, from the *Institut*, will be smoothed away and that we will be permitted to realize the generous hopes which the *Institut* originally and since its founding has inspired in its patrons and members.

The whole is humbly submitted.
Montreal, 23 September, 1869

J. Eméry Coderre
President

4 THE CHURCH'S ULTIMATUM

Le Pays, Montreal
September 27, 1869 [translation]

Having so far placed before our readers the various documents pertaining to the *Institut Canadien* affair, we print today, from *Le Nouveau Monde*, the resolutions proposed by the Diocesan Administrator:

It shall be resolved by the *Institut, speaking in its corporate capacity (comme corps)*, and not by the Catholic part of the members only, 1st. That it submits itself fully and entirely to the two judgments recently given, the first by the Tribunal of the Index against the *Annuaire de l'Institut Canadien pour 1868*, and the second by the Holy Roman Inquisition against the *Institut Canadien* as being a school for pernicious doctrines.

That it be resolved, 2nd. That under the name of pernicious doctrines the *Institut* understands the reprobation of all those which the Catholic Church condemns or reprobates and notably moderate Rationalism, Indifferentism, Progress, Liberalism and Modern Civilization, as understood and condemned by the Encyclical *Quanta Cura* of 1864, matters which the *Institut* can henceforth neither meddle with nor be reconciled to, since the Roman Pontiff refuses himself to do so.

That it be resolved 3rd. That like every other institution having any connection with education and instruction especially of youth, the *Institut* recognises the customary jurisdiction of the Bishop, and recognises further his right to purge its library of all books which he shall judge prohibited by the Church, or by natural morality.

That it be resolved 4th. That the *Institut* submit its constitution and by-laws to the Ordinary that he may strike out all the false principles they may contain or provisions of a nature to favour the diffusion in the *Institut* of *pernicious doctrines,* condemned by the judgment of the Holy Inquisition of Rome already cited.

5 THE INSIDIOUS GOAL OF THE INSTITUT

Le Nouveau Monde, Montreal
September 27, 1869 [translation]

The *Institut Canadien,* coming back again and again as it will to the problem of its condemnation, will find but one solution, namely; the absolute impossibility of joining error with truth and light with darkness; that is to say, the fated, inevitable, and necessary dissolution of this body composed of radically heterogeneous and irreconcilable elements. The more the Catholics attempt to affirm their principles, the more complicated also becomes the question of their union with the Protestants of the *Institut*. Here again, it is purely a matter of figures and all the spirit of tolerance and conciliation imaginable will do nothing; two and two make and will invariably make four, no more, no less, in spite of the principle of complete freedom of thought. It is this that certain members, more enlightened and sincere, understood so well at first, that upon learning of the condemnation of the *Institut Canadien* as a body, a condemnation which has bearing on those very principles which make it what it is and without which it would be another institution entirely, they immediately proposed the dissolution of this baleful society.

It is also our opinion that it is the dissolution of the *Institut* that is necessary and nothing else will do. Never for a moment did we believe in the possibility of a rapprochement or a true reconciliation between the *Institut*, with its present composition, and the religious authority of this diocese. Even supposing that the Catholic party were of such good faith, all its efforts towards reconciliation were destined to be useless in our eyes. We repeat here what we have said elsewhere, It is not in the power of any man to force the *Institut* to yield to Catholic principles, nor is it in the power of the Bishop to yield the principles that form the basis of its resistance.

So, will the good faith of some members change the rebellious elements which today compose and dominate this body? And will it submit to the same yoke those irreconcilable spirits which the principle of complete liberty of belief, thought, and speech has brought together? Will it lead Protestants and the other Catholics to repudiate as pernicious all the doctrines which the Roman Inquisition and the Tribunal of the Index condemn and repudiate as such? In a word, will the *Institut* as a body ever submit frankly and simply to the jurisdiction of the Bishop of Montreal, as completely as if its members were all humble and docile children of the Church? We would like it to be so, but it is folly to so hope. And this is, however, the only possible condition for a rapprochement and true reconciliation: a type of submission that perhaps not even ten members of the *Institut* feel ready to sign, at least if one judges by the committee report on which the *Institut* has just voted.

It is unfortunate, doubtless, but we can do nothing. The intolerance which refuses to join light with darkness is not our doing, nor that of the Bishop of Montreal. It is based on a matter of principle and principles govern us. Is it thus our fault or yours that the *Institut*, with the constitution that it made, and the members that it has received, is absolutely incapable of making a single act of Christian faith and Catholic submission? And should we, because we are a religious newspaper and an instrument of peace evade doctrine and thereby evade truth? Charity is a necessity without a doubt, but are you certain that it is not out of charity that we write these lines, that it is not out of charity for improvident and weak youth that the Bishop of Montreal at first attempted to reform the *Institut* and finally that it is not out of a spirit of charity that Rome, after first having praised his past zeal, today commissioned him to do all in his power to lead the faithful from this den of pernicious doctrines which it itself had just condemned? A strange charity would be that of a mother who gives her children razors as toys and poison as food.

Now the books and doctrines of the *Institut* are just that, and it is as a result of a well understood charity that we fight them with all our strength. . . .

To understand properly the zeal and the manoeuvrings of a certain number of members who demand impossible reconciliation, it is necessary to know that in their opinion the ultimate evil would be the complete triumph of the Bishop of Montreal over the *Institut* and the dissolution of their society, which he has so long condemned. These members still dream of a future for their unfortunate work, a future of which only a few serious spirits have yet dared to speak, all while undertaking nevertheless to achieve it. They want to transform the

Institut Canadien, in the not too distant future, into a large school and the head of professional studies in this part of the country – into let us actually say the word, the Canadian University of Montreal!

To those who smile and think that we exaggerate the ambitions of the leaders of the *Institut,* we permit ourselves to recall what has been accomplished over the last few years in this realm.

Does one ignore the affiliation of the *Institut Canadien* with the Protestant Victoria University? the establishment of its chair of Law? the organization of the course of this faculty? the names of its four professors? the number of students that actually attend it? and the privileges with which it finds itself invested?

The fact is that the *Institut's* school of law, which opened only yesterday, makes everything else very difficult here and not only rivals the University of Laval but secretly undermines it and in reality consumes it. Does one forget the efforts which were made even last year, similarly, to entice our Canadian School of Medicine to amalgamate with the *Institut?* We are told that it is only because of the great courage of a number of professors of this school that the fatal amalgamation did not take place and that the *Institut* did not at once open a new university chair.

What then would have remained of the pupils of the Catholic University and into whose hands would advanced professional studies in Montreal have fallen? The root of the matter is that the University of Montreal has already begun and if we do not want it to be the creation and daughter of the *Institut,* which is Canadian only in name, the time has come to see to it. . . .

---

6 DEATH AND ATTEMPTED BURIAL OF GUIBORD

The Montreal Herald
November 23, 1869

A case which will probably be brought before the courts of law has just taken place in the city. We give the facts simply as they occurred, and which we have taken great pains to verify. Joseph Guibord, a printer, who for about thirty years was in the employment of Messrs. Perrault, died suddenly on Thursday night. An inquest was held on the body, and the usual certificate sent by the coroner to Mr. Rousselot, curate in charge of the parish. The following morning the friends of the deceased went to the Seminary to have the death registered, to arrange for the usual service for the dead, and to obtain an order for interment in the Roman Catholic Cemetery. The officer in charge refused to register the death or to give any order for interment. The usual service was also refused. The reason for this, distinctly and unequivocally given, was that the deceased was a member of the Canadian Institute, it being further stated that orders had been issued that no member of that institution was to receive any of the rites of the Church. As Mr. Guibord had been a consistent adherent of the Romish Church, had fulfilled all the duties required of its members, during the whole of Lent and on Fridays abstaining from meat as ordered, was a pew-holder in St. Peter's Church and a member of two Societies under the control of the priests, and to which only Roman Catholics were admitted as members – the friends thought there must be some misconception. One of his relatives, therefore, went to the Seminary, and asked for an order to have the deceased buried in a lot belonging to the applicant, but he was told this would not be given. To put an end to all doubt on the subject, the widow gave a written order to three gentlemen to act for her, who were to use every means to obtain permission to have the body interred in consecrated ground. Armed with this they called on the Rev. Mr. Rousselot, and formally asked him to give the order. This was again refused. They then demanded of him in his capacity as a public officer to give Joseph Guibord interment, who was born a Catholic, baptised and married in the Catholic Church, and had always been a Catholic up to the hour of his death. The only answer to this was that he had received orders from the Vicar-General to that effect, and he produced the letter, which stated that "no member of the Canadian Institute was to have the Sacraments of the Church administered, to receive the last rites, to have funeral services performed or to obtain interment in the Catholic cemetery." The friends then made a legal tender of the fees usual in such cases, which Mr. Rousselot offered to accept, but said that the body could not be interred in the lot. A request was then made that the body should be allowed to be deposited in the Vaults, but no answer could be returned till the matter had been referred to the Grand Vicar. On the return of the friends for an answer the Curate was present with a witness, and said they must understand that interment was not refused, but that the body of Guibord must be buried in a lot set apart for the burial of unbaptised children, suicides, and people unrecognized by the Church. This was declined by the friends and a notarial protest was served on the *Fabrique*. On Sunday a large concourse of friends and sympathisers attended the body to the Roman Catholic Cemetery, it being in a hearse used for the funeral of deceased Protestants. At the gate the procession was stopped, the coffin taken off and placed on a common sleigh, on which it was taken to the chapel, where the demand was made on the representative of the *Fabrique* to give interment, a legal tender being again made of the fees. This he refused to receive, stating that he had received instructions from the *Fabrique* not to inter the body in consecrated ground, but that he would give interment in the strangers' lot. At the request of some of the friends the lot (a small rough piece of ground, totally uncared for) was pointed out, and Mr. Desroches, the superintendent, repeated the statement that suicides, &c., were buried there, and added in answer to an enquiry that criminals executed without confession were also buried there. . . . The body was then returned to the hearse and taken to the Mount Royal Cemetery, where it was deposited in the vault. . . . Affidavits to the facts have been prepared, and a *mandamus* will be applied for to compel the *Fabrique* to give interment in consecrated ground. The application will, of course, be resisted, and the case, the decision of which will, no doubt, turn upon the duties of the clerical authority acting as a public officer, will be watched with keen interest. . . . It does seem singular that murderers and malefactors should be allowed to repose in holy ground, while the member of a simple literary society should be cast forth into the Potters' field.

---

7 LE NOUVEAU MONDE APPLAUDS THE CHURCH'S STAND

Le Nouveau Monde, Montreal
November 27, 1869 [translation]

Death in the *Institut Canadien*

Yesterday, one of the saddest sights possible was presented to the Canadian Catholic population of Montreal; namely, the funeral of one of the leading members of the *Institut Canadien* who died since the excommunication decree was directed against this unfortunate society. The poor deceased, struck down suddenly in his sleep during the night, had no time to call a priest, and his body, instead of being buried in sacred ground, with the honours and prayers of the Church, had to take the road to the Protestant cemetery.

The tears and supplications of his relations were of no avail, the law took its course and the penalty its terrible effect. What aversions had to be overcome, what sorrow to be added to all the others for this small number of friends who agreed to accompany the members of the *Institut* in forming a cortège for the hearse.

Up until now, it was asked what significance a sentence promulgated by Rome could have on the insubmissive Catholics of America. At the gate of the Catholic cemetery, at the edge of the unblessed grave, among other strange graves, the answer was given.

There was no element lacking at this funeral to make it into an antireligious demonstration and the body of a poor misguided workman heard from his casket not the normal pious oration addressed to him but the following words: we quote from this morning's *Le Pays*:

"A eulogy of the deceased's virtues formed the principal theme of these short speeches. The example of moral courage which he gave to his compatriots would not remain useless. As a silent representative of a noble cause, his memory would remain graven not only on the memory of his friends, but on the history of his country. There are today, added one of the orators, two unique movements in the Church, one that aspires to draw to it those belonging to other faiths, the other, no less active, which seems to have as its mission, the estrangement from the Church of her most distinguished children.

"The deceased, although only a humble workman, belonged to the latter category. He was our co-worker in the good that we wished to do towards the public well-being of our fellow citizens. We respect him for not having deserted this cause on his deathbed and for having left his fellow citizens an example of moral courage which they so need in order to be a match for those foreign sources that beset them."

Burlesque rubs shoulders here with the irreligious and it is not the least distressing aspect of the scene in this cemetery that it recalls the burials of both Belgium and France. To make of the deceased 'one of the most distinguished children of the Church' is ludicrous: to praise him for what is regarded by the Church as the most dreadful misfortune, is irreligious, and we understand that it took four men, three self-styled Catholics and one Protestant to say it.

It is not this that Catholicism means by good and moral courage and if it is necessary, in order to be a match for those foreign sources which beset us, to die excommunicate and to be barred no matter where, we pity the poor Catholics who prefer to be assisted on their deathbed by the *Institut Canadien* rather than by the merciful minister of the Almighty.

By the grace of God, we are not accustomed to hearing liberal thinkers or Protestants holding forth in this country over the grave of a Catholic and using his sad example as a threat and challenge to the religious sentiment of the whole population; we hope that this spectacle will provide some beneficial results and encourage a large number of people to reflect on the disastrous consequences of their revolt against the authority of the Church. This is the first tomb that opens to receive a member of the *Institut*; God knocked suddenly and the forgiving words of a priest could not arrive soon enough to effect a reconciliation. Which will be the second?

---

8 DIVINE v. CIVIL LAW

The True Witness and Catholic Chronicle, Montreal
December 3, 1869

Right To Be Buried in Consecrated Ground

This is the heading of an article that appeared the other day in *The Montreal Herald*, and was provoked by the circumstances we are about to narrate.

A few days ago a man named Joseph Guibord died rather suddenly, and without the services of the priest. The deceased at the time of his death was a member of a society called *L'Institut Canadien,* now under the ban of the Church; and membership in which virtually excludes from all participation whilst living in the Sacraments, and after death in the offices of the Catholic Church which as do all other religious bodies – (the Catholic Church) claims the right of determining her own conditions of Communion.

The friends of the deceased notified the fact of the death to the ecclesiastical authorities, and demanded for him the last offices which the Church renders to her children departed. These, seeing that the said Joseph Guibord by his own deliberate act had knowingly and wilfully refused to submit himself to her when living, were of course refused. His friends were told that they might bury the body of the deceased in the *Côte des Neiges* Cemetery if they so pleased; but not in that particular portion of it which by special religious rites has been consecrated or set apart for the reception of the mortal remains of those who die in peace with the

Catholic Church, and in her Communion. Upon this the friends of the deceased took his body to the Protestant Cemetery where it now lies; and they have also instituted legal proceedings to compel the ecclesiastical authorities to receive it into the religiously consecrated portion of the Catholic Cemetery.

This raises the question stated by *The Herald* of the "Right To Be Buried In Consecrated Ground."

Such a right, legally considered, cannot exist unless in virtue of a special contract. For no one can it be claimed as a legal or natural right, that his body be buried in consecrated ground set apart by religious rites for burial purposes. For the sake of decency and of the public health, the civil magistrate very properly insists that the dead shall be buried, and in ground that may not be disturbed or used for other purposes. He can insist therefore that there be cemeteries; but he cannot insist that the land so set apart or secularly consecrated, shall also be spiritually consecrated; for he has no right or power to compel the performance of any purely spiritual act or religious function.

Now in the *Côte des Neiges* Cemetery there are two distinct things. The whole thereof has been by law set apart, or secularly consecrated for burial purposes; and over and above this, a portion of the ground so secularly consecrated, has been spiritually consecrated by the performance of certain religious rites. The questions then at issue are simply these:– "Has any one, not dying in communion with the Catholic Church, a legal right to be buried after death in that particular portion of the cemetery which by special spiritual acts has been set apart, or consecrated by the Church for the reception of the bodies of those who die in her communion?" And – "Did the deceased Joseph Guibord die in communion with the Catholic Church?"

To the first question we reply – No. No one can claim as a legal right to be buried after death in ground spiritually consecrated.

Of the second question, the Church alone is the competent judge, for she alone has the power of determining the conditions of communion.

Thus the case of Joseph Guibord is very simple. His friends are at liberty to bury him in ground legally or secularly set apart or consecrated for burial purposes; but they have not the right to bury him in ground spiritually consecrated, for the reception of the bodies of those, and of those alone, who die in communion with the Church.

---

9 THE COURT CASE: FREE THINKERS PERSECUTE THE CHURCH

L'Ordre, Montreal
January 25, 1870 [translation]

The free thinkers of the *Institut Canadien* do not yet have the fierce instincts of their European models, but one senses that they are developing them quickly. And if it were not for their weakness in number and influence, they would soon end up by being more than a match for those whose doctrine they follow.

To ruin the authority of the Church and to force it to submit willy-nilly to the whims of the civic authority, that is the objective at which these good apostles of free thinking want to arrive in the name of the great principle of tolerance, of which their leader speaks.

In the case that the *Institut* is setting up against the religious authority regarding the refusal of an ecclesiastical burial for the body of Guibord, the excommunicant, one sees shining through clearly that spirit of aggression and of hatred of the Church which animates these champions of free thought.

To see the persistence with which they wanted to involve our civil courts in this question of an exclusively religious character; to see the audacity with which they wanted to encroach upon its prerogatives, to the extent of destroying its influence, one recognizes more and more the hypocrisy of these "children submissive to the Church" in their deceitful protestations of submission to the judgment of the Court of Rome which has just attacked them.

What surprises and saddens even more in this case, is not even so much the provocative attitude of the members of the *Institut Canadien* in the face of the ecclesiastical authority, but that of a Catholic judge who allows himself to be led astray, to the detriment of the religious authority either by an ignorance of the treaties and laws that safeguard the existence of the prerogatives of our religion in this country, or by an incapacity to understand their purport and spirit, it being outside the limits of his jurisdiction to interfere in matters that are not in the least in the scope of civil courts.

"We ask ourselves," the *Journal des Trois-Rivières* so well put it "after having read the statement on this case of the administrator of the diocese of Montreal, who represents the bishop at this time, (we ask ourselves) after having learned of the order of His Honour Judge Mondelet, if we are in a country where the free exercise of Catholic worship is allowed by solemn treaties, or if we live under the despotism of the Tsar of Russia, or if we revert to pagan times."

This arbitrary interference, which attracted attention in so deplorable a way, in forcing the representative of the bishop to appear before a civil judge to justify a judgment given by him in his capacity as an ecclesiastical judge within the limits of his jurisdiction, is heightened even further by the occasion of the interrogation to which the *curé* of Notre Dame was forced to submit.

The prosecutors thought that by wiles and threats it would be easy to draw from this *slave* long used to the yoke of religious *intolerance* proof of the correctness of their position; but they reckoned without realizing the illumination which exists in this *backwater* from progress and the force and strength which comes from adherence to duty.

One cannot but admire the attitude taken by Master Rousselot in face of those who, espousing the malice of the *Institut*, wished to misuse both his position and the weakness of the court, to obtain answers that only a religious authority had the right to demand from him.

We ardently wish the lesson on law and on jurisdiction, that the court received in this circumstance, will be useful to it at the opportune time.

The testimony of the *curé* of Notre Dame brings into the open the question raised by the case. As of today we begin its publication, and we urge our readers to read it.

They will find there sure evidence to show them what is the domain of religious authority and what is the jurisdiction of a civil court in these matters.

They will see there above all that true liberty, that the noble independence to which all men aspire is not to be found in doctrines subversive to all authority, but in the sacred lessons where the sublime slavery of duty is preached; not in the temples of free thought but in the Church of God.

10 THE COURT CASE: BIASED REPORTING BY CATHOLIC JOURNALS

Le Pays, Montreal
March 28, 1870 [translation]

The counsel's speech proceeds slowly in this case without, however, wearying the interest of the public. The spectator's room is congested each day. M. Cassidy ended on Saturday the slightly disjointed paraphrasing of the points of law submitted by M. Jetté. In the arranging of the defense, M. Cassidy seemed to aim his plea more to the public than to the court. The reporters had to make numerous cuts to give to this speech a true character of reality plus application to the case. The "You are Peter and on this rock I will build, etc.", and "one must obey God before Mammon" took up most of this interminable verbal discourse. Besides it seems to us that it was St. Paul who said "There is no power which does not come from God, and it is He who ordains those on earth and that is why those who oppose these authorities resist the order of God." If this means anything it is that we should obey God Himself in obeying the authority of the judge and to pretend to be God Himself is to scorn his words. These few remarks are sufficient to upset the whole pattern of the speaker's argument.

Those who have attended these debates and who read the *Minerve* and the *Nouveau-Monde* must be very narrow-minded or as dishonest as the newspapers if they resist or indignantly deny that these accounts which are rendered there daily are false and deceitful. Beyond the style of the lawyers of the prosecution which they are pleased to criticize, and which will sustain, we are sure, the comparison with the diction of the lawyers of the defense, they pretend to report the text of what MM. Laflamme and Doutre said, and every assertion thereafter is an outright lie. If they had pretended to be making commentaries everyone would have known what they wanted to say, but when they place parts of the speech in quotation marks, to make it seem that that is the text and that all that is false, they fall into what the French criminal law terms "false documentation." When they are in the service of truth, it seems that falsehood is allowed, at least that is the ethics practiced by our confrères.

A day does not pass that a new falsehood does not find its way into the columns of these newspapers. Thus one day they attributed to M. Doutre the statement that one should congratulate the Indians for having put to death and martyred the Jesuits. The following day they made him say that Catholicism is a pure form of religion of which it is necessary to rid oneself to become free; another day he was to have said that Voltaire and E. Sue are the only books that permit emancipation of thought.

If these newspapers have readers naive enough to swallow these stupidities, these latter are as much to be pitied as the former are despicable. And you will see, that in order not to contradict themselves, these newspapers do not publish any of the speeches which they thus distort. See, as an example of these distortions, the calumnies constantly attributed to Judge Mondelet which remain in all their horror, in spite of the denials given by the Judge himself; see as another example, the suppression of M. Dessaulles' reply to a question which they published fully.

Our colleagues have an honourable institution! They know they cannot descend any lower in public contempt and they flounder in their filth without any feeling of disgust. Let us allow them to do so, and let us rely on the certainty that there is another day tomorrow.

---

11 THE COURT CASE: M. DOUTRE AND THE JESUIT MARTYRS

L'Ordre, Montreal
March 29, 1870 [translation]

"Let us honour the small tribe of Indians who forced the disappearance from this continent of the seeds of this Society of Jesus."

It is M. Doutre, Joseph, who said that. Let's go M. Dessaulles, you have been bettered. The Buies, the Lanctots, the Chiniquys were your competitors, your rivals, but they were worth no more than you. Finally you found your Master. M. Joseph Doutre has excelled you. You will complain of it, that is certain.

You have long proceeded cautiously in your premises. Your duty as Justice of the Peace, of Inquisitor of his Civil Majesty, forced you to hesitate to advance further against those whom you regard as colleagues in this Ecclesiastical Inquisition. But nothing liked that stopped Guibord's lawyer; he had the strength of his conviction, and he used the noose which you had spun to hang this black race which was your pet aversion.

Indeed the souls of the executioners who murdered Fathers Brébeuf, Garnier and Jogues and so many others who with them represent the noblest figures of our history, must have thrilled with pleasure when they saw a "civilized" being of the nineteenth century undertake the justification of their barbarism before a court composed of men belonging to that very religion whose apostles they had tortured and massacred.

One asks oneself what ignorance, what ineptitude, what powerless fury could have inspired such sentiments in this democrat, in this strong spirit, in this progressive individual, in this member of the Institute of progress!

M. Doutre how could you, you who were raised in the shadows of the steeple of the Catholic Church; you who were able, thanks to the solicitude of the clergy, to learn to speak this language which you now use to abuse them; you who owe, like so many others, the position you occupy today to the sacrifices which the religion you vilify inspired, how could you not by one single movement of recognition acknowledge the meaning of what these men did, men who cemented with their blood the stones which serve as the bedrock of your nationality!

You, *frère patriot*, who never find the liberty which our people here enjoy extensive enough, you who pride yourself for so much love, such patriotism, have you never thought of leafing through the pages of your history?

So you have never suspected to whom Canada owes the most beautiful and glorious pages of her annals?

So you have never learnt who was responsible for the most important discoveries, who carried the torch of civilization in the most remote areas of the continent?

You, a man of progress, you push ignorance to the point of not knowing who first spread education among us!

Poor M. Doutre, can the issue dull the human brain to such a degree?

You, in applauding the martyrdom of these men, before whom even the Protestants refrain, struck with admiration of these men whose effects were kept even by their executioners as talismans. You, what have you done for the advancement of knowledge in your society? What have you ever done even to compare with the tasks that these men imposed upon themselves for the maintenance of civilization on our shores?

What products have you pulled from your learned intelligence to advance this progress which you are so anxious to implant among us? What works have you done to raise the level of intelligence of your compatriots whom you find so backward?

Nothing!! . . . No, let us not deceive ourselves, you did do something, . . . ? You endowed the land with *The Betrothed of 1812* . . . ?

You will never be a martyr M. Doutre.

---

12 THE COURT CASE: A POPULAR INTERPRETATION

Le Pays, Montreal
March 29, 1870 [translation]

On leaving the court last evening, a local "Smart Alec" explained the role of the lawyers of the defense to a friend of his. The two speakers seemed most animated:
– Wait then, until I explain to you . . .
– Come on then, explain as you will.
– Well, I tell you, the lawyers share the job.
– That's right, because they share their money.
– So, listen then!
– Go on.
– So, M. Jetté pleads the constitutional, Mr. Cassidy, the spiritual, and M. Trudel, the supernatural.
– Oh! That's it, that is why I understood nothing Monday.
– It is not a question of understanding, believe me!

This conversation, between two common people, is not without significance, and contains a sound measure of wisdom.

We present it as we heard it.

---

13 THE COURT CASE: RELIGIOUS FREEDOM v. GALLICANISM

The True Witness And Catholic Chronicle, Montreal
April 15, 1870

The Guibord Case. – This case, destined to be one of the *causes célèbres* of Canada, has already been discussed and argued at great length before M. Judge Mondelet, whose decision is anxiously looked for, and may be expected in a short time. *En attendant* we propose to say a few words to our readers on the subject.

The case originated in this wise. The deceased, Joseph Guibord, a member of a virulent anti-Catholic society, *L'Institut Canadien*, and as such condemned by the Church, died suddenly in the month of November last. As a member of *L'Institut* he had for some years been excluded from participation in the sacraments of the Church; and having never made his Paschal communion, had necessarily fallen under the condemnation and sentence of excommunication pronounced by the Council of Trent against all who do not communicate at Easter.

His friends demanded that, in spite of this well known, long established and universally recognized law of the Church, his body should receive ecclesiastical sepulture – in the sense of being laid in that part of the Cemetery reserved for those who die members of, and in actual communion with, the Church. . . . The present action is brought – nominally by the widow of the deceased, virtually by the *Institut Canadien* – to compel the ecclesiastical authorities to grant ecclesiastical sepulture to the said Joseph Guibord.

Two questions, and two only, are at issue: one of law, the other of fact.

The question of law is this – "Has any one, not being at the time of his decease, a member of, or in communion with the Catholic Church, a civil right to ecclesiastical sepulture?"

The question of fact is this – "Was the deceased Joseph Guibord, at the time of his decease, a member of, or in communion with, the Catholic Church?"

The first question, that of law, is well answered by the *Evening Telegraph* of the 8th instant, as follows:–

> "If Guibord died out of the pale of the Church of Rome, he has no more right to be interred in the Roman Catholic cemetery than the writer of these lines would have."

This answer will we think commend itself to all. There remains therefore only the question of fact – "Was Guibord in communion with the Church at the time of his decease?"

Who is to decide? The question of fact is purely a spiritual question, and therefore belongs exclusively to the domain of the spiritual judge. The latter replies, that the deceased Guibord was not, at the time of his death, in communion with the ecclesiastical body of which he is the mouthpiece. The civil judge is invoked to declare the contrary; in other words, to determine the spiritual status of the deceased!!!

For be it remembered that there is no dispute as to the latter's civil status, or his civil rights thence accruing. No one contests Guibord's civil right to a civil burial in the cemetery; all that the ecclesiastical authorities contend for is that they be not compelled to give ecclesiastical burial, in a particular part of the cemetery, to the remains of one who died outside of the pale of their Church.

The cause was pleaded on the 17th ult., and the discussion was continued for many days. On the part of the *Institut Canadien* it was argued by its advocates that the old penal laws of the Plantagenets, and the Tudors were in force in Canada; and that therefore no sentence of excommunication was valid, unless ratified by the civil power. In the name of Civil and Religious Liberty the sanguinary codes of Henry VIII, and of his daughter Elizabeth, were invoked to repress the spiritual pretensions of the Church of Rome in Canada. This was M. Laflamme's chief line of argument; but we would remind him that it is a ticklish and dangerous one to pursue. . . .

Penal laws are as it were a two edged sword, and it would fare badly with M. Laflamme, and his friends of the *Institut*, were the *Six Articles* of Henry VIII, or the bloody statutes of his daughter to be vigorously applied in Canada. Nevertheless we feel grateful to our liberal friends in that they have thus exposed the inherent badness of their cause, which can only be supported by appeals to the tyrannous legislation of a tyrannical age.

M. Doutre who followed M. Laflamme, bearing in mind we suppose the instructions of the attorney to his Counsel – "No case: abuse the other party's lawyer" – pitched into the Jesuits with hearty goodwill, and in a style which must have gladdened the hearts of the frequenters of the *salons* of the Pompadour, and other illustrious strumpets of the last century, if they be still cognisant of what is passing in this upper world.

MM. Jette, Cassidy, and Trudel appeared for the defence, and our only regret is that we can not lay before our readers their masterly replies. This the limited space at our command forbids; but we take this opportunity of expressing our admiration of, and gratitude for, the manner in which they repudiated the slavish principles of Gallicanism or Erastianism, and vindicated the fundamental principle of religious liberty: That is to say, the absolute independence of the Church, within her own domain, of the State or Civil power. . . .

14 JUDGE MONDELET'S DECISION: A VICTORY FOR CIVIL LIBERTY

Le Pays, Montreal
May 3, 1870 [translation]

At eleven o'clock yesterday morning, His Honour, Judge Mondelet, took his place on the bench to pass judgment on the notorious Guibord case.

Since ten o'clock, numerous lively groups, debating the probable judgment, congested the approaches to the Palace, or paced feverishly along the narrow alleys of the square which extends in front of the building.

At half-past ten the majority of seats, of the reserved benches, were occupied and the circumference of the wall surrounding the room was filled minute by minute with worried and curious heads.

An indescribable air of solemnity seemed to hover over this vast room of the Superior Court. Each watched the countenance of his neighbour, examining his features and his attitude, as if to read there, to discover there his personal thoughts. Even the lawyers whom the experience of victory and of defeat had accustomed to these contests, and who normally awaited the decrees of the court with a fairly indifferent attitude, had

lost their usual impassiveness, and whether it was the magnetic influence emanating from all these brains, from this gathering of hearts, or genuine concern, the result of a decision of such serious consequence, the lawyers seemed moved and subdued by the irresistible effect of the prevailing mood.

Let us first announce that the decision of His Honour, the learned judge, Mondelet, a decision extensively explained, was in favour of the plaintiff, Mme. Guibord, and consequently a decision in favour of the *Institut Canadien* of which the deceased, Guibord, was a member before his death.

This noteworthy judgment, which will undoubtedly serve as a precedent, will establish, once and for all, the position of the law on these delicate matters of the powers of the two jurisdictions which have been engaged in a constant struggle since the establishment of the legitimate political power of the state.

Some readers will perhaps think that we wantonly exaggerate the significance of this case, and that it is nothing. The courts of Lower Canada have already passed judgments against the pretentions of ecclesiastical authority in parallel cases which certainly added to the uncertainty of the controversy even more; but in none of them has there been such a confusion, such a mixture of diversified elements, and such an effort to discredit the law and justice in the midst of violent appeals to political opinion and the naive but respectful credulity of the mass of Catholics.

In this judgment it is a matter of particulars, of individuals reduced to their appropriate force, having to defend themselves as much against their own doubts, their hesitations and their weaknesses, as to struggle against these powerful influences that intrude upon the very privacy of their own home. In the Guibord case, a long-standing institution had to be dealt with incidentally, an institution resting on the principles of wise liberty, the foundation of which goes back to a time when such unfortunate conflicts were not known; an institution to which all those who enjoy self-education, who enjoy broadening the scope of their knowledge, in an *ad hoc* location, belong and do still belong, discussing literary and scientific subjects, embellishing their spirits, raising with these communal studies their level of intelligence and their hearts above the vulgar preoccupations of material life. It is this institution, so slandered, so defaced and a party to the suit in this debate, that above all makes this case so interesting.

Well, we say it today, it is with as much profound sadness as true joy that we record the triumph of the great principle of civil liberty, recognized and sanctioned by the law. We sadly resent that in this land of America, in the shadow of English law, we were obliged to run to the courts to obtain a just verdict, the denial of which, however the case was obscured, would have delighted many believers, people more lost than guilty. It is this belief that saddens us, for this difference of views reduces and diminishes not only the group of people desirous of good, of advancement of social and political progress, but also, because it weakens and disintegrates the nucleus of a formerly hardy nationality which, imperceptibly, but in a very few years, if these divisions continue, will disappear – overrun, submerged by the element that surrounds, encircles, and hems it in from all sides. Whatever happens, Canadians at the moment are still masters of their destiny; it is up to them to choose between two very different alternatives.

The decision that has been rendered brings us real joy because the judgment clearly demonstrates to the members of the *Institut Canadien*, as to general opinion, the justice and legality of a cause of which many, in the minds of numerous persecutions, had learned to despair. Finally, we rejoice at what His Honour the judge, M. Mondelet, who is considered to be one of the most honourable, the most enlightened, the most knowledgeable of our magistrates, understood and applied as much with scientific care as with a sense of justice, with impartiality and considerable reason, the principle of law. Perhaps the judgment will be laid before the Court of Appeal, but it will hardly be able to alter the decision without taking into account in its considerations the principles which negate all civil law and

that anarchy which is exalted into a system; for what no power can ever reverse is the acquisition and the possession of those rights which are today regarded by all civilized people as the heritage of mankind; it is to this indestructible monument, cemented by the blood and tears of thousands of martyrs, erected to the cause of liberty and tolerance and progress, that the judgment pronounced in the Guibord case is connected as a single stone in a colossal pyramid.

Seen on a small scale in a practical way, the decree of His Honour the judge, M. Mondelet settles the difficulty between the *Fabrique* and the parishioner, nothing more, nothing less. Considered from the point of view of principles, it has a higher and further bearing; it pronounces on a dispute, prolific with disagreements and settles in its sphere, one of the most arresting problems of our time in the Catholic world, the separation of Church and State. Henceforth, the Guibord case will be part of the judicial annals of Lower Canada; it marks an epoch and renews the chain of traditions.

---

15 MONDELET ABOLISHES TRADITIONAL LIBERTIES OF ROMAN CATHOLICS

La Minerve, Montreal
May 3, 1870 [translation]

The Guibord case took neither a very long, nor a very decisive step. The judgment of His Honour M. Mondelet the Judge was awaited only as a base for future operations. Between the two irreconcilable principles that are debated all over the world, one to bring to it order and peace, the other to divert for its own advantage, all influence, all domination, all those situations which assist arrogance and egoism, there is no plateau where they are able to halt by mutual consent. It is necessary that they roll on down to the very bottom and we have but to wait to see who will be crushed. These two great enemies have been in combat since the tree of the Garden of Paradise let fall those two fruits, good and evil. Yesterday order got the worst of it but we expect that insubordination will not remain triumphant long.

His Honour M. Mondelet, the Judge, gave a pronouncement learnedly elaborate and we do not want to raise the slightest suspicion about his motives. The judgment of any court is right in our view and in all the presumptions of integrity and capacity. That is why we don't want to begin again a speech for the defense that has been exhausted; but we will be allowed to draw conclusions from the sentence of the Honourable Judge. Until this day we thought that the liberties and privileges of the Catholic Church were admitted and established in Canada. His Honour's decision reverses these pretensions and history will decree that this restriction of liberties which he proclaimed at the demand of so-called Catholics who call themselves liberals and who guarantee to their school the benefits of all licence, denies society the advantage of all true liberty.

The Church has its organization. It seemed to us that the legalization of its existence authorized the maintenance of its rules. Nobody can exist without having the right to regulate himself. No institution can exist in which all the world ends up being its master and where the masters end up being puppets.

If the consecration of the privileges of the Catholic Church is not a mockery, and if the fundamentals and necessary doctrine unique to Catholicism is submission, it is the right of the Church alone to know and to say when it is satisfied, and who respects its teachings.

From the moment when no one forces citizens to become Catholic it seems to us just that no one can force the Church to accept so-called Catholics who are not only not Catholics but also wage a most dangerous and perfidious war against it. And when the Church has established laws outside of which she does not recognize members, how is it that the whim of a stranger declares to be what is not and can impose this decision on it.

We know that a vestry or a priest is not the Church and we know that the priest who is able to assert to a judge that such is Catholic doctrine and assert it with a great de-gree of force is to that degree erroneous in his interpretation. But what a remarkable thing it is to pretend to be a Catholic in order to enjoy certain Catholic privileges when, on every occasion, one attacks Catholic doctrine and what a sad position to be in to be proving that one has always been a good Catholic and, all the while, to be blaspheming against its doctrines and institutions.

It was pleaded that Guibord was not undeserving of the Church and that he was always worthy of the privileges due to Catholics; and to uphold this argument one is forced to arrive at the proposition that Guibord should have been buried in a Catholic cemetery because the Church is an intolerant and usurping power whose pretentions and arrogances must be destroyed, and must be reduced to impotence.

This is what we regret in this case. One has left in obscurity the pretentions of those proceedings to batter against that immortal Body – left them in that obscurity in which they want to be enveloped.

In those pretentions, the arguments of the prosecution are but personal but the judgment of the court is a solemn act, and regarding this point we profoundly regret the severe words that His Honour addressed to the Church. As Catholics we are obliged to object. His Honour has only the right to judge the point of law, but as soon as the learned judge transports his sentence into the domain of valuation we are justified in complaining against that which so cruelly wounds our sentiments.

If the judgment of His Honour remains the interpretation of the law of the country, one can say that the free exercise of Catholic worship is abolished in Canada – that free exercise which was permitted by the Protestants and which no honest Protestant has yet attempted to reduce.

16 MONDELET'S TYRANNY

L'Ordre, Montreal
May 3, 1870 [translation]

The judgment rendered in the Guibord case was as expected.

The malicious insinuations, the thinly disguised rancour that was obvious despite numerous pleas of impartiality by that ranter who has been making a mockery of the bench for too many years now, could leave not the slightest doubt about his opinions which were conceived even before the speeches for the defense and the arguments of the lawyers of the case, and which formed the basis of the judgment passed down.

The *Institut Canadien* can momentarily congratulate itself, for having discovered in him the instrument necessary to conclude satisfactorily the conspiracy that its members had so long woven against ecclesiastical authority.

These free thinkers had no trust in right, they had recourse to that brute force that a judge has at his disposal to enforce the execution of his orders.

They knew full well what advantage could be taken of this power placed in irresponsible hands.

They knew well beforehand how avidly this unfortunate fellow who, under the pretext of independence, turns at the mercy of every wind; this judge, who today reverses the judgment he passed yesterday, who is seduced by praise and prejudiced by any remark, would accept the role that had been given him to play.

They knew well beforehand that this man who, ever since he has been on the bench, has accumulated insults in order to prove he is above public opinion, who has opposed his colleagues and good sense, for just as long, under the pretext of independence, would joyfully grasp at this new opportunity to assert his alleged steadfastness of character.

They succeeded, but they should hasten to make merry, for their triumph will not last long. And before they put Guibord's remains in the Catholic Cemetery, the other members of the *Institut* may well have time to fulfil their three score years and ten in his company.

For, happily for society, if governments are sometimes unfortunate enough to place in a position of such responsibility, fellows who bring so little to it, at least the law offers palliatives, and to those whom arbitrary action attacks in this way, the law provides recourse to appeal.

The case is going to be appealed to the Court of Revision, and only there will it be possible to see in reality if civil authority is disposed to respect religious authority, or if, in spite of the treaties that guarantee the latter, and in contempt of the beliefs of the majority of the population, it will force the exact meaning of the law to authorize its tyrannical intrusion into a question of exclusively religious jurisdiction.

If such a denial of justice can be perpetrated, which we have no desire to believe, religious authority, thus persecuted, will have no alternative but to scorn this judgment that cannot affect it.

To submit thus would be to accept the claims of civil law to superiority over divine law.

What we say, is that we hope and are convinced that the *Fabrique* which has the honour in the battle of fighting for the flag of religion, will have the courage of its convictions.

And if civil authority, persisting in this course of action, endeavours to enforce the execution of such a judgment, only one course of action would remain open, and that would be abstention.

Even if the constabulary, even if the police, even if all civilians support the execution of the sentence, even if Guibord's remains are escorted by those same men who escort criminals to prison, the *Institut* would triumph, but its victory would be a victory of shame, and the stigma of anathema that shrouds the memory of this excommunicate, will become more apparent. And from this spot that will be chosen in the Catholic Cemetery to inter these pathetic remains, other Catholics will remove the bodies of their dead, just as in life they would have remained aloof in their spirit and in their hearts from schools of error and houses of profligacy.

We give below the analysis of the indictment of Judge Mondelet that we borrow from the *Nouveau Monde*.

His Honour, Judge Mondelet, began, at eleven o'clock this morning, to render judgment on the Guibord case.

After entering into a consideration of the extensive preliminaries, and having analysed the proceedings, His Honour the Judge entered into a consideration of the legal questions.

First of all, did the Court have any jurisdiction in this case?

In demonstrating the origins of the Superior Court, the judge finds that this was beyond doubt.

To discover which is the law that governs the country in the matter of interment, the judge examines the various articles of the surrender of Montreal and of the Act of Cession, which guarantee the freedom of the Catholic religion, and says that too much importance must not be attached to the words *Roman church and Roman rites.*

The Treaty of Cession did not abolish the old French law, on the contrary, it is precisely that law which is guaranteed and insured for us, and consequently the appeal as well as the violation exists here as it existed in France.

He cites diverse judgments and the opinion of Sir George Etienne Cartier who claims that the Catholics of Montreal can force the *curé* of Notre Dame to administer Baptism, Marriage and Extreme Unction, in spite of the division of the town into canonical parishes.

Does the Bishop of Montreal have the right to forbid the granting of ecclesiastical burial to the remains of Guibord, and could the *curé* legally obey him?

This refusal is justified neither by the law, nor by canon law, nor by achievement.

Thus, the judgment will order that Guibord's remains be granted burial *according to law and according to custom.*

The judge's pronouncement was not a sentence, but an indictment against the Venerable Bishop of Montreal and the Chief Administrator.

17 A DECISION FOR FREEDOM AND PROGRESS

The Daily Witness, Montreal
May 4, 1870

The decision in the Guibord case marks an epoch in the history of Lower Canada, and is fraught with consequences of the utmost moment in connection with the relations of Church and State and their influence over the rights of individuals. The most remarkable feature of this case, and the most hopeful for the cause of liberty, is the circumstance of its being a contest between the Roman Catholic Church and a numerous and influential party of its own adherents, professing entire belief in all its doctrines, but who offer resistance to the ecclesiastical tyranny which has tried to crush *l'Institut Canadien* and to smother free thought and independent scientific enquiry in Lower Canada. It is a most encouraging sign when a reform is begun and carried out inside of an institution itself. There is now some prospect that Roman Catholics in Canada will enjoy a share of the freedom already secured to their co-religionists in France, Austria, and Spain, who by their own efforts have burst asunder the fetters of ecclesiastical bondage. . . .

Leaving matters of creed and doctrine aside, we cannot but think that every true friend of freedom and progress will rejoice at this decision of Judge Mondelet, and hope and pray that it may ultimately be confirmed.

18 L'ORDRE DEFENDS ITS ATTACK ON MONDELET

L'Ordre, Montreal
May 10, 1870 [translation]

The Herald is scandalized by the manner in which we spoke of Judge Mondelet, with respect to his conduct in the Guibord case. For their benefit, we will repeat what we have already replied to *Le Pays.* Deplorable as the verdict may be, from our point of view, we will certainly refrain from criticizing the judge presiding over this case. He himself refrained from particularly ill-inspired and offensive comments when he realized how much the questions raised had stirred up thought on all sides.

The proportions he had allowed this debate to take, the principles upon which he himself had provoked discussion and which enveloped and at the same time exposed to the battle the most established and traditional teachings of the Catholic Church, the invariably hostile position which he had adopted against the claims of the defence, the numerous obstacles which he brought forth as if for the mere pleasure of embarrassing the counsels for the defence and to impede the development of their argument – all this had, despite his numerous protestations of impartiality, prepared popular opinion for the verdict which was inevitably returned. In fact, in view of all the harm M. Mondelet brought upon himself in warding off the blows of the defence against the claims of the *Institut*, many people began to wonder what would be the outcome of this revived battle of the three Horaces and three Curiaces.

We did not therefore, denounce the tribunal, but rather M. Mondelet's confusion of the attributes of a judge with his sympathies for free conscience and free thought. We did not attack him as the judge, but as the adversary of religious authority. . . . And we did not believe that we owed more respect for him than that which he demonstrated to the religious court; which is in fact superior to the one over which he presides to the same degree as is religious to civil authority.

We realize that *The Herald* will find this statement of principles amusing: but we will not take exception to this. . . .

We hold sacred the teachings and authority with which the divine founder of the Catholic Church has entrusted those whom he constituted his successors. The Church has invariably expelled from its bosom those who have chosen to disregard this authority or to reject one small particle of its truth.

If one wishes to remain Catholic, one must therefore accept the entire body of this doctrine, and reject none of it; or else withdraw from it and renounce all the privileges which one formerly regarded as one's own.

Simple good sense can dictate nothing else, and *The Herald* has had the good judgment to recognize this in the past. From the moment, it states, that a man professes membership in a church, he must clearly conform to the discipline of that religious body, just as he would to any other society of which he were a member, and in the case of an infraction (or violation) he must accept the set punishment.

Very well! Is this not the claim of the defence in this case?

But we, along with *The Herald*, cannot push this comparison further, and we deny the civil courts the right to regard theological questions as part of their jurisdiction: and we question their competence in this area. In certain matters of a secondary nature the Church has, in effect, the appearance and attributes of a corporate body, within a society: but it is more than a corporation, it is a legitimate power and authority. The moment its existence is recognized and accepted in a country, one accordingly grants it the right to exist in its own way.

Moreover, it is accepted in principle within the Church, that it has always denied the right to earthly authorities to intrude in questions of dogma and discipline. In deciding upon the merit of Guibord's case, and on the validity or insufficiency of the reasons for the refusal of burial, has Judge Mondelet not passed beyond the limits which he should have respected?

But, in order to put the case in a more favourable light, they have spoken only of Guibord's rights in the cemetery as a Catholic parishioner of Montreal. Without commenting on the absurdity of this proposal, we would immediately state – what the defence has invoked through Trudel – that the title of Catholic and parishioner owned by the deceased Guibord has never entitled him to a common share in the wealth of the Church; that cemeteries, like churches, are not the property of the people, but of the religious authority; and that this right is widely acknowledged – in that no religious body may dispose of ground used as a cemetery or of a church without the permission of the bishop; and that this principle is accepted and practiced everywhere. Judge Mondelet's decision, apart from the bad light which he deigned proper to throw on it, was therefore injurious to ecclesiastical jurisdiction. To want to compel the Church to bury Guibord's body in the Catholic Cemetery, is to violate the right of ownership, as sacred for the public body as for the individual.

We as Catholics are, therefore, justified in our objection to this decision; which not only offends in our eyes the inviolability of property, but attacks the immunity of the Catholic Church – which is guaranteed by treaties, without reservation for jurisdiction or exceptions of doctrine.

---

19 MONDELET'S DECISION UNCONSTITUTIONAL

L'Ordre, Montreal
May 11, 1870
From Le Journal des Trois-Rivières
[translation]

. . . If the decision of His Honour, Judge Mondelet is precise, and if the explanations he provided for the decision are correct, one must naturally come to the conclusion that the Catholic Church is not free in Canada, and that civil power can restrain freedom of worship, and can force the church to grant burial, to administer the sacraments, when it is impossible for the church to do so when the doctrines it teaches do not permit. Now up until today, we had believed that in keeping with the treaties of the surrender of Canada to England, the Catholic Church had absolute freedom of worship in this country.

We will not amuse ourselves by discussing the judge's motives in rendering his decision, which we had already expected. The reasons he gives have already been fully discussed, and are for the most part hopeless for all devout Catholics who are upright in spirit, and free of prejudice.

His Honour disapproved of those, in France, who used the police to force a priest to administer the last Sacraments to a sick person. But this is merely an extreme consequence of the principles upon which the court leaned to render its decision. If in one particular case you can coerce the Church into violating the laws which govern it, you can do so equally well in another case. If you can force the Church to grant a burial, when divine law forbids it, you can also oblige the Church to administer all the sacraments. There is no happy medium. It is the principle of freedom and independence of the Church that is in question here. If civil courts have the right to tell the Church that it misapplies its dogma and its discipline, when through the voice of its regularly established judges it claims the opposite, it is no longer free or independent. These courts could force it to do whatever they wish. . . .

Pilate had one day in which to judge the Saviour of mankind. It was painful for him to condemn Jesus, and he even declared that he was washing his hands of the innocent blood of this virtuous man.

Judge Mondelet did not judge the Saviour of the world, but one of His ministers; and he, [Judge Mondelet] who so often referred to himself as the slave of the law, the servant of Caesar, and of civil power, did not even judge with the idea of washing his hands on the condemnation he pronounced. . . .

. . . It is Parliament's duty to oversee the conduct of the judges. It has the obligation to see that the Constitution remains intact. Well, the decision of His Honour, Judge Mondelet violates the Constitution, and negates the treaty that guarantees of freedom of worship. Consequently, we demand the dismissal of the judge, by the Federal Ministers, and we demand that all men in public life give back the rights, liberty and independence of the Catholic Church in this country.

20 THE DUTY OF TRUE CATHOLICS

*The True Witness And Catholic Chronicle,
Montreal
May 13, 1870*

It would be presumptuous on our part to discuss a point of *law* with a learned jurist like Judge Mondelet; but on a matter of *fact*, we may be permitted to hold and maintain our own opinion.

In the long and elaborate judgment pronounced by the said Judge in the Guibord case, and reported at length by *Minerve*, the Court asserted that neither in the Roman Ritual, nor in that known as the Ritual of Quebec, is there anything to justify the refusal of ecclesiastical sepulture to the deceased Guibord.

Now in both Rituals, ecclesiastical sepulture is expressly forbidden to all who fail in the performance of their Paschal duty – that is to say, the duty or obligation imposed by the Lateran Council, of confessing and receiving the Eucharist at Easter time.

The Quebec Ritual says:

"Ecclesiastical sepulture is to be refused to those . . . who without a legitimate excuse shall have failed to accomplish their Paschal duty, unless at least they manifest signs of contrition."

The Roman Ritual says that ecclesiastical sepulture is to be refused to those who shall not have confessed and communicated at least once a year, and at Easter, and who die, making no signs of contrition.

Thus both the Quebec and the Roman Rituals agree in this; that therein ecclesiastical sepulture is expressly forbidden to all who wilfully abstain from confessing and receiving Holy Communion at Easter. But for some years the deceased Guibord had so abstained; and therefore to him ecclesiastical sepulture could not have been accorded, without a flagrant violation of the laws of the Church, as laid down in the two Rituals cited by Judge Mondelet.

If we take exception to the matter of the arguments on the Guibord case offered by *The Montreal Herald* of the 9th inst., we take none to the manner in which these arguments are put forward; for we gladly acknowledge the courteous and gentlemanly tone of the writer, whom we will strive to imitate in this respect.

"If," says *The Herald*, "Guibord had committed a religious offence for which excommunication was the legal punishment according to the recognized rules of the Church, to which he belonged; if he had been regularly excommunicated, not inferentially but expressly and personally after such fair opportunity of defence as the rules of equity require; if, moreover, the denial of ecclesiastical services at his burial were a part or a consequence of the sentence – these hypotheses being all answered in the affirmative we take it for granted that the refusal of such ceremonies would have been justifiable, and would have been maintained by the Courts."
– *Mont. Herald*, 9th inst.

Although Guibord had never been excommunicated expressly by name – and to do so might expose the person pronouncing excommunication to a legal action for defamation – in his case, it was not necessary; because the law under which he had fallen was the old established, publicly proclaimed, and universally accepted law of the Church, since an epoch long before the Reformation; and the denial of ecclesiastical sepulture is by that law expressly enjoined as one of the penalties on all without exception who violate its precepts. By that law, the Bishops, and priests are as much bound as are the laity: nor could either violate it, without incurring the extreme censures of the Church.

That law, to which the Church attaches so much importance, that THREE times every year for centuries past it has been read publicly from every Catholic pulpit, so that no one to whom it applies can plead ignorance of it – is contained in the canon of the Lateran Council *"Omnes ultriusque senus"*; and is to the effect that all persons, having attained years of discretion shall under pain of excision from the society of the faithful whilst living, and the refusal of *ecclesiastical sepulture* after death, receive the Sacrament of the Eucharist once a year at least, at Easter, and from their own parish priest, in their own parochial church. So well is this law known that it has given rise to a French idiomatic phrase, – "*faire ses Pâques.*"

Now this law Guibord had for some time, for years we believe, habitually and deliberately violated. For a length of time he had refused to approach the Altar and to receive Communion – *faire ses Pâques*; and as having died without absolution for this wilful, deliberate, and obstinate disobedience to the universally known law of the Church, accepted and acknowledged as binding in England before the Reformation, and in all Catholic countries to-day, Guibord was expressly excommunicate, and by the laws of the universal Church, *ecclesiastical* sepulture was expressly denied to him. No priest, no Bishop could authorise the giving of ecclesiastical sepulture to Guibord, even if he wished to do so, without himself becoming disobedient to the laws of the Church, and incurring her censure; for the law is binding on all without exception. This is the whole state of the case. Guibord, when living, refused to comply with the laws of the Church as to Paschal Communion, and was therefore by those laws incapable of receiving ecclesiastical sepulture when dead.

One other point in *The Herald*'s article we take up. The part of the cemetery in which it was offered to bury the body of Guibord is not "ground marked with opprobrium" – it is not even destined for the reception of the bodies of criminals – for the latter, if penitent, are buried just where other Catholics are buried. It is a part of the cemetery which, though as well protected against intrusion, or desecration as any other part, is not specially blest, and which is reserved for all those who die unbaptised, or cut off as Guibord was by the decree of the Lateran Council, from the society of the faithful. The child of our most respected Catholic citizen, dying without baptism would be buried there tomorrow; it conveys therefore a false impression to speak of it as "ground marked with opprobrium."

The Herald will pardon us for correcting him on some matters of fact, and will we trust accept our thanks for the courteous manner in which, when treating of matters wherein Catholics are particularly interested, he expresses himself.

---

21 IS SPIRITUAL CARE A CIVIL RIGHT?

The True Witness And Catholic Chronicle, Montreal
May 20, 1870

We cannot understand, perhaps because we are Papists, and therefore the slaves of logic and consistency, how men can abhor a religion which they profess, or profess a religion which they abhor. The members of the *Institut Canadien* profess to be Catholics, members of the Catholic Church, and yet, without ceasing, they revile her doctrines, repudiate her discipline, and insult her ministers. Why then do they continue to call themselves children of such a Church? Why seek after death to be interred amongst those whose society whilst living they repudiated, and whose belief they scouted as a vulgar superstition? Why ask for services for a corpse from a priest whose ministrations the living man spurned with contumely? If we held the opinions of a member of *L'Institut Canadien* we should deem it an outrage to be buried with Romanists, and an insult to our remains, to have the mummeries of Popery performed over them.

And yet we see this same *Institut*, whose prophet is Voltaire, the avowed enemy of Christianity, setting the machinery of the law in motion to obtain for one of their members deceased, who whilst living, deliberately and obstinately abstained from participation in her Sacraments, and who therefore was not in Communion with her – certain purely religious ministrations from the Catholic priest, whose ministrations whilst living he had deliberately and to the last moment of his existence, rejected! And this is done in the name of civil and religious liberty! We contend that the action

48

of the *Institut* is a direct attack upon all liberty, and should, as such, be opposed by men of all denominations.

Let us be logical and consistent. If the individual has rights, which the civil magistrate may enforce, to the spiritual services of the ministers of religion, it follows as a logical consequence that the latter, or minister of religion, must have spiritual rights over the individual which the civil courts are also bound to enforce. But here in Montreal, neither priest nor Bishop has any spiritual rights over any individual which the civil courts can enforce. Neither priest nor Bishop can compel any man against his will to take part in any manner in any act of Catholic worship, in any ceremony of the Catholic religion. The individual, though baptized by a Catholic priest, though admitted to the participation of the Sacraments, is free at any moment, and for any reason that seems good to him, without formal notice or warning of any kind given, to repudiate all connection with the Church; nor has the Church or her ministers any claim of any kind over him of which the civil courts can take cognisance. By parity of reason therefore, the Church should be equally free to repudiate, or reject from her bosom, any individual, without thereby being responsible for her conduct to any civil tribunal. If, however, the latter be invoked to enforce the performance of purely religious, or spiritual functions in behalf of the individual whom she has repudiated, why should not the same tribunal undertake to compel the spiritual allegiance which every baptized person owes to the Church? Rights and duties are always reciprocal terms. Where the one cannot be predicated, so neither can the other. But the Church in Montreal, as represented by the Bishop and the clergy has no spiritual rights, that the civil courts can take cognisance of, over the individual; so therefore neither has the latter any claims to the spiritual or religious services of the said Bishop and clergy which the civil courts are competent to enforce. Now the action of the *Institut Canadien* to compel by law the parochial clergy of Montreal to perform certain religious services, and to recite certain prayers to God over the mortal remains of Guibord, implies that the latter had *rights* which the civil courts can enforce, to certain spiritual ministrations: it implies therefore, as the corollary of this proposition – that the deceased owed certain spiritual *duties* to the ecclesiastical authorities, which the same courts were in like manner competent and bound to enforce. Yet there is not a member of the anti-Catholic society, whose course of action we are criticising, but would repudiate this logical and necessary consequence of his own premises. Again therefore that society stands self-convicted of the grossest inconsistency. Here, in short, is their thesis. The Catholic Church in Montreal has no rights than can be pleaded in a civil court to compel any man to accept her spiritual services, or to submit to her disciplinary rules; but the individual has civil rights to the spiritual services of the Catholic priest which the civil magistrate is bound to maintain. This is absurd. . . .

Even the Montreal *Witness* repudiates, as a monstrous absurdity the proposition that the individual has a civil right to the Sacraments of the Church. What have our Courts of Law, he asks, to do with the Sacraments? Well, carry out and apply this principle! What have our Courts of Law to do with any religious services or spiritual functions of any kind? On what grounds can you pretend that though the civil courts cannot issue a *Mandamus* to the priest to give sacramental absolution to this man, or administer the Eucharist to that man, they are competent to compel him to bless a grave, or to recite certain prayers prescribed by the Ritual, over the remains of another man? Do you not see, we say to our opponents, that you are commanding the impossible, and decreeing blasphemy? You cannot, even with your jails, nay not even if to incarceration you add the thumbscrew and the rack, compel a man to bless, or pray from his heart! and every uttered blessing, every proffered prayer which is not accompanied, or rather preceded and dictated by the requisite interior or spiritual intentions, is a sacrilege and a blasphemy – a mockery of God!

By this simple fact, the limits of the civil power are sharply defined. It cannot – and no one is bound to the impossible – it cannot in the nature of things, make a priest bless, or pray from his heart, *ex animo*, or with the requisite dispositions: and in the nature of things it has no right to compel any man to mock God with prayers which do not proceed from the heart – for this is sin.

22 THE SUPERIOR COURT REVERSES THE DECISION

L'Ordre, Montreal
September 10, 1870 [translation]

Good sense has finally reconciled itself with our civil courts.

The outrage that was so cruelly inflicted upon it by Judge Mondelet in the Guibord case, was fully and justly repaired by Judges Berthelot, McKay, and Torrance.

In the first place, all the quibbles and invectives of the judge, as well as the sophisms, calumny and absurd claims of the lawyers of Guibord's widow, were demolished without pity.

The length of the observations made by the three Honourable Judges before the reading of the judgment, reversing the ordinance of the first court, prevent us from giving any kind of interpretation from that day forth.

In the observations of Judge McKay, as in the case of those of Judge Berthelot, the principle that the ecclesiastical authority is the only competent one in matters of dogma, morals, and discipline is completely accepted.

Judge McKay does not recognize the Superior Court as having the attributes of an ecclesiastical court.

Also, he says that the practice of the division of cemeteries is universally acknowledged, that it is reasonable, and should be a part of the law.

Rarely has the court been given the opportunity to listen to such logical and scholarly grounds for judgment, as the judgment which was rendered on this occasion.

All the parties in the case are treated with the greatest respect.

The tone, sobriety, and dignity with which this report is worded, is in contrast to the intemperate and thoughtless outbreaks and hazardous assumptions contained in Judge Mondelet's report.

This formal recognition of the rights and liberty of the Church in Canada should gladden the hearts of all good Catholics.

It should also have the effect of abating the arrogance of the leaders of the *Institut Canadien vis à vis* the clergy, and to open the eyes of those who, up until now, were led by ignorance more than malice in their actions.

They tell us there will be an appeal against this judgment.

We rather doubt it.

23 FILTHY BOOKS IN THE INSTITUT'S LIBRARY

Le Nouveau Monde, Montreal
September 22, 1870 [translation]

We acknowledge receipt of the much vaunted "Catalogue of Books in the Library of the *Institut Canadien*". Our thanks to the person who sent it to us.

We frankly suspected a little withholding of information, some trifling fib, when M. Dessaulles proclaimed, in reply to published reports, that the Library of the *Institut* did not contain any truly bad books at all. But we did not think him capable, having the list in question before his eyes, of denying as he did, a hundred times, that there was not one obscene volume in this catalogue.

To listen to him, there were no other books there than what is found in all libraries, however little they may be worthy of the name: some treatises of abstract learning, some works on public law, some systems of natural philosophy, and a few learned dictionaries – which no one, he adds, can do without, even if they are *forbidden*. Very well! This very statement is today proven false, and, according to the public allegation of M. Boisseau, what constitutes the foundation of the library, and gives it its real character, are not works of heretical *knowledge*, but obscene novels. We repeat, it is before and above all, a library of evil novels that the Bishop of Montreal condemned in condemning the *Institut*, and a source of impure poison that he shut off from his flock.

We have done a little survey of M. Boisseau's Catalogue; well, from his list, it appears that, for the 291 volumes of *religion*, *philosophy*, and *political economy* that the *Institut* includes, the number of these *Novels* augments it to the comparatively exorbitant number of 1,049 volumes, of which 129 are of such a character that we do not want to stain this white paper with their titles, nor to mention their names to Christian readers. Alexandre Dumas, Alphonse Karr, Eugene Scribe, Emile Souvestre, Paul de Kock are nothing, as bad as they sometimes are, compared to the impure, obscene, and sordid products we can only allude to.

There are some books that will be the eternal shame of literature: some novels that, according to what Chateaubriand says, a man can only read while trembling, or that, as expressed by the cynical Jean Jacques Rousseau, a young girl cannot peruse without losing her modesty – they would be sufficient in themselves to corrupt an entire city. Here, according to M. Boisseau, is the true character of the essence of the Library of this platonic *Institut*, where the spirit, says M. Dessaulles, soars so high that one would think it escapes meaning. And he would like the Church to keep quiet about this danger – that the Bishop of Montreal should allow the young people to be exposed to the moral philosophy of the *Institut*, let the poison penetrate into the bosom of our families; in short, that he reconcile himself and administer the Communion, with his Bishop's hand, to the excommunicated purchasers, owners and readers of these books?

Come now.

---

24 A MEMBER OF L'INSTITUT ATTACKS LE NOUVEAU MONDE

Le Pays, Montreal
October 27, 1870 [translation]
Correspondence between *Le Nouveau Monde* and the *Institut Canadien*

Montreal, the 25th of October, 1870

The Editor:

After twelve years and more of vain attempts to break the back of the *Institut Canadien*, there appears to be a willingness to talk sense. It's the story of the man who does not succeed in smothering a victim in an attempt to take either his purse or his life: and would then avail himself of arguments to obtain a loan of money from him. The victim, having emerged victorious from the fight, is naturally difficult to persuade.

The most dishonest, annoying, arbitrary and irritating of methods have marked the conduct of people, blinded by their pride, who believed that it was enough simply to lift one foot to crush an association made up exclusively of mature and educated men, equally imbued with notions of right and of duty.

They have not succeeded, and *Le Nouveau Monde*, mouthpiece of the persecutors of the *Institut*, is at this moment searching for the causes of their failure, and of the conclusions to which this prolonged battle has led us.

It would take too long to recall the manoeuvres contrived against the *Institut*, the unseemly and odious abuses of religious authority which they did not hesitate to employ in such instances. But all these stratagems were so manifestly unveiled during the course of the Guibord trial, that it will be expedient to recall how this issue came to light.

It is known that the contents of the *Institut*'s library was the original pretext for the bad will of the Bishop of Montreal against the *Institut*.

Well, it has been proven that the catalogue of books had been in the hands of the Bishop for six long months, so that he could indicate those which appeared dangerous to him: and that he returned this catalogue without indicating a single book. You may explain this refusal any way you like, the fact remains that the question of the books was only a pretext.

When this fact was presented in Rome, the Bishop could not make *them* accept the good excuses which are fed to simpletons here, and a change of face took place. The *1868 Yearbook* had just been published. The issue here was *tolerance* in a mixed society. The doctrine practiced by the Catholics in the United States was unpopular in Rome. By means of this tract they procured a declaration that the *Institut* taught *pernicious doctrines,* and as long as such doctrine was taught there, it was necessary to keep the Catholics, and above all, the young people, away from it.

That was the last official action directed against the *Institut,* and we draw the attention of sensible men chiefly to this.

During the examination of the Diocesan Administrator, Vicar-General Truteau, at the Guibord trial, he was asked to indicate the pernicious doctrine that the *Institut* was accused of teaching, and would have to cease teaching in order to see the end of its troubles with the religious authority. In reply, he referred to document B or document D, which do not say a word about it. To circumvent his evasiveness, they asked him the following questions, and got the following responses:

Question: Have the members of the *Institut* ever had, to your knowledge, recourse to any source other than the highest ecclesiastical authority of this Diocese at the time (himself), from whom they could acquire information which would, in your opinion, entail the denial of the sacraments of the Church and of ecclesiastical burial?

Reply: I do not believe that they could have had a better source of information than myself. As we have informed the members of the *Institut* of all the reasons for which they were condemned, I do not believe that they could have had other sources of information. The Bishop was probably acquainted with the issue longer than I, as it

is he who applied himself particularly to this issue.

Question: Can you, from memory and without referring to any document, indicate the doctrines qualified as pernicious in the said Exhibit D?

Reply: *I do not remember them at the moment.*

This reply must illumine an electric light, and make it shine in everyone's eyes!

The Bishop's deputy, the highest diocesan authority at this time, declares, under oath, that he does not remember why the *Institut* is condemned!

Is it surprising that we should know more than he?

Is it surprising that the class that reads, the young people who seek out, question things and study, no longer wants to allow itself to be mystified?

Le Nouveau Monde is investigating the reasons why the questions of Catholic discipline, dogma, etc., have become the object of study for certain members of the *Institut.* It is very simple: because they are forced, in spite of themselves, to be concerned with it. Constantly harassed under the pretense of religion, driven back even from the resting place of the dead, they wondered what all this meant. They wanted to ascertain whether they were right or wrong in resisting; and when they were convinced that all the wrong was on the side of their adversaries, they felt inspired by a most sacred duty – not to participate in this profanation of God and everything sacred. They now have Vicar-General Truteau's testimony that they were right all along.

Le Nouveau Monde wonders why these religious questions have almost taken the place of political issues among certain members of the *Institut.* If they don't already know, I will tell them.

Through the calumnies and prejudices spread by the patrons of *Le Nouveau Monde* against the liberals, a blind fanaticism has taken the place of reason in a notable sector of the Canadian population. In another sector of this same population, corruption, patronized by friends of *Le Nouveau Monde,* has eclipsed the sense of morality. The result is the ostracism of the men of greatest ability and integrity in the nation, and the triumph of nonentities and hypocrites, ready to sell their country for a plate of beans. With talent, studiousness, and integrity, having been driven from the political sphere, they had to find an outlet for intellectual activity in some other sphere; and this was the result of that very ostracism. It is you who have created the casuists and the theologians, when they would have been happy to serve their country in the political arena.

What have you done with the young people who have been following you for the last fifteen years? Show us your young people now. No one has meddled with them except you. Where are they?

Stop now! You are fighting the impossible. Rome itself, with all the elements for success at her disposal, has not been able to make of the Romans what you are attempting in vain to make of the Canadians. The human spirit will not give in that way. You seem to be at the height of victory against it, all things being equal. But the Romans wept with joy upon seeing the arrival of Savoy's flag, they kissed the hands of their liberators. You had 150 voices against 150,000. Stop there, I beg of you. The sun revolves no matter what you may say about it: you will not do away with it. In the same way, the *Institut* will live on in spite of all of you: it will thrive on your persecutions when it has no other stimulant.

A Member of the *Institut*.

---

25 THE APPEAL: CAN A CATHOLIC JUDGE BE IMPARTIAL?

The Montreal Herald
December 3, 1870

Yesterday morning the Guibord case came up before the Court of Queen's Bench in Appeal, when Mr. Doutre, Q.C., presented a petition, excepted to Chief Justice Duval, and Justices Caron, Drummond, and Monk, on the ground that, being Catholics, they were liable to favour the respondents, and that they could not render justice to the appellant, without violating ten distinct propositions of the Syllabus; and that the respondents, themselves, allege that the question at issue is, whether the Church or the Queen's authority have supremacy. Then the judges excepted to, are respectfully called upon to declare in writing, according to law, whether they consider themselves bound in conscience, by the dictates of the Court of Rome, as contained in those propositions.

In presenting the petition, Mr. Doutre said that he hoped the measure he was going to adopt would not be looked upon as implying want of respect and confidence in the high character of the Judges; but after due consideration he thought it essential before arguing his case, to know whether the Judges felt themselves competent to hear him and give justice to his client. The condition of the Catholics since the cession of the country has been altered by decrees of new dogmas, some of which if they are adhered to by Judges, would prevent the Catholic Judges from applying the law of the country. By Chap. 83, 14th, George 3rd, which confirmed the treaty of cession, the Catholics are granted free exercise of their religion, but subject to the supremacy of the Sovereign. Several articles of the Syllabus declared it to be a heresy to believe that any Sovereign had authority over the laws decreed in Rome, and that in a conflict of jurisdiction in mixed matters, it was another heresy to recognize in Civil Law the power of pronouncing on jurisdiction. The right exercised by the appellant, which was fully recognized and practised in France at the time of the cession under the name of "Appeal against Abuses" (Appel comme d'Abus), is especially mentioned in the Syllabus to be proscribed, and it is worthy of anathema to attempt to make use of that recourse. The judge that would receive such an action and pronounce favourably upon it would be liable to anathema and excommunication. I know very well, said Mr. Doutre, that none of the judges consider themselves bound by anything but the laws of the country; but in the natural state of religious exaggeration my own conviction in that respect is not a guarantee that will be sufficient for my client and the public. I have no doubt that the answer the Judges will give to the facts mentioned in this petition will be such as to suggest the withdrawing of the exception. This opportunity is a precious one, and should not be lost for defining clearly the position of our Catholic Judges in these mixed questions, otherwise their judgments would lack moral weight, and would leave a suspicion that they are not free in the exercise of their judgment.

Chief Justice Duval remarked that it was, perhaps, giving too much importance to the imbeciles who think that Catholic Judges recognize any authority but that of the Queen and the law enacted under her authority, but the petition would have consideration.

---

26 THE CASE FOR A STRONG UNION OF MONTREAL LITERARY SOCIETIES

Le Pays, Montreal
April 22, 1871 [translation]

At the Thursday night session, 20th instant, the members of the *Institut Canadien* took into consideration the plan of merger proposed by the "Mercantile Library Association". There were many people at the meeting, including some of the most influential of the *Institut*. After the reading of a letter from the Honourable John Young submitting, to the President of the *Institut Canadien,* the resolution adopted by the Mercantile Association, and the latter's reply, the following resolution was proposed by Joseph Doutre Esq., and seconded by N. Aubin Esq.

"That a delegation composed of the Honourable L. A. Dessaulles, J. Doutre and A. Boisseau be authorized to enter into negotiations with the societies of the *Mercantile Library Association,* the *Mechanic's Institute*, and other literary or reading societies, with the aim of uniting these societies with the *Institut Canadien,* under the same charter and a common administration; with the condition that persons of French origin who are able to take part, enjoy the same rights and freedoms that they possess under the charter of the *Institut Canadien,* and that they be instructed to report to the *Institut* which will take the appropriate action in this matter."

In introducing this motion, M. Doutre gave a short résumé of the history of the *Institut Canadien,* recalling to mind that this institution had originated in the midst of national struggles which, fortunately, no longer exist. He pointed out that a similar proposal had been debated around the year 1852; but with the memory of these struggles still fresh, union of the divided forces of the societies that were formed to propagate and popularize knowledge had been prevented. Instead of dividing itself into national bodies, the population had chosen, in the course of time, the more rational basis of political principles and divided itself into conservatives and liberals. The French split and the English did the same. Each faction had to endeavour to obtain alliances that would have the effect of diminishing national prejudices and racial hatreds. Each had its own peculiar viewpoint on questions related to social, scientific and industrial matters. The French have too many of those illusions that Lamartine called reality seen from afar; the English, on the other hand, examine reality in such a way that they often lose sight of the distant, but real horizon. We would be mutually useful to one another; the French would abandon unnecessary speculation, the English would pursue truth further beyond purely material facts, and all that without losing any of the advantages attached to a separate existence. The French would have their day for the exclusive use of their language, and the English would take part in our debates to demonstrate their progress in our idiom. The English would also have their sessions, where we could show off our familiarity with their grammar and dictionary. Instead of selecting a book out of 7,000 volumes, we will have 25,000 at our disposal and the prospect of multiplying (increasing) the books and journals (newspapers). Instead of spending from $8,000 to $10,000 a year in administration costs, $2,000 would be sufficient to cover our common (joint) expenses, and the remainder could be used for the acquisition of new books and journals. Instead of three or four languishing societies, we would have one single strong body, capable of protecting those who wish to elevate themselves morally, and racial prejudices would disappear forever. Our struggles would take on an essentially intellectual character; merit and knowledge would become our sole claim to superiority. . . .

The Motion was unanimously adopted.

---

27 THE SUPERIOR COURT'S VERDICT UPHELD, BUT L'INSTITUT GIVEN LEAVE TO APPEAL TO THE JUDICIAL COMMITTEE OF THE PRIVY COUNCIL

The Gazette, Montreal
September 8, 1871

By the judgment of the Court of Appeals yesterday in this *cause célèbre*, the decision of the Court of Review has been unanimously affirmed, in other words, the highest Court of the Province has refused to interfere to compel the Fabrique to inter the remains of Joseph Guibord in any manner other than was offered by them in the first instance. We have said the judgment was unanimously affirmed, but although the five Judges of the Court of Appeals have arrived at the same conclusion, they are very far from travelling in company towards that conclusion. In fact, not one of the five has taken precisely the same view of the case as any other of the five. The opinions of the Bench were given at great length, the entire day being consumed in the delivery. This is not surprising when we remember at what length the case was argued, and how great the interest attaching to it. . . .

At the conclusion of the judgment, an application was made, and immediately granted, for leave to appeal to the Privy Council; so that this long agitated case cannot yet be said to have received a final decision.

---

28 PROGRESS OF THE DISPUTE SO FAR

The Montreal Herald
September 9, 1871

As a matter of law and logic, we can hardly say that the elaborate judgments delivered in this affair are as satisfactory as they are ponderous, especially as, although all the judges but one have agreed in rejecting the demand of the plaintiff, they have done so upon so many, and apparently inconsistent grounds, as to leave nothing but confusion in the minds of less learned persons. Judge Mondelet, sitting alone, held the proceedings to be regular, and the demand of the plaintiff good on its merits. In the later proceedings, four of the judges have decided against the action on its merits, and the remainder against its form. But of those who take the ground that the Court could not order the burial of Guibord with religious rites, which they held to be implied in the demand of the plaintiff, some say that they would have ordered civil burial, if that had been the thing asked for. We suppose by that they mean burial in the part of the cemetery where the plaintiff claimed a resting place for her husband, though without the usual religious rites. This view is, on the other hand, contested by one at least of the judges, who considers the consecration of the ground to be a religious rite, and that, therefore, the ground thus consecrated is beyond the pale of the law. Some of the judges say that a Catholic citizen of Canada had once a right to the intervention of the Courts, in order to compel the ecclesiastical authorities to perform their due functions on his behalf, but that he lost that right by the cession of the country to a Protestant Sovereign, which seems, if it be so, to be rather hard on the citizen, thus deprived of his wonted protection, if protection be necessary, and without fault on his part, since he could not help the cession. It also places him on a different footing from the Protestant citizen, for at the arguments a precedent was quoted for the Plaintiff to show that the Anglican authorities of Quebec in a similar case did not question the authority of the Court. We do not presume to decide among such a conflict of high authorities. The question, however, may hereafter be raised frequently, and therefore, it is important for a part of our population that it should be authoritatively decided. That can only be done by the Privy Council, where it is said the suit will be carried. Possibly, however, the Plaintiff may not have the necessary funds for so distant a litigation, and in that case everything will remain in the obscurity, which has been created by the difference of opinion which we have noted.

29 THE JUDICIAL COMMITTEE OF THE PRIVY COUNCIL UPHOLDS L'INSTITUT

Le Bien Public, Montreal
November 22, 1874 [translation]

There was great excitement in the city Saturday afternoon, due to a despatch from London announcing that the Privy Council had returned a verdict in favour of the appellant in the Guibord case.

Here is the text of the telegram received by M. Jetté, which this gentleman was very willing to communicate to us:

London, 21st of November, 1874
Order given to bury in the main lot of the cemetery. No ceremonies. Is neither public sinner nor excommunicated by name.
– Ashurst

Thus, the Privy Council orders the priest and the *Fabrique* of the parish of Montreal to bury Guibord in the Catholic Cemetery, but without ceremonies; on the principle that Guibord was neither a public sinner nor was he excommunicated.

One must avow that it is rather ludicrous to see an English Protestant court decide what are the elements of excommunication that will authorize the Catholic Church to refuse ecclesiastical burial to one of its members.

The fact that English judges are called upon so often to judge from the viewpoint of French law, that they must necessarily know less than our own judges about the case brought before them, is bad enough. But that they should be called upon to settle questions of canonical law and high theology, is just too much. Those poor judges, they must be the first to realize how ridiculous it is that they are forced to study such questions, and to inform the Catholic Church of its rights and duties.

It is thought that the Privy Council has no doubt adopted the opinion that the French law we inherited used to grant and still grants to civil courts the power to intervene and judge in such matters.

Whatever legal viewpoint the Privy Council adopts, it is no less true that an intervention by a Protestant and naturally prejudiced or incompetent tribunal in such questions is a strange anomaly.

Yesterday, the Reverend M. Rousselot, parish priest of Notre Dame, read out the judgment in the Guibord case in his sermon. He accompanied this reading with remarks that do not appear to have been very well understood. Here is the correct meaning of it:

He said that the judgment of the Privy Council ordered him to bury the deceased in the main lot of the cemetery, without ceremonies. He would have no objection to burying him in the section they had just bought to enlarge the cemetery, and which is not blessed; but he would never consider burying him in the consecrated part of the cemetery. In any case, the *Fabrique* and ecclesiastical authorities would await the actual text of the judgment, before deciding exactly what line of conduct they would agree to.

It is evident that the Privy Council understood that the main section of the cemetery meant the consecrated part; thus, it can be expected that the ecclesiastical authorities will not comply with the judgment.

30 A POX ON BOTH THEIR HOUSES

The Globe, Toronto
November 23, 1874

This protracted suit has at length, after many and wearisome delays, been decided by the Highest Court of Appeal in favour of Guibord's representatives, and of course against the ecclesiastical authorities of the R.C. Church. The deceased Guibord is declared to be entitled to burial in consecrated ground and with ecclesiastical rites, let the Church through its proper officials say to the contrary what they choose. The proviso is put in that the *curé* is not obliged to officiate at said funeral, but in that very innocent phrase, there may lie one or two more lawsuits. . . .

On what grounds can this decision be based but on those which all really free Churches have long repudiated, viz.: that the different Churches are all in subjection to the State, and that Church office-bearers can be dragged into Courts of Law as often as any member may think himself aggrieved by the decision of his ecclesiastical superiors, under whose authority he has voluntarily placed himself, and from whose jurisdiction he can deliberately withdraw himself at any moment. If it is argued that Churches, like other corporations, must keep within their own regulations, and that the civil authorities may at any moment be legitimately appealed to in order to determine whether these Churches have obeyed their own laws or not, then here again a subjugation of the Church to the State would be implied which none but the rankest Erastians of any Church would acknowledge or submit to. If the decision is based upon the assumption that the Roman Catholic Church of Quebec is a State Church, and as such subject to the State in a way and to an extent she would not otherwise be, then we can so far understand the decision: but, on the other hand, it would then puzzle us to see on what ground the Roman Catholic Church is recognized as a State Church, except, to be sure, it is that she has the power of collecting tithes, and can claim all individuals born within her pale as under her jurisdiction and responsible for her pecuniary imposts, unless there has been on the part of such, a formal and public withdrawal from her communion.

The members of the Institut in fact may find that in gaining this victory they have gained a loss, unless they are prepared for the manly and independent course of withdrawing from the Roman Catholic Church altogether, looking upon the idea of consecrated ground as a pious figment, and upon being buried in such earth as of no importance whatever. We would never wish to say a single word that would grate harshly upon the ear of any pious, conscientious man, and wish always to treat with tenderness even the delusions and misconceptions of the perfectly honest and sincere. But surely no human being, let him do his best, can discover the slightest difference between earth that has been consecrated and what has been left as mere common ground. It is about time that men were rising above such ecclesiastical fictions, and coming to the conclusion that every part of God's earth is holy. A man's body will lie as peacefully and as securely in any common cemetery as in earth that has been even saturated with ecclesiastical rites of consecration. The civil courts *cannot* FORCE ecclesiastical ones to perform any religious rite however insignificant. And the sooner this is recognized and acted upon by all parties, so much the better. In short, the false notion of a State-endowed and State-favoured Church lies at the bottom of all these wretched complications.

The world will never be free from these politico-ecclesiastical discussions and collisions till the Church is supported only by the free-will offerings of those who actually believe in its dogmas and voluntarily place themselves under its rules. Even then, some may think such collisions would be possible. Wherever property or character is involved the State no doubt may claim a right to interfere, and may do its best to redress the grievance and protect the injured. But civil rulers, if wise, will be very chary about mingling themselves up in disputes and contentions which had their origin in mere voluntary organizations, into which individuals knowingly and deliberately entered of their own accord, and from which they can at any moment withdraw without let or hindrance. . . .

---

31 AN INFRINGEMENT ON THE RIGHTS OF THE CHURCH

La Minerve, Montreal
November 23, 1874 [translation]

The lawyers of both parties in the Guibord case received Saturday the news we announced two months ago, to the effect that the Judicial Committee of the Privy Council in England declared itself against the *Fabrique* including costs, and had ordered the interment of the Guibord family in the main part of the Montreal cemetery.

The *National* and its colleague, furious at having been outdone by us, then had the delicacy to accuse us of having fabricated the dispatch: one can see what was involved.

The judgment was not pronounced at that time, but in England, as in Canada, the decisions of the courts were known before their official publication. . . .

To put in a less concise and more explicit manner than in the telegram, the Court decreed:
1. That permission is granted to Guibord's heirs, that is the *Institut Canadien*, to demand that the *Fabrique* bury Guibord, not in the cemetery for children who die without being baptized, but in the main cemetery.
2. His Reverence the Parish Priest of Notre Dame is ordered to be present at the interment, but simply in his capacity as a civil officer, without being obliged to don the Surplice or to pronounce prayers.
3. The Court determined that M. Guibord was neither a public sinner nor an excommunicate.

M. Doutre received two dispatches that confirm the one we have just provided. We learned from another source that if His Reverence the Priest does not conform to the injunctions of the Court, he will be liable to a fine of $2,000. We give you this rumour with all caution.

A serious question immediately presents itself. Guibord owned a plot of land at the cemetery, where his wife was buried. This land, which was consecrated ground, is the property of the *Institut Canadien*. Allowing that he accepts the Court's judgment, will the priest bury Guibord in this spot?

Under what law did the judges decide that Guibord was not a public sinner and that he was not excommunicated in name? Do they claim to govern the Church, and to be more knowledgeable than the Church itself about what it decided?

This judgment will bring grief to all Catholic souls: it will be regarded as an infringement on the rights of the Church, as an attack against its liberties, as an insult against reason. It seems to us that a man of common sense should never demand privileges for an individual after his death, which he did not make an effort to secure during his lifetime; it would be the same as forcing a priest to pray over the grave of an atheist in order to reclaim the efficacy of prayers that he had denied while living. . . .

---

32 THE ESTABLISHED CHURCH OF LOWER CANADA

The Daily Witness, Montreal
November 27, 1874

The Guibord decision is England's protest against the claims of Rome to dominate all States. Rome was once contented, if not satisfied, that a Roman Catholic Church should exist as the State Church of each country, receiving its support and fulfilling its duties as such, under the laws. Now it will not hear of any reciprocal rights; all nations must pay homage and tribute, but none shall say to her "What doest thou?" The chief grounds of objection put forth by the clerical organs to the decision of the Privy Council are, first, that the Judges, being Protestants, were disqualified on that account to decide without bias in such matters, and, second, that, even if they were

Roman Catholics, no civil tribunal has the right to judge the Church in regard to ecclesiastical affairs of any kind, whatever. With their usual zeal they cast gratuitous abuse on the members of the Privy Council that were concerned in disposing of this appeal, just as they did in the case of the Roman Catholic Judge Mondelet for daring to reverse Judge Routhier's decision. Thus while the ecclesiastical authorities put in appearance before the Civil Courts and plead their cause with the best ability that can be procured, it is with the hope that the decision will be in their favor. They deny at once the authority and the honesty of the Court if it is not. That the decision confirms the status of the Church of Rome as a State Church in this province, is, they declare, no consolation to them, as they virtually occupied that position before. They bewail, however, the fact that, having these legal privileges, their flocks, and each individual member thereof have rights that the law will compel them to respect, and that the courts will even look into and examine the value of any plea that any one has been excommunicated or otherwise ecclesiastically banned before it will allow him to be deprived of his rights as member of the Church. . . . If the clergy in Canada does not like it, let them renounce the revenues awarded them by the State, tithes, &c., and become like other churches, dependent on the bounty of their followers, and their position and influence will be greatly improved – the clergy will not be so ready to alienate the attachment of members of their congregations by arbitrary conduct, while the members on their part will feel the gentle influence of persuasion, instead of being goaded by force, and both will like each other better. It has always been the physical support lent her by the State that has been at the bottom of the haughtiness and cruelty displayed by Rome, and which cowed her followers and sealed up their voice of protest. As this State support deserted her a notable change became apparent in her policy, and she now appeals to her people with sweet, persuasive accents to support her against the State. . . .

33 TRANSCRIPT OF THE PRIVY COUNCIL'S JUDGMENT

The Montreal Herald
December 8, 1874

JUDGMENT OF THE JUDICIAL COMMITTEE OF THE PRIVY COUNCIL ON THE APPEAL OF DAME HENRIETTE BROWN V. LES CURE ET MARGUILLIERS DE L'OEUVRE ET FABRIQUE DE NOTRE DAME DE MONTREAL, FROM CANADA.

The suit was for a *mandamus* to *les Curé et Marguilliers de l'Oeuvre et Fabrique de Montréal*, upon receipt of the customary fees, to bury the body of Guibord in the "Cemetery of La Côte des Neiges," conformably to usage and to law, and to enter such burial in the civil register.

La Fabrique had the control of this cemetery. The cemetery is divided into two parts, separated by a paling. In the smaller part are buried unbaptised infants and those who have died *sans les secours ou les sacrements de l'Eglise*, persons who had committed suicide, and criminals who had suffered capital punishment without being reconciled to the Church. In the larger part are buried ordinary Roman Catholics with the rites of the Church. Neither portion is consecrated as a whole; but it is the custom to consecrate separately each grave in the larger part, never in the reserved part. The cemetery is thus divided into a part in which graves are, and in which they are not, consecrated. Guibord was a parishioner of Montreal of unexceptionable moral character, and both by baptism and education, a Roman Catholic, which faith he retained up to the time of his death. In 1844 a literary and scientific institution was formed for the purpose of providing a library, reading-room, and other appliances for education, incorporated by 16 Vict., c. 261, under the name of the *Institut Canadien*. Guibord was one of the original members. In 1858 certain members of the Institute proposed a Committee for the purpose of making a list of books in the library, which in their opinion ought not to be allowed to remain therein. An amendment, however, was carried to the effect that the Institute contained no improper books, that it was the sole judge of the morality of its library, and that the existing Committee of Management was sufficient. On the 13th of April in the same year the R.C. Bishop published a Pastoral in which he referred to what had taken place at this meeting, and after praising the conduct of the minority, pointed out that the majority had fallen into two great errors: first, in declaring that they were the proper judges of the morality of their books, whereas the Council of Trent had declared that this belonged to the Bishop; secondly, in declaring that the library contained only moral books, whereas it contained books which were in the Index at Rome. The Bishop further cited the Council of Trent, that any one who read or kept books forbidden on other grounds would be subject to severe punishment; and he concluded by making an appeal to the Institute to alter their resolution, alleging that otherwise no Catholic would continue to belong to it.

The resolution was not rescinded. In 1865 several of the Roman Catholic members of the Institute, including Guibord, appealed to Rome against this Pastoral. They received no answer. But in the year 1869, the Bishop of Montreal issued a Circular with the answer of the Holy Office and the decree of the Holy Congregation of the Index condemning the annuaire of the said Institute for 1868.

This was dated 16th July, 1869. He also sent a Pastoral letter from Rome, which contained the sentence or answer of the Holy Office, as printed in the case before us.

The Pastoral letter drew attention to the fact that two things were especially forbidden by this Decretum. – 1. To belong to the Institute while it taught pernicious doctrines. 2. To publish, keep, or read the *Annuaire*. And the Bishop also pointed out that any person who persisted in keeping or reading the *Annuaire,* or in remaining a member of the Institute, would be deprived of the Sacrament, *même a l'article de la mort.* The Institute held a meeting on the 23rd September, 1869, and resolved:–

1. *Que l'Institut Canadien, fondé dans un but purement literaire et scientifique, n'a aucune espèce d'enseignement doctrinaire, et exclut avec soin tout enseignement de doctrines pernicieuses dans son sein.*

2. *Que les membres Catholiques de l'Institut Canadien, ayant appris la condamnation de l'Annuaire de 1868 de l'Institut Canadien par décret de l'autorité Romaine, déclarent se soumettre purement et simplement à ce décret.*[1]

These concessions produced no effect. The Bishop in a letter, dated Rome, 30th October, 1869, to the Administrator of the Diocese (which that officer received on the day before Guibord's death), denounces these concessions as hypocritical, and gives five reasons why they are insufficient, the third of which is –

3. *Parce que cette soumission fait partie d'un rapport, dans lequel est proclamée une résolution tenue jusqu'alors, secrète, qui établit la tolérance religieuse qui a été la principale cause de la condamnation de l'Institut.* The letter concludes:– *Tous comprendront qu'en matière si grave il n'y a pas d'absolution à donner, pas même à l'article de la mort, à ceux qui ne voudraient pas renoncer à l'Institut, qui n'a fait qu'un acte d'hypocrisie, en feignant de se soumettre au Saint Siege.*[2]

This *principal ground of condemnation* of the Institute, viz., that it had passed a resolution which established the principle of religious toleration, was entirely new, does not appear in any former document, and, it would seem, could not have been known by Guibord. It should also be mentioned, to complete the necessary history, that Guibord, about six years before his death, being dangerously ill, was attended by a priest, who administered unction to him, but refused to administer the Holy Communion unless he resigned his membership of the Institute, which Guibord declined.

Guibord having died suddenly, the widow caused a request to be made to the *Curé* and Clerk of the *Fabrique* to bury him, and tendered the usual fees. Previously M. Rousselot, the *Curé,* having heard of the death, had applied to the Administrator for his directions. He replied that he had yesterday received a letter from the Bishop directing him to refuse absolution *même à l'article de la mort* to members of the Institute; he could not, therefore, permit *la sepulture ecclésiastique.* The *Curé,* therefore, refused to bury Guibord in the large part of the cemetery, but offered to allow him interment in the other part, without religious rites. The agent of the widow offered to accept burial in the larger part without religious services; but this was rejected. On the 23rd of November the widow presented a petition to the Superior Court, and prayed that a *mandamus* might issue as above stated. . . .

It now becomes necessary to determine the merits of the case, and the grave questions of public and constitutional law raised. . . . In order to do this, it is desirable to consider the status of the Roman Catholic Church in Lower Canada. It is certain that before cession the Established Church of that Province, was the Roman Catholic Church; its law, however, being modified by what were known as *les libertés de l'Eglise Gallicane.* There seem also to have been regular Ecclesiastical Courts, and besides them there was vested in the Superior Council the jurisdiction recognized in French jurisprudence as the *appel comme d'abus.* . . .

The following are the public documents which show how the Roman Catholic Church in Lower Canada was dealt with on the conquest and cession of the province: . . . [Here their Lordships cite sections from the Act of Capitulation, the Treaty of 1763, and the Quebec Act of 1774.]

From these documents it would follow that although the Roman Catholic Church in Canada may have ceased to be an Established Church in the full sense of the term, it continued to be a Church recognized by the State; retaining its endowments, and continuing to have certain rights . . . enforceable at law. It has been contended on behalf of the Appellants that the effect of the Cession, and subsequent legislation, has been to leave the law of the R.C. Church as it existed before the Cession, to secure to the Roman Catholic inhabitants, all the privileges which their fathers, as French subjects, enjoyed under the head of the liberties of the Gallican Church; and further, that the Queen's Bench, created in 1794, possessed, and that the existing Superior Court now possesses, as the Superior Council heretofore possessed, the power of enforcing these privileges by proceedings in the nature of *appel comme d'abus.* Considering the altered circumstances of the Roman Catholic Church in Canada, the non-existence of any recognized ecclesiastical Courts such as those in France which it was the office of an *appel comme d'abus* to control; and the absence of any mention in the recent Code for Lower Canada of such a proceeding, their Lordships would feel difficulty in affirming the latter of these propositions. . . . Their Lordships do not, however, think it necessary to express any opinion as to the competence of the Civil Courts to entertain an *appel comme d'abus.* . . . Nor do their Lordships think it necessary to pronounce any opinion upon the difficult questions raised touching the *status,* of the R.C. Church in Canada. It has, undoubtedly, since the cession, wanted some of the characteristics of an Established Church; whilst it differs materially in several important particulars from such voluntary religious societies as the Anglican Church in the Colonies, or the Roman Catholic Church in England. The payment of *dîmes* and rateability to the maintenance of cemeteries, are secured by law. These rights of the Church must beget corresponding obligations, and may give rise to questions between the laity and clergy which can only be determined by the Courts. It seems, however, unnecessary to pursue this question, because even if this Church were a voluntary religious society resting only upon a consensual basis, Courts of Justice are still bound when complaint is made that a member of the society has been injured to inquire into the laws of the authority which has inflicted the alleged injury. . . .

If the act [of refusal of ecclesiastical burial] be questioned in a Court of Justice, that Court is bound to inquire, whether that act was in accordance with the law and discipline of the Roman Catholic Church, and whether the sentence, if any, was regularly pronounced by an authority competent to pronounce it. It is worthy of observation that in the Courts below, it was ruled, apparently at the instance of the Respondents, that the law, including the ritual of the Church, could not be proved by witnesses, but that the Courts were bound to take judicial notice of its provisions. The application of this ruling would be difficult, unless it be conceded that the ecclesiastical law in Lower Canada is identical with that which governed the French province of Quebec. If modifications have been introduced since the cession they have not been introduced by any legislative authority. They must have been the subject of something tantamount to a consensual contract binding the members of that religious community, and, as such, ought, if invoked to be proved. It seems, however, to be admitted that the law upon the point is to be found in the Quebec Ritual, which was accepted before the cession and does not differ in any material particular from the Roman Ritual cited in the Courts below. The Quebec Ritual is as follows:—

On doit refuser la sepulture ecclésiastique – 1º, aux Juifs, infidèles, hérétiques, apostats, schismatiques, et à tous ceux qui ne font pas profession de la religion Catholique. 2º, Aux enfants morts sans baptême. 3º, A ceux qui auraient été nommément excommuniés ou interdits, si ce n'est qu'avant de mourir ils aient donné des marques de douleur, auquel cas on pourra leur accorder la sepulture ecclésiastique, après que la censure aura été levée par nos ordres. 4º, A ceux qui se seraient tués, etc. 5º, A ceux qui ont été tués en duel etc. 6º, A ceux qui, sans excuse légitime, n'auront pas satisfait à leur devoir pascal, etc. 7º, A ceux qui sont morts notoirement coupable de quelque péché mortel, etc. 8º, Aux pécheurs public qui seraient morts dans l'impénitence; tels sont les concubinaires, les filles ou femmes prostituées, les sorciers et les farceurs, usuriers, etc.[3]

The refusal of ecclesiastical burial to Guibord is not justified by either the 1st, 2nd, 4th, 5th, or 7th of the above rules.

To bring him within the 3rd rule it would be necessary to show that he was excommunicated by name. That such a sentence might be passed and that it might be the duty of the Civil Court to give effect to it their Lordships do not deny. It is true that there are now no regular Ecclesiastical Courts, such as existed when the province formed part of the dominions of France. It must, however, be remembered that a Bishop is *judex ordinarius*, according to the canon law; and may hold a court and deliver judgment. And it must further be remembered that, unless such sentences were recognized, there would exist no means of determining the many questions touching faith and discipline which may arise. There is, however, no proof that any sentence of excommunication was ever passed against Guibord *nominatim* by any Ecclesiastical authority. Indeed, it was admitted that there was none; their Lordships are therefore relieved from the necessity of considering how far such a sentence might have been examinable. . . . In the course of the argument it was suggested, rather than argued, that the refusal of ecclesiastical burial might be brought within the 6th of the rules, and justified on the ground that, without legitimate reason, he had failed to communicate at Easter. But this failure was not the ground on which ecclesiastical burial was denied; and, so far from wilfully abstaining from receiving the sacraments, those sacraments were refused when he desired to receive them. The cause of refusal finally insisted upon was that Guibord was *un pécheur public* within the 8th rule. . . .

It is impossible to avoid a suspicion that it had originally been intended to rely on an *ipso facto* excommunication, and that this subsequent defence of *pécheur public* was resorted to when it became manifest that a sentence of excommunication was necessary, and that none had been pronounced. What is this category of *pécheur public* to include? Is the category capable of indefinite extension by means of an *et cetera* in the Quebec Ritual? Or if the force of an *et cetera* is to be allowed to bring a man within the category, must it not be confined to offences *ejusdem generis*? Guibord's case did not come within any of the enumerated classes.

. . . To allow a discretionary addition to, or an enlargement of the categories specified in the Ritual, would be fraught with the most startling consequences. For instance, the *et cetera* might be expanded so as to include any person being in habits of intimacy with a member of a literary society containing a prohibited book; any person visiting a friend who possessed such a book; any person sending his son to a school in the library of which there was such a book; going to a shop where such books were sold; and many other instances. Moreover, the Index, which forbids Grotius, Pascal, Pothier, Thuanus, and Sismondi, might be made to include all the writings of jurists and all legal reports of judgments supposed to be hostile to the Church; and the Roman Catholic lawyer might find it difficult to pursue his profession.

Their Lordships are satisfied that such a discretionary enlargement of the categories would not have been deemed within the authority of the Bishop by the law of the Gallican Church as it existed in Canada before the cession; and it is not established that there has been such an alteration in the law of that Church founded on the consent of its members, as would warrant such an interpretation, and that the just conclusion of law on this point is, that the fact of being a member of this Institute does not bring a man within the category of a public sinner to whom Christian burial can be legally refused.

It would further appear that, according to the ecclesiastical laws of France, a personal sentence was in most cases required in order to constitute a man a public sinner. . . .

It remains for their Lordships to consider what is the substantive law upon which the Respondents rely in their contention that Guibord is to be considered a public sinner within the terms of the Quebec Ritual. They place their principal reliance on Rule X of the Council of Trent:–

It is forbidden to the faithful to read or to have any books prohibited by this Index, for if any will read or have them he falls immediately under sentence of excommunication.

Various observations arise on this citation, which seem to deprive it of all authority in the present case. In the first place it is a matter of historical and legal fact that the decrees of this Council were never admitted in France to have effect *proprio vigore*, though a great portion of them have been copied into French Ordonnances. In the second place, France has expressly repudiated the decrees of the Congregation. . . .

No evidence has been produced to establish the grave proposition that Her Majesty's Roman Catholic subjects in Lower Canada have consented to be bound by such a rule as it is now sought to enforce, which, in truth, involves the recognition of the authority of the Inquisition, an authority always repudiated by the law of France. . . . The conclusion to which their Lordships have come upon this difficult case is that the Respondents have failed to show that Guibord was, at his death, under any such ecclesiastical sentence as would, according to the Quebec Ritual, or any law binding upon Roman Catholics in Canada, justify the denial of ecclesiastical sepulture. It is suggested that the denial took place by the order of the Bishop or his Vicar-General; that the Respondents are bound to obey the orders of their ecclesiastical superior; and that no *mandamus* ought to issue against them. Their Lordships cannot accede to this. They apprehend that it is a rule in every system of jurisprudence that an inferior officer can justify his act or omission by the order of his superior only when that order has been regularly issued by competent authority. The argument would, in fact, amount to this; that even if it were clearly established that Guibord was not disentitled to ecclesiastical burial, nevertheless the mere order of the Bishop would justify the *Curé and Marguilliers* in refusing to bury him in that part of the cemetery in which he ought to be interred; or, in other words, the Bishop, by his own absolute power in any individual case, might dispense with the application of the general ecclesiastical law, and prohibit upon any grounds, revealed or not revealed, the ecclesiastical burial of any parishioner. There is no evidence that the Roman Catholics of Lower Canada have consented to be placed in such a condition. Their Lordships do not think it necessary to consider whether, if the parties and circumstances had been different, they would or would not have had power to order the interment of Guibord to be accompanied by the usual religious rites, because the widow finally forewent this demand, and Counsel have not asked it, and also because the *Curé* is not before them in his individual capacity; but they will humbly advise Her Majesty that the Decrees of the Court of Queen's Bench and of the Court of Review be reversed; that the original Decree of the Superior Court be varied, and that, instead of the order made by that Court, it should be ordered that a peremptory writ of *mandamus* be issued, directed to *Les Curé et Marguilliers*, commanding them, upon application, and upon tender of the usual fees, to prepare, or permit to be prepared, a grave in that part of the cemetery in which the remains of Roman Catholics, who receive ecclesiastical burial, are usually interred, for the burial of the remains of the said Joseph Guibord; and that, upon such remains being brought to the said cemetery, they do bury the said remains in the said part of the said cemetery, or permit them to be buried there. And that the Defendants do pay to the Canadian Institute all the costs, except such costs as were occasioned by the plea of *recusatio judicis*, which should be borne by the Appellants. Their Lordships cannot conclude their judgment without expressing their regret that any conflict should have arisen between the ecclesiastical members of the Roman Catholic Church in Montreal, and the lay members belonging to the Canadian Institute. It has been their Lordships' duty to determine the question in accordance with what has appeared to them to be the law of the Roman Catholic Church in Lower Canada. If, as was suggested, difficulties should arise by reason of an interment without religious ceremonies in the part of the

ground to which the *mandamus* applies, it will be in the power of the Ecclesiastical authorities to obviate them by permitting the performance of such ceremonies as are sufficient for that purpose, and their Lordships hope that the question of burial, with such ceremonies, will be reconsidered by them, and further litigation avoided.

[1] "1. That the Institut Canadien, founded with a purely literary and scientific aim, has no doctrinaire teaching of any kind, and carefully excludes all teaching of pernicious doctrines from its midst.
"2. That the Catholic members of the Institut Canadien having learned of the condemnation of the Institut Canadien's *Annuaire* for 1868 by decree of the Roman authority, declare their total and unequivocal submission to this decree."
[2] "3. Because this submission forms part of a report in which is set out a hitherto secret resolution establishing religious toleration, which has been the principal ground of the condemnation of the Institute . . . Everyone will understand that in matters as serious as this, no absolution can be given, not even the last rites to those who are unwilling to renounce the Institut and who have acted hypocritically in pretending to submit to the Holy See."
[3] "Church burial must be refused – 1o, to Jews, infidels, heretics, schismatics, apostates, and to all those who do not profess the Catholic religion. 2o, To children dead before baptism. 3o, To those who have been by name excommunicated or placed under interdict, unless before dying they show signs of repentance in which case they may obtain Church burial after censure has been lifted by our orders. 4o, To suicides, etc. 5o, To those killed in duels, etc. 6o, To those who, without legitimate excuse, have not fulfilled their Easter duty. 7o, To those who died notoriously guilty of some mortal sin. 8o, To public sinners who died impenitent, such as adulterers, prostitutes, witches, mountebanks, usurers etc."

34 THE GUIBORD CASE AND THE PRIVY COUNCIL

Le Nouveau Monde, Montreal
December 16-21, 1874 [translation]

The Privy Council's judgment in the Guibord case is interesting to study, from whatever point of view. . . .

Such men, accustomed to receiving great cases from the four corners of the globe, living among the élite of the educated class of the British Empire, could not regard a case like the Guibord affair from the narrow point of view in which the majority of the liberal magistrates of our little province, Gallican or Protestant still place themselves. The Lords of the Privy Council approach, one after the other, the great questions of public law, of ecclesiastical and civil law which present themselves in this case: and one never sees them evading these questions through improper procedure or subtleties, nor are they visibly biased in their decisions.

The first of these issues, and the most important, is without a doubt that of the *Status* of the Catholic Church of Canada; without dwelling on the terms of surrender, the Quebec Act (1774), or the Treaty of Paris (1763), which grant the free exercise of the Catholic religion, "as far as the laws of England allow, under the Supremacy of the King as laid down by a statute passed in the first year of Queen Elizabeth," they openly recognize the liberty of the Catholic Church in this country. The status of this church in English Protestant Canada is not, and cannot be that which existed in French-Catholic Canada.

"It follows from the documents that, although the Catholic Church had ceased, at the time of the conquest, to be an Established Church of the State, nevertheless it continued to be a Church recognized *by* the State, retaining its privileges and continuing to enjoy certain rights (like the Tithe) which the law gave it the means to enforce."

Such was not the opinion of the *Institut,* which maintained that the treaty and subsequent acts of the English Parliament had left the Catholics within the provisions of the Gallican law . . . "under the protection of the Gallican Church." The Superior Court of the time, according to this school of thought, possessed the powers of the French *parlements* to hear appeals "by writ of error" from the decisions of the ecclesiastical courts. One remembers how many of these ridiculous or despicable judgments, rendered in France on the strength of these "appeals by writ of error," were collected by the Honourable Judge Mondelet, following M. Doutre's example, some forcing the priest to give the last sacrament, guarded by two soldiers, to pitiable public prosti-

tutes, impious persons, etc.

If Guibord's lawyers do not venture to demand more such monstrosities, it will not be because their principles will prevent them.

Starting from the principle enunciated in the case of *Long v. The Bishop of Capetown,* their Lordships acknowledged that there is not a State Church in the colonies; not even the Church of England, which is on the same footing as the other Churches, neither better nor worse.

The noble Lords, pushing their principle further, declared that the Bishop of Canada or his officer, if he established one, could excommunicate *namely* or *by name* any one of his Diocesans (inhabitants of his diocese), and "that it would be the duty of the civil courts to recognize this sentence, to respect it and to make it effective"; for, "according to canon law, the Bishop is always *Judex ordinarius*, having the power to hold court, judge and condemn, if he has not established an officer to carry this out."

"And, furthermore, one must remember that unless such sentences are recognized, there will be no means to conclude the various questions about the faith and the discipline which can be set up among the Catholics of Canada, concerning the recognized canons of this Church."

This declaration of the highest Court of the Empire is very valuable to us, and we must record it.

Many a time we will need to invoke it against the narrow-mindedness of our magistrates, who would want to prevent the ministers of the faith from making the slightest allusion to public sinners or scandal mongers; and who will always have recourse to damage suits to punish the ministers and teach them a lesson about Christian charity and the way to uphold the morality and discipline of the Church.

What outcries of peacocks would we have heard if the Bishop or the priest had dared, from the high pulpit, to declare M. Doutre, M. Dessaulles, M. Guibord excommunicated for heresy, or schism or as public sinners! There would not have been enough gold in the country to make amends for the "harm" that such a denunciation would have caused them. Wrong, says the Privy Council. Who then will maintain the discipline and the faith in the Church, if not the Bishop? – and if his diocesans are recalcitrant and violate the rights of the Church, he can excommunicate them *by name, and the civil courts will recognize, respect, and carry out such sentences.*

We repeat, it is absolutely essential to point out especially, this great liberty of the Church, which is formally recognized by Her Majesty's Privy Council.

After all that, one naturally wonders how and why these same Lords came to the conclusion to reverse the verdict in the Guibord case, and order that he be buried in a common cemetery, in spite of the Bishop's decree. . . .

---

35 LE NOUVEAU MONDE'S EXTREME ULTRAMONTANISM

The Daily Witness, Montreal
December 22, 1874

The *Nouveau Monde* in criticising the conclusions of the judgment by the Lords of the Privy Council in the Guibord case seems to do little else but repeat the arguments used in the case by counsel on its own side of the question. It is easy to understand this when it is remembered that this paper looks at the question from the extremist Ultramontane point of view, which cannot tolerate the bare idea of popular rights or responsibility to the civil law as modifying or offering checks to the development of its aims. Constitutional government as developed in England and other free states where the law is supreme, and claims the right to remedy injustice wherever found, is altogether insupportable to Ultramontanism, which indeed is perhaps only another name for arbitrariness in Church government. It has been seen that the law of France recognised neither the decrees of the Council of Trent nor those of the Roman congregations. This law was in force, and formed part of the ecclesiastical law in Canada at the time of the cession.

Has it ever been formally abrogated or modified? Of this the Privy Council could find no proof. . . .

---

36 THE EAGLE AND THE ARROW

The True Witness and Catholic Chronicle, Montreal
December 25, 1874

The full text of the decision of the Judicial Committee of the Privy Council in this long pending case, being now before the public, we think that many of our readers may be pleased to have a short account of the circumstances which led to this long litigation. . . .

To understand the merits of the case we must needs say a few words about the *Institut Canadien.*

The *Institut Canadien* is a literary society founded some thirty years ago in Montreal with the avowed object of furnishing the public with a reading room, a library, and other appliances for educational and scientific purposes. About the year 1858 several of the then members of the Society not being pleased with many of the books contained in its library, proposed the naming of a Committee charged with the revision of the catalogue, with the object, we suppose, of eliminating any peccant matter the said library might be found to contain. A warm discussion ensued, and finally it was voted by a large majority of the *Institut,* that the library contained no improper books, and that the *Institut* itself was the sole judge of the morality of its library. Under these circumstances the matter came under the cognizance of the Bishop, who took the side of the minority of the members of the *Institut;* declaring that its library did contain many most immoral books, which no Catholic, which no Christian, which no man with any respect for the natural law, should read, or put into the hands of young persons of either sex. His Lordship therefore declared that the *Institut* had incurred the censures pronounced by the Church until its library should be purged of the books which he denounced as immoral.

To judge of the merits, in a moral point of view, of this action of the Bishop, we must take some allusion to the contents of the library of the *Institut*. It contained no doubt many good and valuable books; but it also contained others of a most objectionable character – books to which not only all Catholics and all Christians must object as contrary to Christianity; but to which every decent man who respects the natural virtues of chastity and moral cleanliness, must, no matter what his views of religion, also object.

Of these objectionable books we will mention some that have mostly struck us on a perusal of the Catalogue of the library of the *Institut*. We find therein, for instance, all Voltaire's Works; his filthy, his unmentionably obscene *Romans* which not only throw ridicule upon all revealed religion, but which are very cess-pools, throwing out day and night a stench sufficient to poison the moral atmosphere of the entire world. A singular circumstance connected with this portion of the *Institut*'s library we must mention. One of the books contained in a *complete* collection of the *Works of Voltaire* (which the *Institut* announced as being in its possession) comprises of course the ineffably beastly *Pucelle*; but though, by implication from its catalogue, acknowledging the possession of this work, the *Institut* pretends that it is not on the shelves of its library. By what sort of moral or intellectual jugglery this extraordinary feat of having, and at the same time of not having, a book is accomplished, we cannot pretend to explain. We may form a shrewd guess as to how the trick is done; but we leave it as a puzzle for our reader's ingenuity. *En attendant*, we must continue our analysis of the *Institut*'s strictly moral library.

In the catalogue we find amongst others, a long array of the works of *George Sand* in which are sung the praises of impure and illicit love, together with a fine assortment of the books of that very filthy old satyr, *Paul de Kock*. That our readers may form some estimate of the moral value of these works, with which the *Institut* adorns the shelves of its library, and whose perfect morality it maintained against the Bishop, we may mention that, in a celebrated Protestant literary *Review, Blackwood's Edinburgh Magazine*, the writer of the first is spoken of as the "Sappho of Adultery"; whilst the other is dismissed with the curt remark that the lascivious old beast is evidently so destitute of all moral sense whatsoever, as to be ignorant of the word decency. These, not to be tedious, were the works which the Bishop condemned as immoral, as highly unfit to be put into the hands, or placed under the eyes, of the *jeunesse* of Montreal, and which brought about the quarrel betwixt the Church and the *Institut Canadien*, which culminated in the excommunication of the members of that society.

Would Protestants divest themselves for a moment of their bitter anti-Catholic prejudices; would they for a moment grant that it is possible, barely possible, even for a Catholic Bishop sometimes to be in the right – we would fearlessly leave the decision in the case as betwixt Mgr. Bourget and the *Institut Canadien* in their hands. – Nay! we would go further, and would confidently expect from every Protestant father, from every Protestant mother, from every man who respects the natural laws of chastity, of moral cleanliness, and of conjugal fidelity, a vote of thanks to the Bishop, Romanist though he be, who denounced as immoral, the works of one whom eminent Protestant authorities have branded as the "Sappho of Adultery," and of that lewd old reprobate *Paul de Kock*. As it is, the sympathies, we are sorry to say, of the ultra-Protestant and evangelical community have all been on the other side.

And yet the question here at issue was not one of dogma; was not indeed merely a question in the supernatural order; it involved not only the issue: Are the works of Voltaire without restriction – for even in Voltaire's works we must make a distinction – wholesome food for a community calling itself Christian, and against which the Christian minister of religion has no cause or right to raise his voice? But are the novels of George Sand, the aforesaid *Sappho of Adultery,* are the tales of *Paul de Kock*, books fit to be put in the hands of any young person? Are they not morally corrupting? And is not he, or it, which lends his or its aid in making young persons acquainted with this peculiar style of literature, * * * * ? Our readers will each one for himself, fill up the blank as his moral feelings may dictate. . . .

We cannot, in concluding this brief history of the case, but express our regret that the very able counsel for the *Institut* should, in the course of the proceedings, have indulged in such very severe language against the Church and her ministers in Canada, as that which in the reports we find attributed to him. . . . He should have remembered that, if to-day he stands before the public, as a prominent member of a learned and honorable profession, it is, under God, to the Church, to the Bishop, to the priests whom he is severe upon, that he owes his social and professional position, and other worldly advantages; that they, when he was in very humble circumstances, took him by the hand, brought him into their colleges, educating him gratuitously and out of their abundant charity giving him that intellectual life which he now devotes to the service of their enemies; that in fact, he is the creature of their bounty, and the work of their hands. . . . The wounded eagle felt – so the fable tells us – her anguish redoubled as she reflected, that the arrow which had struck her was feathered or tipped with the spoils of her own wings; may not the learned counsel for the prosecution make a personal application of this fable of the Eagle and the Arrow?

---

37 A RIOT AT THE CEMETERY

The Gazette, Montreal
September 3, 1875

Attempts to Bury the Remains of
Joseph Guibord –
A Fiasco – A Mob Interferes –
Disgraceful Scenes –
The Cortège Hurriedly Retires – Force to
be Employed.

Towards two o'clock yesterday afternoon a number of people, women and men, assembled about the vault in the Mount Royal Cemetery, where rested the remains of Joseph Guibord. Mr. Doutre, the Messrs. Thibeaudeau, and Mr. A. Boisseau, Secretary of the *Institut Canadien*, were early on the ground, and Messrs. M. A. Galt, Robertson and MacCrea, Trustees of the Mount Royal Cemetery Company, and Mr. Turner, the Secretary, who attended in order to see that no disturbance took place – and an infraction of the peace was among the possible contingencies. Happily, however, in this quarter the utmost tranquility reigned, and it was imagined that the interment would be effected without trouble or disagreement – hopes which were subsequently painfully disappointed. . . .

The vault was opened in presence of an eager crowd, which pressed about the doors despite the sickening odor which floated from its gloomy recesses; several attendants quickly entered, and in a few moments appeared with the coffin which was enclosed in a rough box rudely painted of a dark red color. It was placed in the hearse, a very unpretentious vehicle, with a plain heavy cross rising from its centre, and drawn by two black horses, covered with black trappings; the coffin was enveloped in a British flag, but why, it would be difficult to explain. The hearse, on leaving the cemetery, was followed by some fifty persons on foot and several carriages, and perhaps one hundred persons, chiefly of the laboring class, including women and children, were present on the grounds. The cortege was obliged to make a lengthy detour to reach the Cote des Neiges Cemetery, which immediately adjoins the Protestant Cemetery, being easily accessible for pedestrians. The distance between the burial grounds was hurriedly traversed; but on arriving at the Roman Catholic Cemetery, an excited crowd was found at the gates. Groups had been gathering in the vicinity during the previous half hour, the ringleaders haranguing their friends and gesticulating violently, as they spoke about the attempt about to be made by the members and friends of the Institut. They stood in and near the gates, closely scanning the roadway, in order that they might not be taken unawares, and a large number of carriages arriving on the trot, followed, as they correctly imagined by the hearse, they were strongly disposed to shut the gates and to forbid any further entrance until it should be their royal pleasure to act otherwise. The carriages rolled up to the gates in spite of the shouts and murmurs of the spectators, and several were admitted, but as by this time the dreaded hearse was rapidly approaching, hoarse cries of – shut the gates – arose, and no sooner said than done. They were closed very hurriedly and very bunglingly, and had firmness and decision been shown, in lieu of hesitation and weakness, in all probability these disturbers of the peace would have been easily cowed; but this was not to be. The gates were nervously barred as the hearse drove up the roadway, and stopped; nothing was done for several minutes – and in the interval, the rioters became emboldened. The driver of the hearse, a young man named Seale meanwhile kept his seat, although his position was far from enviable. Encouraged by the want of determination to effect an entrance, if this were possible, these disturbers of order, who were all French Canadians, and all apparently residents of the neighborhood, essayed more overt acts. They set to work to strengthen their position by propping the gates on the interior; and several, the ringleaders in the movement, ran about shouting like madmen: *Ils n'entrent pas – ils n'entrent pas; Jésus Christ, ils n'entrent pas; Mon Dieu, ils n'entrent pas; Vierge, ils n'entrent pas. Il y a des bouledogues ici,* screams another – *ils n'entrent pas.* Imprecations were showered upon the head of Mr. Doutre, and a rush being made for the horses, the driver deemed it prudent to leave the spot, narrowly escaping an upset the while, as he was forced to leave the roadway, and turning sharply to pass between a tree and the gate, the frightened animals on the point of breaking loose of all control, a shower of stones thrown by the crowd assembled in the cemetery fell about the vehicle, but fortunately no damage was sustained. Mr. Doutre and his friends did not seem to know what to do under the circum-

stances, and decided opposition was certainly a contingency for which they should have been well prepared. Half an hour, or more was passed in inaction; the ring-leaders could not calm the excitement under which they labored, and their actions gave color to the suspicion expressed that they had fortified their effervescent courage by means of liquor; Mr. Doutre, Mr. Thibeaudeau and Mr. Boisseau stood at some distance from the gates, conversing about the situation, as if it was all a bewildering surprise; they stated that word had been sent to Desroches, the guardian of the cemetery, in the hope, that he might be able by persuasion to induce the mob to disperse; and it was said that he did endeavor to do so, but without the slightest avail, as the rioters would listen neither to warning nor reason. Matters were becoming monotonous, when the shouts, threats and imprecations were renewed, a portion of the mob ran to woods, the spot where all the friends of the *Institut* and of the deceased were supposed to be standing, and their most forcible argument, stones, which unfortunately were but too plentifully strewn in the neighborhood, were again brought into requisition, being hurled into the crowd regardless of consequences; several persons were severely injured, and the hearse was again obliged to retire to a considerable distance; even the sight of the horses, who were far from being contented with their novel position, seemed to inflame these peaceful subjects of Her Majesty with fresh religious zeal, and a stronger desire to prevent a defilement of holy ground. Another half hour passed; and finally defeated by a mob Mr. Doutre and his friends, preceded by the hearse, and followed by a long train of carriages, drove rapidly away in the direction of the city, the spectators being wholly in the dark as to their intentions. Many supposed that the assistance of the military would at once be obtained; others imagined that they would return supported by a squad of armed policemen or volunteers; the problem was solved when the procession was seen defiling up the roadway to the Protestant cemetery, and the coffin having been restored to its resting place, the friends of the deceased departed, altogether uncertain as to what would be the next step in this disagreeable drama.

The rioters were disposed to imagine that the departure was a ruse to throw them off their guard, and they refused to open the gates on any consideration. Possibly they are still on duty. The only mode of obtaining entrance into the cemetery, in the meantime, was through a gate at some distance above. An officer of the Fabrique was found at the chapel. He explained that he came up to receive the dues, which are always paid at this spot, and represent the Fabrique; and he stated that he had requested the mob to cease its disgraceful proceedings. Asked whether the counsel of the Curé or of any of the clergymen would not be effectual, he was of opinion that even the remonstrance of their pastors, would be of no effect whatever. He was also inclined to throw the blame for the entire disturbance upon the shoulders of the friends of the deceased, for the reason that if no announcement had been made as to the time when the interment would be attempted, the mob could not have assembled to offer resistance to this proceeding; but to this representation was made the reply that the friends of the deceased would scarcely care to "sneak" into the cemetery as if ashamed of the act of depositing in a grave the bones of the man whose cause they had so warmly espoused. . . .

A couple of hundred persons may have taken part in the riotous proceedings; and perhaps a couple of thousand, inclusive of women who were spectators of the disturbance; they were dotted over the grounds and the rocky heights opposite the main entrance were occupied, as an excellent position from which a capital view could be secured; the road was lined with carriages, for however slender may have been the apprehensions of Mr. Doutre, many citizens were clearly of a decidedly different opinion. . . .

38 LA MINERVE'S PROVOCATIONS

The Daily Witness, Montreal
September 3, 1875

. . . The conduct of Guibord's friends and those who have sympathized with them in refraining, despite the great provocation offered, from any attempt to enforce the law at their own hands, and resolving to bide the action of the constituted authorities, is undoubtedly a great moral victory for the friends of civil rule and order, and throws entirely on the shoulders of the Ultramontane party in this Province in general, and possibly certain shining lights among them in particular, all responsibility for what may afterwards happen in the enforcement of the law, which will now have to be carried out, no matter at what cost. . . . It is a notorious fact that the friends of the cause deprecated to the utmost any attempt at what might be construed as a public demonstration, and beyond the discussion that a case of so much interest gives rise to, no invitation was made calculated to cause an undue assemblage at the funeral. As it turned out, the latter did not exceed the dimensions of an ordinary respectable cortege, and the arrangements were all with the expectation of peace and quietness. On the other hand, the *Minerve* seems to have been well posted as to coming events, having prophesied that the interment would not be allowed to take place, and, as one of its own confreres, which does not take the Guibord side, remarks, while hypocritically pretending to deprecate any disturbance was doing what it could to bring on one. The Landswap organ having chuckled as much as it could over the discomfiture of the funeral party – a discomfiture all the sweeter to it that they comprised several opposed to its corruption politics – feels nevertheless that the issue is a compromising one for the particular interests of the Province that it claims to represent, and accordingly protests against making *all* the French-Canadian population responsible for the resistance made by "a small group." If it thinks this "small group" has done wrong it takes care not to say so.

On the contrary it defends them to the utmost, stating, in defiance of overwhelming testimony to the contrary, that they were "calm and peaceable," except a few isolated cases of stone-throwing and vociferation. This "little group," however, in other parts of the report becomes a "foule" (crowd), and when the funeral party are obliged to retire it swells to the dimensions of "the public," who, the *Minerve* asserts, at the moment the cortege began to move, saluted it with jeers and hisses. If anything could make the French-Canadian population responsible for this riot it is such a report as *Minerve*'s. It says the covering of the coffin with the British flag was "unusual," but that ought surely to have insured it from the insult of having stones thrown at it, if the cross over the hearse – an emblem held sacred by Catholics – failed to do so. The contempt manifested for both seems to show that the crowd in the cemetery were as destitute of the "religious feeling" attributed to them as they were wanting in respect for the law of the land. The people of England have been well indoctrinated by their press in the details of this Guibord case, and this riot will be serious news for them after the eulogiums of Lord Dufferin on the people of this Province, especially the French-Canadian section.

---

39 THE QUEEN'S LAW OR MOB RULE

The Montreal Herald
September 3, 1875

This affair yesterday assumed a new phase and one of a character very different to any which it has hitherto passed through. Heretofore the question has been one involving directly at least only the members of a particular Church, though a Church which from its numbers and wealth is more conspicuous than any other in the country. Within that religious community the dispute was of a mixed religious and legal character, and it was one which apparently could in the last resort only be decided in due course of law and by the tribunals, just like a suit for tithes, Church rates, or any matter of a similar kind which might be in controversy. It was a question, to our apprehension, of implied contract, the layman asking for the enforcement of his rights, just as in suits of the kind we have mentioned, the clergy seek to enforce rights which the law confers upon them. At present we have a new problem presented to us – it is whether a mob shall set the law, when regularly administered, at defiance. The public has, no doubt, regarded with interest, as all intelligent persons must do, an affair so remarkable, and embracing such profound and various affections and claims as those which attach to the ecclesiastical proceedings against the deceased, Guibord, and the subsequent effort to vindicate his freedom of action. But, as we have said, this interest has been, except to Roman Catholics, that of spectators. It is otherwise now. The matter of the most consequence which is to be determined at present is whether the Queen's law or mob law is to prevail. Whether Guibord is, or is not buried, is a matter of only speculative concern to the community in general; but it is a matter of life and death to any community whether a proceeding directed by the highest constitutional tribunal shall be violently interrupted, without any adequate force being employed to put down the rioters. In the face of that question the rights and wrongs of the original cause of dispute, even the justice or injustice of the decision, wholly disappears; for after all there must be some end to controversy, and if any unauthorized body of violent men can make their will prevail over the law in one case, they may do so in all. . . . We know not what steps may hereafter be taken; but we trust that at all events we may have an end put to such disgraceful and disastrous acts as those to which we refer.

---

40 A PLEA FOR CIVIL OBEDIENCE

The Gazette, Montreal
September 3, 1875

We had strong hopes that common sense would for once assert its sway, and that the burial of the remains of Guibord would have been permitted to take place yesterday without molestation. That, we believe, was the desire and intention of the Fabrique, and certainly of the more intelligent and influential of our Roman Catholic fellow-citizens, and we are bound to say there was nothing in the conduct or demeanor of those who have espoused the cause of Guibord to justify any other course. There was an utter absence of anything like an imposing demonstration on their part, and their willingness to accept, in the meantime, the simple burial without religious ceremonies, showed an absence of all attempt at glorification in their triumph that should have secured for them other treatment than that which a comparatively few thoughtless enthusiasts, in a mistaken interest in the cause of the Fabrique, extended to them yesterday. That nothing more serious than an unseemly demonstration occurred is matter for congratulation; but the effect of the resistance cannot be otherwise than unfortunate. . . .

. . . The authorities will, we hope, take such measures as will ensure the quiet performance of this burial, and in doing this they will have the hearty sympathy and support of all classes of the community. Whatever our opinion of the facts may be, however little people may sympathise with the effort to secure for a man's remains the ecclesiastical privileges which during his life-time he voluntarily despised, there ought to be and we hope there will be among intelligent men – men who value the peace and prosperity of this community, and who, recognizing the differences of race and religion that prevail, are anxious to do nothing to disturb the harmony which has generally characterised us – no difference of opinion as to the duty of all loyal subjects to pay a loyal obedience to the behests of the highest Court of the realm.

41 THE CHARACTER OF THE LATE JOSEPH GUIBORD

The Daily Witness, Montreal
September 4, 1875

. . . A high ecclesiastical dignitary of this city lately said, in conversation with a well-known French-Canadian gentleman upon the present difficulty, that he regretted exceedingly that the censure of the Church should have fallen upon Guibord, for that, having known him for upwards of twenty years, he was the last man who deserved such a misfortune. The same clerical authority stated that as far as honesty, public and private virtue, and integrity in the broadest sense of the term, were concerned, Guibord was without reproach. Guibord was a man of more than ordinary ability. When the catechism and hymns for the use of Indians in the North-West were published, l'Abbé Garin, amongst others in charge of the mission, consulted Guibord as to the best mode of putting the Indian language into type, and of forming the matrices. Although the Indian language was entirely unknown to him, Guibord undertook the difficult task of putting these works into print, and accomplished it so well that for ten years he furnished the Roman Catholic mission in the North-West with the catechism and hymns for the use of the Indians. In recognition of these services l'Abbé Garin and his coadjutors were accustomed to bring Guibord some of the finest mink and otter skins that could be obtained in the North-West. When visiting Montreal Guibord was one of the first whom l'Abbé Garin, Bishop of Anemour and others called upon, and the effusions of sentiment that passed between them gave no promise that the pious and simple-hearted printer would in future become the object of the anathema of his church. Guibord was foreman of Mr. Perrault's printing establishment, and was greatly beloved by his employers and fellow-workmen for his kindness and many good qualities. C. O. Perrault, Esq., Vice-Consul of France, from whom we obtain several of these particulars, says Guibord's punctuality was proverbial among those who knew him. The lawyers in St. Vincent street where he then worked were accustomed to say in reference to this habit of his: "It is not one o'clock yet, for Guibord has not passed." Mr. Perrault considered him as one of the first printers in the Dominion. He had great mechanical ingenuity, and was, in fact, a scientific printer. He was the first who introduced stereotyping into this country, and the first book stereotyped in Canada was done under his supervision. Mr. John Lovell states that he was personally acquainted with Guibord since 1826, and during all that time he never knew him to have erred through strong drink or bad company, or have been guilty of a dishonorable act. At the time of his death he was the oldest printer in Canada except Mr. Lovell. Guibord was sixty-two years of age when he died. . . .

. . . A few days before his death Guibord met one of his fellow members of the Institut in the street, and asked him what was the news about their appeal to Rome. The answer was that no news had yet arrived, but the Institut hoped that justice would be done them. "I hope so too," said Guibord, "for I feel that I am going fast, and unless this matter is settled before I die there will be a row (*tapage*) about my grave. I am a poor man, and they will no doubt bury me along with those that have been hanged if they can." "Have no fears about that," returned his fellow-member, "your friends will see that you are no worse treated than a rich man." The case of Guibord is another illustration of the curious fact that the greatest sufferers from the intolerant bigotry of the Roman Catholic clergy, have been men of superior excellence belonging to their own church.

42 THE GOOD THIEF

La Minerve, Montreal
September 6, 1875 [translation]

Our Protestant newspapers, even the most respectable, certainly lack the necessary information to judge rightly the actions of ecclesiastical authority, at the very time when they pretend to be righteous.

It appears that they cannot explain how it is that ecclesiastical burial was refused Guibord, when it is sometimes granted to freemasons and other members of the *Institut Canadien*.

For informed Catholics, the difference is not at all mysterious. It is the priest that helps the dying man to settle the question. If the freemason gives signs of repentence and promises to retire from the society if he returns to health, he will be granted ecclesiastical burial. Thus it is with the members of the *Institut Canadien*; everything depends on the intention manifested *in articulos mortis*.

The priest therefore represents the grace of God. A man could have been a great criminal throughout his entire life, a monster in the eyes of society, without having truly comprehended the enormity of his crimes – until finding himself face to face with death. If he then sincerely confesses and begs forgiveness, the faith tells us that he can be saved.

Two thieves are crucified beside Our Lord Jesus Christ; one of them is pardoned for his crimes and receives the promise of heaven, and the other dies in agony and despair. Why this difference? Why does the one enter immediately into the joys of paradise, while the other remains in suffering? Because one repents and begs for mercy and the other does nothing about it.

With such an example, have Christian journalists the right to blame the Catholic Church for dealing differently with the repentent sinner and the one who is not? Therefore, gentlemen, do not be shocked if you sometimes see the freemasons receive ecclesiastical burial. Rather, have faith that they have played the "good thief."

43 RELIGIOUS FANATICISM COULD PROVOKE REPRESSION

Le Bien Public, Montreal
September 6, 1875 [translation]

We have often expressed our opinion on the Guibord case. We have said that it was an ecclesiastical question that should never have come before our courts. But we have always maintained, and we still maintain, that from the moment our courts have spoken, we must comply with their decisions; even to the point where the law is changed.

To endeavour to resist the carrying out of a judgment of the court by force, and above all a decree of the Privy Council, is an act of unpardonable folly.

All the newspapers, all those who have influence on public opinion, must exert themselves in an effort to pacify the people.

What will result from the resistance to the burial of Guibord? Do people believe the authorities are going to yield? But, is it not known that the English government will send an army, if needed, to carry out the judgment. There may be bloodshed and numerous arrests, severe punishments, but that would not prevent Guibord's being buried.

The Catholics are quite right to feel their religious feelings are being offended, but sensible people will understand that they must suffer in silence and try to find ways to render such conflicts impossible in the future.

It is unfortunate that the Protestant and Catholic newspapers do not realize the danger in provoking religious fanatacism at this moment.

La Minerve made a supreme effort, this morning, to manifest its religious zeal in the matter of the Guibord case; and to stir up the Catholics against the Protestants – chiefly against the reformers. It would like to persuade people that the English Tory party is all . . . but on the side of the religious authorities in this case. Well, there is only one opinion among the Protestants, whatever party they belong to, which is that Guibord be buried; and that those who are opposed to the fulfilment of Her Majesty's decree be severely punished.

But let us hear what the *Leader,* political ally of *La Minerve* and *Le Nouveau Monde,* has to say.

The *Leader,* Tory mouthpiece in Toronto, ally of *La Minerve* and *Le Nouveau Monde,* writes the following on the subject of the tentative interment of the deceased Joseph Guibord: "The city of Montreal has again been debased by the supremacy of mob rule. When Guibord's body was transported to the Roman Catholic cemetery yesterday, the inebriated rabble closed the doors, cursed the dead body of Guibord, pelted the wagon with stones, and drove away the friends of the deceased. The authorities, nevertheless, allowed these shameful events to take place; even though they had been informed that a riot was brewing, the objective of which was scornfully to reject the decree of the Privy Council of England authorizing and ordering the interment of Guibord's remains in the cemetery. Clearly, the police authorities as well as the volunteers of Montreal are a collection of poltroons if they will allow a pack of ignorant French-Canadians to scorn a decree of the highest court of the Empire."

---

44 A PLEA FOR MODERATION ON BOTH SIDES. L'EVENEMENT, SEPTEMBER 3, 1875

*in the Globe, Toronto
September 7, 1875*

While we are sorry to see that some of the French papers of Quebec which express any opinion on the disturbance connected with the attempted interment of Guibord rather favour the rioters, and would like it if these were yielded to so that mob-law might be left possessed of the field, others take a different view. Among these *L'Evenement* [of Sept. 3] says:–

This incident is all the more to be deplored, as the religious authorities had taken a more becoming attitude. In face of an order which violated her liberty and obliged her to tolerate an act which wounded her conscience, the Church had determined to allow it to pass, and to oppose to the outrage no other resistance but that of the mute protest of the wounded moral sense. Why, then, should the excesses of a crowd, led astray by an indignation very natural perhaps, have caused us to lose the benefit of such a wise resolution? We had hoped that we had finished with this sad Guibord affair, but it is only too evident that things will not remain as they now are, and that the interment in the Catholic cemetery, for an instant delayed, will not the less take place, and with a reduplication of the scandal. Violated at first by the order of the Privy Council, liberty will be anew violated by the *emeute*. It is thus that the first violation of liberty brings along with it others, and involves complications only to be avoided by each power respecting the rights of the other.

The Catholic Church is mistress within her own fold. She has the right to grant or refuse Christian burial to whom she pleases, and it is absurd and tyrannical for the State to interfere, and to pretend to know better the obligations and rules of the Church than she does herself. But the State *has* interfered, *has* pronounced, and it is neither for the dignity nor interest of the Church to offer resistance to law. The ecclesiastical authorities have fully understood this, and it is deplorable that an irresponsible body of men should take upon themselves to avenge religion for an outrage which could not touch it. It is equally certain that the friends of Guibord have been exceedingly ill-advised in not resting content with the sort of triumph which they gained at London, but have wished to impose upon our religious population the spectacle of an interment made in holy ground in spite of the authority which there watches over the inviolability of the grave and the repose of the dead. They have light-heartedly provoked the popular feeling, and it is only owing to the good character of our population that the outburst has not been more violent. They have played with the most powerful elements to a greater extent than prudence could sanction. For our part we protest energetically against an enterprise which can have no other result than to put in peril both the good feeling subsisting between the populations and the interests of religion. There is surely altogether too much ado

being made around the grave of Guibord; and even from the point of view of those who have espoused his cause, it is risking too many and too precious things merely to have the satisfaction of putting in the ground the little which remains of a man who was never anybody of any consequence whatever.

---

45 M. DOUTRE'S MADNESS

Le Nouveau Monde, Montreal
September 7, 1875 [translation]

What can one say, or think of this man, who, for the pathetic glory of extending his madness beyond endurance, would not hesitate for an instant to endanger the lives of thousands of his fellow-citizens; to watch the blood of his compatriots flow in a riot, and to change this peaceful city into a field of fratricidal carnage.

Among all the sinister figures surrounding Guibord's coffin, the most repulsive is, in our judgment, this French-Canadian who, betraying everything – his faith, his nation – today appeared in public at the head of a gang of infidels, led them to the sacred field of the dead, opened it to this alien gang, and invited them to desecrate the earth in which the dead lie in the eternal peace of the grave.

In truth, it is hard to believe that this religious city harbours such a man in its bosom.

---

46 HOW THE CHURCH MAY BE AVENGED

Le Nouveau Monde, Montreal
September 8, 1875 [translation]

(i) Vengeance of the outraged Church

The Church endures violence, but never sanctions it. And particularly in the Guibord case, it does not count on violence to avenge its dignity and rights, so shamefully trampled underfoot. We can comprehend the just indignation of the Catholics: we also realize that, in such circumstances, it is not easy for them to remain calm spectators to the outrage being committed against their Holy Mother, the Church; but however much they might wish to do violence in the name of their justifiably indignant feelings, they know how to imitate the submissiveness of the Church; they do not respond at all to provocations from the enemies of their faith; for the Church has in its hands the weapons of a just revenge; the ground it has blessed and consecrated to serve as a resting place for our dead, can also be execrated and secularized, if sacrilegious hands dare to desecrate it.

They should not then be alarmed at the idea that the remains of their beloved relatives will be put in contact with those of an unruly child whom the Church was obliged to excommunicate and to dismiss from its bosom. Between the small piece of consecrated ground that they would usurp to bury his body, and the rest of the sacred ground where the remains of the faithful lie in peace and harmony with the Church, the Church will place a demarcation which will stand as a monument of shame and disgrace to its fanatical oppressors.

(ii) Our English Protestant Fellow-Citizens

We do not know if it is really the desire of some English Protestants to incite such hostile attitudes between themselves and the Irish and French-Canadian Catholic population to bring about a regrettable blow-up between the two groups. To witness the persistence with which the majority of their newspapers insult sentiments most dear to us, exaggerate all the facts, as if on purpose, and overwhelm with insults and outrages men who have never done anything to deserve such conduct – one would truly say that they hope for nothing else but the upheavals of a war that would destroy the peace and harmony this country has enjoyed for a great many years. . . .

If there are (as we doubt not), men of gallant soul and intelligence among our English compatriots, who do not believe that they themselves, any more than the country, have anything to gain in a conflict of race and religion; we ask them to use their influence to silence the aggressors on their side, – as we, on our own, endeavour to forget the resentment that they have caused.

Rightly or wrongly, the Catholic population is becoming more and more firm in the conviction that certain Protestant circles have chosen to push domination to its farthest extreme and to take advantage of every occasion when they believe that they can, with impunity, disregard the rights of Catholics and trample them underfoot.

In Manitoba, in New Brunswick, this spirit has been manifested in the most open manner, and the Catholic population of these provinces still suffers from the unfortunate policy that such a spirit has engendered.

In this province, this tendency towards dissension and the disregard for laws, that place us *vis-à-vis* the power of the *Anglais,* on an equal footing, is becoming more and more accentuated.

We therefore wish that those Protestants who have the habit of constantly getting mixed up in the interests and affairs of our Church, would henceforth concern themselves exclusively with their own affairs; and abstain from entering into an area that they only contaminate with their ignorance and bad faith.

As for us, as Catholics, we have always avoided interfering in their affairs. We willingly leave them to collect all the disloyal priests, perjured ministers, and apostates on whom the yoke of the Roman Catholic Church has weighed too heavily.

We have never penetrated into their churches to interpret the sermons of their preachers, and used it to foment dissension among the various persuasions.

We have desired liberty for the Protestants, just as we demand it for ourselves: and we intend to have it.

And let it be well understood, we are determined to preserve this liberty, and we will preserve it.

If peace and harmony are destroyed, the responsibility should not fall on us, but on those who would so maliciously have provoked the hatreds and conflicts among the population.

Our English Protestant fellow-citizens must understand that they will suffer at least as much as we from these dissensions, and it is in their interest to take pains to prevent them.

Hence, it is not simply a question of mere sympathy or moderation that presents itself, but an issue in which the material prosperity of the country is at stake.

If defiance and resentment are permanently introduced into our social structure, we will have what took place in Ireland and elsewhere; occult organizations forming on all sides, arming themselves for vengeance and ruin, defying authority and the law.

Is this what these fanatical, unbelieving sects really want?

---

47 A CATHOLIC WRITES TO THE EDITOR OF THE MONTREAL HERALD

The Montreal Herald
September 8, 1875

To the Editor of the Montreal Herald:

Dear Sir, – Would you kindly grant me a portion of your valuable space to reply to your correspondent "Peace," merely in justice to the other side of this much vexing Guibord question.

Your peace-loving friend states, or at least endeavours to prove, that because Guibord acted in accordance with his conscience, the Catholic Church had no just right to visit him with her censures. In support of this theory, he quotes certain words of Dr. Newman, on *Conscience*, which only have value as a portion of a treatise; apart from their explanation by the venerable Doctor, they can be used for any argument. It is an old saying that the Devil can quote Scripture to suit his purposes. "Peace" forgets that conscience is composed of a very elastic material and can be moulded to any form, or stretched to any capacity be means of habit. Thus the man who in the beginning of life would scruple to steal a three cent stamp, can gradually accommodate the capacity of his conscience to the extent of millions. I am afraid if conscience be taken as the standard whereby we measure a man's crimes, we will soon have a crop of consciences with the stomach of Wantley's dragon.

As an Irishman, I deny the right of England to rule my country, but if I go over to Ireland to-morrow, and join some society whose aim is to sever the links that bind my country to England, even though I may be actuated by conscientious convictions, the chances are, that some unconscientious peeler would clap me and my conscience into durance vile. No doubt "Peace," and all his loyal friends, would say that miserable peeler did his duty, and that I had no right to have a conscience of so peculiar a construction, as to deny British supremacy in all sublunary matters. Most decidedly, assuming that the English have a right to govern Ireland, they would be justified, in their view of the matter, in granting me free lodgings in one of their inimitable stone jugs, even though my conscience was terribly opposed to anything of the sort. The law never examines what a man's conscientious ideas may have been, when he breaks the statutes "made and provided," but simply judges the fact on the evidence and punishes accordingly.

Now, Guibord was a Roman Catholic, outwardly a member of that Church and acquiescing in her doctrines and dogmas. He becomes a member of the *Institut Canadien,* and meanwhile the Roman Catholic Church condemns that institution as dangerous to faith and morals, and informs the Catholic members that they must leave that society, or, persisting in their course, be accounted guilty of rebellion against the Church, and subject to the penalties prescribed in such cases. Mr. Guibord elected to remain a member of the Institute, and thereby became guilty of rebellion against the Church, and incurred the penalties of excommunication and forfeiture of Catholic burial, – that is, burial with Catholic rites in consecrated ground. Mr. Guibord may have been influenced by conscience; but that is a matter between him and his God. Canon law, like Civil law, is guided by facts, and the evidence supporting them; and in the case of Guibord the fact proven on evidence was, that Guibord denied and resisted the authority of the Church despite the pains and penalties prescribed for so doing. According to the laws of the Church he was found guilty and punished. If a rebel to the State be punished by the State irrespective of his conscience, wherefore should not a rebel to the Church be punished by the Church according to its laws? "Peace" asks, "Why did the Fabrique plead to the action?" Why? Because trusting in the justice of their cause, they expected a judgment in their favor, which would prevent future disturbers from giving similar annoyance. Because in the beginning, as now, the people would have resisted the burial of Guibord, and the Fabrique hoped that the judgment they had expected, would be a final defeat to the Doutres and that ilk, and the fanatics who cheered them in their rebellion, and thus avoid all cause of animosity.

To speak of the Privy Council of England judging a Catholic case on canonical principles, is as absurd as would be the submitting of the case of the Rev. Mr. Machonochie to the judgment of Cardinal Manning and a council of English Catholic Bishops. "Let us have peace," cries your peace loving friend, but when these few defamers of their own mother revolted against the Catholic Church, why were they patted on the cheek and supported by wealth and influence? We will have peace, no doubt, but it will be, I very much fear, dearly bought. You have raised your idol, gentlemen, and you may well shudder at the ugliness of his countenance.

The Catholic clergy, who have been pointed at as the enemies of law and order, the disturbers of the peace, etc., are now called on to allay the phantom their fanatical enemies have raised. You call on all Catholics of position to aid: – Aid what? The desecration of our graveyards? Would it not be more delicate to leave Catholics to act as they consider proper, without volunteering advice in a matter so delicate? Have we not been outraged enough? We will do our duty, and that duty has been expressed by His Lordship the Bishop of Montreal and the Rev. Mr. Rousselot. We must smother our indignation if needs be, but let those who have brought things to this pass, hide their heads and try to learn the forbearance they are so pat at preaching.

Yours truly,

J.P.S.

---

48 SPIRITUAL AND TEMPORAL POWERS

The Globe, Toronto
September 8, 1875

In a recent letter thanking a German author for the dedication of his work, Mr. Gladstone wrote as follows: – "Germany now holds the first place on behalf of the world in asserting the necessity of limiting the spiritual power to spiritual things." It does not follow from this that Mr. Gladstone, whatever his admiration for the work that has been accomplished in Germany, would endorse all the means used for its accomplishment.

If the proposition holds good that the spiritual power should be limited to spiritual things, not less strong or less worthy of acceptance is the rule that the temporal power should be limited to temporal things. If the State has the right to be held free from the aggression of the Church, none the less has the Church the right to immunity from the interference of the State. Perfect liberty in all that relates to matters spiritual is of as great importance as perfect liberty in matters temporal. The intrusion of the temporal power upon religion in any of the forms in which it is represented, is not only an error, but an absurdity. It is an error, because it involves an attempt to manacle or hinder what in its very nature should be absolutely free; and an absurdity, because, although it may harass, or annoy, or persecute, it cannot compel the submission of that which is beyond all chains, or prison-houses, or penalties. Where these principles are well understood, as they are in our country – wherever, in fact, spiritual liberty is complete and unquestioned – collisions ought to be impossible. Temporal authority should have no cause of aggression where it has no ground for jealousy; spiritual authority, on the other hand, has no occasion for one iota more liberty that it enjoys in the right to administer its own affairs exclusively and without question.

The charter of this state of perfect freedom is, of course, to be found in the law under which the rights of both are established and maintained. To the law both may appeal, and to the law both must submit, as a condition of the freedom they enjoy. We do not say that every one must give a mental assent to the terms of every decision of the law. The defeated suitor can generally discover a flaw in the judgment against him, but he has nothing to do but to obey nevertheless. And to defy or to resist the solemnly declared arbitrament of the law is an offence more or less grave according to the form the resistance assumes.

We have been thus careful to note the precise relations in which, under a free constitution, Spiritual and Temporal authority stand towards each other and towards the law, because it is necessary to a correct appreciation of the issue raised by the attempt to resist the decree of the highest legal authority of the realm which has recently occurred at Montreal, and may be said, in fact, to be still proceeding. The action of the Quebec Courts – sustained by the opinion of the Judicial Committee of the Privy Council – is represented on behalf of the defendants in the recent suit to be an invasion of ecclesiastical authority – an usurpation, in fact, on the part of the temporal authority. But it is really nothing of the kind. It is not the temporal authority, but the law of the land, that is asserted; that very law which is equally available to protect either civil or religious rights and liberties. If there were any attempt to strain the law, or to infringe in the slightest degree on the perfect liberty of the Catholic Church, as a Church, in any matters pertaining to faith, or doctrine, or discipline over its own members, the Fabrique would have every friend of civil and religious freedom on its side. But the law has decided that the Fabrique, claiming to speak and act on behalf of the Church, has exercised a prerogative not its own, for which it has not valid ecclesiastical authority, and that it has done a wrong for which it must make reparation in the only way in its power. . . .

This authoritative judgment demands, therefore, not merely the negative assent, but the active compliance, of the Fabrique. As loyal citizens, relying for the protection of their own rights and privileges upon the law, it is their bounden duty to sustain, strengthen, and uphold the authority of the law. If they would – had the law given them the right so to do – have excluded the bearers of the body of Joseph Guibord from their cemetery, they should, the judgment being the other way, exclude the crowd of lawless persons who have illegally constituted themselves the guardians of the ground for the time being. But having said this much – and we believe the great body of Roman Catholics in Canada will agree with us – it is none the less important that the right of the Roman Catholic Church, or any other religious body, to make laws for and within itself which no other authority shall question should be maintained. Hence the need for discriminating between an act done according to the law or rules of the Church, and one committed without the sanction of their own laws by a member or members of the Church. . . .

---

49 BISHOP BOURGET TO THE EDITOR OF THE GAZETTE, MONTREAL

The Gazette, Montreal
September 9, 1875

Bishop's Palace
September 8th, 1875

To the Editor:

Sir, – As there have been disturbances some days since at the Catholic Cemetery of Cote des Neiges, I consider it a fitting opportunity of informing you of the following facts:–

1st. Measures had been taken that, if the body they were attempting to bury in the aforesaid cemetery, had been so interred in defiance of the laws of the Church, the place where it lay should be immediately interdicted, and looked upon henceforth as a cursed spot to be held in execration. For the Bishop considers himself in duty bound above all others, to see that the mortal remains of the faithful children of the church rest together in peace, overshadowed by the Redeemer's Cross, till that last day when, calling all men back to life, He will judge them with the full pageantry of His might, and render to every one according to his deeds.

If, therefore, fresh efforts are made to introduce the aforesaid body into the consecrated precincts, I request all Catholics to remain quiet like true children of the church and loyal subjects of Her Majesty the Queen.

I exhort them, at the same time, to unite their prayers with mine, with those of the clergy, of the religious houses, and of every pious family to obtain from the Father of all Mercies that these events turn to the advantage of religion.

2nd. As far as circumstances allowed, I had sought the protection of the municipal authority, that all in its power might be done to prevent demonstrations of violence which, however just the intention of prompting them, are always very much to be deplored.

3rd. I have to return thanks to Providence that the meeting on this occasion was little more than a mere popular protest in favour of the reverence due to the dead who have slept in the Lord and subject to the Sacred Laws of His Church.

4th. I deem it time to invite every one to sign petitions to the Queen begging of Her Majesty to enjoin that the rights possessed by the Catholics of this large city, not to be molested in the exercise of their Holy Faith be respected by all those whom Providence has called to share her royal authority.

I remain, Mr. Editor,
Very truly, your obd't serv't.,

+ IG. Bishop of Montreal.

50 M. DOUTRE IS THE DISCIPLE OF A MANIAC

Le Nouveau Monde, Montreal
September 10, 1875 [translation]

We ask our readers to forgive our talking so often of this worthless individual, but, in a word, we are not at liberty to dispense with doing so. Erostratus was a madman, but in setting fire to the temple of Diana, he managed to bequeath his name to posterity.

M. Doutre aspires to that kind of glory. He also undertook to destroy a Church, and that Church is the Catholic Church.

Observing him in his mad struggle, Erostratus must seem to everyone like a wise man, beside this maniac.

In his mania of destruction, he at least knew enough to undertake only what he needed to attain his ends, but his disciple does not have this same foolish wisdom.

When peace is finally restored in the wake of his latest fit, and when the Church has punished the sacrilege he chose to commit, he will not even be left with the satisfaction of exciting the abhorrence of his fellow citizens; he will be nothing to them but an object of ridicule and contempt.

He is well aware of this, and already he is making fresh endeavours to keep his name before the public, to arouse more sympathy among the fanatical imbeciles who pay the price for this sinister comedy, by provoking new protests on the part of the Catholics whose delicate sentiments and most dearly held beliefs he has been offending for such a long time.

To this end he does not hesitate to insinuate, the cowardly hypocrite, that the venerable Bishop of Montreal, the clergy of the Diocese, and the Catholic population would like to raise the arm of an assassin against him. Through the ungodly newspaper which serves as his mouthpiece he has, by repeated invitations, encouraged his compatriots to help him profane the holy places where their dead are resting, he who knows that this population could not be a witness to this odious crime without manifesting the keenest indignation, and therefore deliberately laid them open to emotions he knew they would be almost powerless to repress; he who knew beforehand the great number of lives he would expose to danger, and in spite of that paid heed only to his instincts of evil, his hatred for the Church. This person now has the gall to declare that these provocations came from the Catholics themselves, that it was the clergy that stirred up the indignation of the faithful against him. He extends his malice, baseness, and need to slander us to the point of stating that we wanted to hand him over to murderers!

Oh! No, even supposing that something resembling vengeance ought to be directed against this man, we should be more than amply avenged by the overpowering shame and scorn that crush him right now to even consider punishing him in some other way. . . .

No, Doutre is worth more to the Church alive, rather than dead like his client, or encamped with the British. He serves as a lesson for those who think they can be Catholic and at the same time disregard the teachings of the Church. It is a lesson to the laity, just as Chiniquy serves as a preventive for the clergy. The rage against the Church that possessed them both (Doutre and Guibord), the incessant need they both manifested to spite their venom on the faithful clergy, on the sincere Catholics – is sufficient to demonstrate to all what excesses those who rebel against religious authority are led into.

---

51 ARCHBISHOP LYNCH OF TORONTO TO THE GLOBE, TORONTO

September 10, 1875

(To the Editor of the Globe)

Sir, – Would you permit me to say a word in the Guibord case? It may occur in Toronto at some future time a branch of a condemned tree might be forced to take root in our midst, and we might, perhaps, prevent mischief by explaining in anticipa-tion, what we should do in such a contingency.

But first let me cite a case in point. Suppose the Fenian organization, properly so-called, were established here and put under the ban of the Church, as is the Institut Canadien; and suppose one of the members at his last moments refused to renounce the society and accepted in preference to die without the Sacraments of the Church, would the Privy Council of the Queen absolve the memory of the man, and force us to give him ecclesiastical burial? I presume not; nor would the Protestants, especially the Orangemen, willingly acquiesce in what they would consider an unjust decree of a Catholic Sovereign, in a like case, where they would be the aggrieved.

I know the mind of our Protestant friends, and give them credit for desiring to know both sides of the question. They, perhaps, would like to know what is really the Institut Canadien, about which there is so much trouble. The French Canadian, in coming under British rule, gained one immense advantage – he was cut off from revolutionary France at a time when infidelity commenced to permeate and ruin all classes, especially the lower, of French society; and hence the descendants of French immigrants grew up a religious and loyal people. But, in the course of time, well-to-do Canadians revisited France, and brought back the seeds of irreligion and too much independence. To foster and perpetuate these evil plants they formed a Society called the Institut Canadien and filled their library with books fetid with the most rampant infidelity, such as was destroying the faith and morality of France. The Bishop of Montreal, as a good pastor of souls, as a good father, who would not place bad books in the hands of his children, wished to have these books removed, or, at least, locked up, so that all comers would not have access to them; and the Bishop further required that a priest of his appointment should watch over the morality of the library and the members of the Institut. Was this beyond the faculties of a Bishop of the Catholic Church in his treatment of those who professed to owe him obedience, and who wished to receive from him the Sacraments? No sane man would say that it was. The Institut Canadien would not comply with the reasonable demands of the Bishop, consequently his Lordship was obliged to warn them if they continued to disobey he would be obliged to cut them off from communion with the Church. The Institut Canadien retained its library and continued its opposition, and were consequently proscribed. The evil ceased to become greater, because good Catholics no longer join the Society.

I ask any of our Protestant friends of the various religious communities, Would you not, if the case were yours, refuse communion to the man who would disobey the formal injunction of your Synod or Conference?

But now comes the question respecting the bodies of excommunicated persons after death. But not wishing to intrude too much on your space, I propose, if you permit me, to continue these remarks in another communication in your issue of to-morrow.

I am, Sir, your obedient servant,

John Joseph Lynch,
Archbishop of Toronto,

St. Michael's Palace, Sept. 9th, 1875.

---

52 THE CIVIC AUTHORITIES AND THE RIOTERS

The True Witness and Catholic Chronicle, Montreal
September 10, 1875

We cannot but deplore the scenes that occurred in front of the Catholic Cemetery on Thursday last, when it was attempted therein to bury the mortal remains of Guibord, late of the Institut Canadien. A noisy and violent crowd barred the entrance to the Cemetery, and proceeded to such acts of violence that it was deemed prudent to return with the coffin to the Protestant vault. For this violence there can be no excuse, religion is neither profited nor honored thereby and the Catholic Church does not require the aid of rowdies and stone-throwers. We, therefore, as Catholics, condemn without reserve all attempts to oppose by physical force or threats of violence, the carrying out of the judicial sentence in the case of Guibord.

At the same time, and without pretending to palliate the conduct of the rioters, we cannot but censure the conduct of the friends of the deceased – inasmuch as they evidently did their best to provoke strife, by appealing to national and religious prejudices. As an instance of this we cite the fact that the coffin of Guibord was enveloped in a British ensign. What does this mean, says the Montreal *Gazette* very pertinently: the answer is obvious, the intent was to introduce the national element into the Guibord affair and to appeal to national prejudices against French Canadianism. No other interpretation of the display of the British Flag over the corpse of Guibord is conceivable, and that display was intended to be an act of defiance to another nationality. That this justified the violence we do not pretend, but, to a considerable degree it accounts for it.

Of course the Montreal *Witness* – it wouldn't be the Montreal *Witness* if it didn't do so – boldly asserts that the ecclesiastical authorities of Montreal not only connived at, but incited to, the riots which all Catholics deplore. Now, the fact is as our readers will see from an article which we copy below, from the Montreal *Gazette*, that the impugned ecclesiastical authorities, the Bishop of Montreal to wit, and the Curé of the Parish having had hints that violence might be anticipated on the occasion to which we refer, wrote to the civil authorities advising the timely employment of the police. If the advice was not taken it is surely most unjust to blame those who tendered it as having been either actively or passively parties to the riots.

Up to the time of going to press we know not what steps have been taken to carry out the burial of Guibord; even the date is uncertain; but it is to be trusted that when again it is attempted to remove the remains they will be attended with such a display of force as shall make even the semblance of resistance impossible.

---

53 ARCHBISHOP LYNCH DEFENDS THE CHURCH

The Globe, Toronto
September 11, 1875

(To the Editor of The Globe.)

Sir, – There is a *quasi* consent that each religious community should have a cemetery especially consecrated or set apart for the burial of the bodies of the members who died in communion with them, and it would be considered an outrage for the State to force them to bury with religious ceremonies the body of one of their members who, while he was alive, was excommunicated from their Church.

But the State steps in and says, this man bought a lot in the cemetery, and it can now be used for his burial.

But the lot was sold with this condition expressed or understood, for the burial of those only who died in communion with the Church, so that, like any other sale of a lot under condition, when that condition is wanting the land is forfeited. The Catholic Church provides for the burial of those who die out of her fold, for in every cemetery a place is set apart for the burial of such persons.

It appears to me that the State, in the case of Guibord, who died out of the pale of the Church, is manifestly interfering in matters not of its competency, and consequently need not be obeyed, for conscience sake; but this interference is rather to be tolerated to avoid a greater evil. If the Guibord case happened here I would hold myself neutral; the State could use its power of force and bury the body in our consecrated cemetery, but certainly not with any active assistance on our part. I would then order the grave or plot to be fenced in, and I would then proceed to re-consecrate the rest of the cemetery.

I might be asked, Do we think that the ashes of a notorious sinner who died unrepentant would injure the souls or bodies of those whose bones lay in the cemetery? I would answer no – nor would the bones of mad dogs or other unclean animals contaminate the cemetery. This is a subject to which we may return again. But such would shock all sense of humanity and public decency; then why make any trouble about the Guibord case?

We don't make the trouble; the trouble is caused by the State forcing the body of an excommunicated man into consecrated ground not under the direct jurisdiction of the State. The clergy hold themselves neutral, as they should. The State is strong enough to force its enactments, even when they are unjust. If the State think well to shoot down the people, it is the State's own business; and if the people resist and expose themselves to be shot, that is their own business too; if the clergy wish to help the State, and advise the people to keep quiet, that is their own business also. The Church tolerates without resistance at present the robbery and spoliation of its most sacred property, as witness the persecution in Italy and Germany, but then she does not help her enemies in their spoliation.

The Catholics of Montreal feel outraged at having their cemetery about to be desecrated by the introduction of the body of an excommunicated man. I don't wonder at it, but I would say to them, don't expose your lives in resisting the State; if you are commanded to renounce your faith, then suffer martydom rather than obey imperial mandates, as the early Christians did.

You ask again, "Why consecrate cemeteries?" This is a question that all religious bodies may answer as well as myself. Are we disposed to sympathize with the irreligious father who, speaking over the body of his own son, gloried that he was unbaptized, and that his body was now some use to humanity, inasmuch as it fertilized the earth – dung to dung?

Our idea of the sanctity that hallows the body after death is based upon the words of St. Paul, "Know ye not that your members are temples of the Holy Ghost, who is in you, whom you have from God, and you are not your own. For you are bought with a great price: glorify and hear God in your body." (1 Cor., vi, 19, 20) And again, "If any man violate the temple of God, him shall God destroy, for the temple of God is holy, which you are." (1 Cor. iii, 17) And again,

"I know that my Redeemer liveth, and in the last day I shall raise out of the earth and I shall be clothed again in my skin and in my flesh, I shall see God." Job, 19.

Hence the bodies of the just will be joined to their glorified souls and enjoy the beatific vision of God; hence our reverence for the bodies of the dead; hence the vice of impurity is so execrable to God.

I am, Sir, with much consideration, Your obedient servant,

John Joseph Lynch,
Archbishop of Toronto.

Toronto, Sept. 10, 1875.

54 THE GLOBE COMMENTS

Toronto, September 11, 1875

Archbishop Lynch and Bishop Bourget have both made their appeal to the public on the Guibord case. They have pleaded their cause in the presence of the public of Canada, and have asked for a verdict in their favour. We are always pleased when clergymen of any denomination take this, rather than the *ipse dixit* plan of settling difficulties. It is in every respect more becoming, and it gives all the weight both of the teaching and example of these reverend gentlemen in favour of freedom of enquiry and liberty of discussion. We may not be able to sympathize with them sometimes in their lines of argument; we may not acknowledge as correct either the premises from which they start or the conclusions at which they arrive. But their arguing the matter at all is what we cannot but invariably and cordially applaud as a movement in the right direction, and as a sign full of hope for the future. It is an acknowledgement that in these days unreasoning and unreasonable authority cannot hope to hold or retain its power. It must tell not only that it has decided thus and not otherwise, but it must give the reason for its decision being of a certain character and its commands pointing all in a certain direction. If Bishop Bourget does not so fully take the argumentative line as his right rev.

brother of the West, yet his missive is, in its way, not less significant, and in the interests of free thought and free speech not less encouraging.

. . . Throughout the British Empire, we are pleased to think, Churches are legally recognized simply as voluntary associations, into which men enter of their own free will, and in which they cannot be retained after they desire to walk out. In Churches, as in all other voluntary associations, there are certain recognized laws by which the proceedings of their officials and members are held to be regulated. With these the State meddles not, so long as these are in the harmony with the law of the land, and are administered according to the fair, honest meaning of the words in which they are couched. . . . What has the law to do with such voluntary associations? Simply to hold them to their own rules, so that every member when he joins may know that he or she shall be treated according to these rules, and not according to the whim or arbitrary decision of the office-bearers for the time being. . . .

The case, as put by Archbishop Lynch, is not fairly stated. It begs the whole question, for it takes for granted the very thing that is to be proved, and the thing which in Guibord's case has all along been stoutly denied. The claim of right to regulate what every one of the members of the Church shall read is one at once foolish and untenable, which the more it is pushed will be the more ignored and defied. We assure the Archbishop that there is not a Protestant clergyman in Canada who would wish to interfere with individual liberty, or would claim the right to say what the members of his Church should read and what they should avoid. Advice, direction, remonstrance in certain cases, there might be, but more than that would never be dreamed of by the greatest Protestant bigot, or the most arrogant Protestant ecclesiastical tyrant who ever preferred to be surrounded by intellectual slaves rather than to have the loyal adherence and attachment of the mentally and the spiritually free. Does the Archbishop mean to say that he and his ecclesiastics regulate the reading of every Roman Catholic in his diocese? He knows he does not, and he equally knows that he could not. Is there any such attempt made in any country in Europe? In France for instance? or Germany? or England? or Italy? Notoriously the reverse. The Church, on the contrary, deals very tenderly with great numbers, not only of those who may read heretical books, but who avow very free, if not infidel, opinions. Indeed, we question if there is any one country, except, perhaps, Lower Canada, in which the R.C. Church has sought to bring such pressure on the members of any literary association as it has attempted with the Canadian Institute. What may be the character of the books objected to we do not know, but sure we are that for one who would have read them, if the Institute had been left to its local insignificance and comparative feebleness, there are now scores, aye – and scores – of Roman Catholics, in good standing with the Church, who will not be satisfied till they know all about this literary poison of which they have heard so much. Archbishop Lynch may speak in a general way of the *fetid infidelity* of many of the publications. It may be so, but it is just equally possible that some of the writings denounced are among the master-pieces of the English language. In any case, however, the struggle of any clergy, we care not whether Protestant or Catholic, to regulate the reading of their people, and that by holding over them the terrors of the Church, is as alien to the spirit of genuine Christianity as it is to that of true freedom. It has always failed, and as long as human nature is what it is it will always fail. Let clergymen elevate the taste of the community to such an extent that bad books will not be sought for, and will become in this way scarce and harmless. Let them warn the ignorant and instruct the unwary. But if they are wise let them not stake their position and influence as religious instructors on their power to prevent some book, or magazine, or newspaper which they dislike being taken by their people, and its contents considered and discussed in all their bearings. If they do they will assuredly play a losing game, and besides will only intensify the evil they seek to *stamp out.*

The proposal of Bishop Bourget to curse the ground in which Guibord will assuredly be buried is more like the proceeding of a weak bigot than of a large-minded, charitably disposed, Christian prelate. It is a poor, round-about way of seeking to show resistance to the law of the land, and is virtually an incitement to further violence in the way of desecrating Guibord's burying-place after the law has taken its course, and put that grave under its protection. The Bishop's proposed course would besides, in our opinion, be as illegal as the resistance to Guibord's interment has been declared to be, and though it would do the poor remains no harm, it would be, while professedly obeying the law in the letter, setting it completely at naught in the spirit. Resistance to Guibord's interment is now to be withdrawn. The only dignified course for the ecclesiastical authorities in the circumstances is loyally to bow to a decision which they may still claim to be both illegal and oppressive, but which they can say they are too good subjects and too good Christians either actively to obey or passively to resist.

55 THE GUIBORD CASE AND CATHOLIC POLITICAL LIBERTY

The Daily Witness, Montreal
September 13, 1875

It was to be expected that the Ultramontane press would studiously misrepresent the decision of the Privy Council in the Guibord case as an encroachment upon the rights and liberties of the Roman Catholic Church in this province. We can understand and even sympathize with the indignation of those honest Roman Catholics who have been accustomed to regard this question only in the light which the Ultramontane press and clergy have judged convenient to throw upon it. We doubt, however, if there is one really intelligent and manly lay member of that Church thoroughly understanding the merits of the case and its bearing upon individual rights, who does not consider the decision of the Privy Council as a palladium of his religious liberty, and a wholesome check to the alarming assumptions of the ecclesiastical power. For such it assuredly is, and as such it will be in time very generally recognized. It is a conspicuous defence of every lay member of that Church against the caprice or tyranny of the clerical authority. It violated no recognized law of the Church, but rather it vindicated that law when it had been broken by the mere whim of a Bishop. . . .

. . . Surely all intelligent Roman Catholics must see that the decision of the Privy Council was just and in accordance with the laws of their Church – that it is a protection of the people themselves against the arbitrary and unjust exercise of authority by the ecclesiastical power. In this case the Bishop had been for years engaged in a contest with l'Institut Canadien. He had succeeded in driving from it the greater part of its members. The stubborn resistance of the remainder vexed and angered him, as through a long life, he had been accustomed to implicit and unquestioning obedience. In the heat of strife he was betrayed into an arbitrary act, not warranted by the laws of his Church. Who but blind Ultramontanes will say that the will of the imperious Bishop should triumph rather than that justice should be done to the poor printer?

Roman Catholics will find in this country, as they found in many others, that their rights and liberties are much safer in the hands of the civil power which they themselves help to control, than if left at the mercy of a priesthood entirely independent of the civil power. Under the present order of things the State is the supreme dispenser of human justice, and a Roman Catholic layman may appeal to the State against the unjust or illegal action of his priest or bishop. The Ultramontanes pretend that the doctrines of the Liberal party in this province are hostile to the Church and dangerous to religion. Suppose Bishop Bourget should carry his censures of that party only a little farther than was done in his pastoral letter of May last, and were to issue another *mandement*, declaring all Roman Catholic Liberals as "public sinners," and *ipso facto*

excommunicated, would those Roman Catholic Liberals feel disposed to submit without a murmur? When upon one of them dying, his body should be denied ecclesiastical burial by Rev. Curé Rousselot and the Fabrique, would not his friends and relatives gladly appeal to the State for that justice which the Bishop denied them? They would claim that the Bishop had acted in contravention of the laws of the Church, that by no decrees of Councils or of the *"Congregatio"* had the profession of Liberal principles yet been held to constitute a man a "public sinner," and they would perhaps, as being a minor point, insist that according to the laws of the Church, for an excommunication to be valid, it should mention the individual by name, whereas the sentence had been a collective one, passed upon the Liberal party as a body. This hypothetical case is sufficiently parallel to the Guibord case to show Roman Catholics the true bearings of the latter upon their own interests, and also to show how false is the cry raised by the Ultramontanes that the decision of the Privy Council is a persecution of the Church.

---

56 THE PROTESTANT PRESS AND THE GUIBORD AFFAIR

La Minerve, Montreal
September 13, 1875 [translation]

The Guibord case has caught the minds of many people, and caused ink to flow from many a pen. Halifax, Toronto and New York seem to be as actively concerned as Montreal, if we are to believe their newspapers. However, it's of no concern, because if our Protestant brothers looked twice at the matter, they would understand that it is none of their business.

Ultimately, the issue can be stated in the following manner. In Canada, are religions not free to regulate, according to their own understanding of them, matters of internal discipline, and to repudiate those individuals who do not wish to submit to their teachings? During his lifetime, Guibord, in cold blood, and in complete knowledge of the situation, chose between alternatives offered by his bishop on orders from Rome: either leave the Institut Canadien to live in the Catholic community, or leave the Catholic community to live in the Institut Canadien.

Without doubt, there is only one way to be Catholic, and that is the one defined by the Catholic Church. We can refuse to accept this, but then we must leave the Catholic bosom. If nobody is obliged to remain Catholic, we do not see that this belief, wherein the ideas and principles are so clearly defined, need be obliged to receive those who do not wish to respect its laws.

In the current dispute, what do we observe? On one side, all the Catholics, on the other the unbelievers and the Protestants who are adamant that Guibord died a Catholic? What interest do the Protestants have in this case?

Do they claim Guibord as one of them? Far from that. They are compelled to class him in the category of Catholics. For them, the Catholic religion is infamous, detestable, dangerous, and yet they make war over a corpse to see that this corpse is granted a Catholic repose. M. Doutre, the apostle of Guibord, is he Catholic? Are we permitted to ask this gentleman if he believes in the Catholic Church, and its Commandments, and if he cares to observe them. Does he accept the Catholic hierarchy and all its authority? We are not prepared to reply for him, but if he would reply to us that he rejects the bishop speaking *ex cathedra*, that he does not go to Mass nor Confession, and that he is not concerned with Baptism, nor carry out one Catholic practice: can we not ask him what is his goal in using such animosity in claiming the honours of a religious man for a corpse, for which he cannot personally make a case, and which hardly worried Guibord himself during his lifetime.

But would you reply along with the Protestants: Guibord had acquired a right to the plot of land, in the cemetery bought and paid for by him, and the courts made it right. The Church, or rather the *Fabrique* received the price of a plot for his family from Guibord. The *Fabrique* as the administrator of the material investments of the Church, is not supposed to examine the conscience of the would-be purchaser. It takes for granted that this man intends to die in the bosom of the Catholic Church, and that as a consequence he will take the necessary steps: and if he does not carry out these provisions, he will keep the plot for those members of his family who have done so. If there were not certain requirements for admission to a Catholic Cemetery, there would be no need for a Catholic Cemetery. One vast cemetery would do for all faiths. It is for this reason that the Protestant Cemetery receives thousands of different sects, each claiming to be worshipping God in a different manner.

It would seem to us that it is up to Catholic ministers alone to indicate whether the deceased have fulfilled the moral conditions of entry into a Catholic Cemetery. In comparison, the material conditions which are the responsibility of the *Fabrique* are of little consequence. Otherwise, the property owner whose family has renounced Catholicism could have Protestants buried in a Catholic Cemetery. What we do not understand, is that civil law became involved in examining the spiritual rights of the deceased in an ecclesiastical burial.

This is where the real question arises for us. In general, the newspapers properly accepted the remarkable letter of His Excellency the Bishop of Montreal. This letter relieved the Catholic conscience of a great burden, and filled them with joy. In the face of legal power, the Bishop made it known that there was only one way left to escape the use of violence, and that was by declaring the cemetery profaned. His Excellency, in respect for authority, pleaded with the faithful to abstain from all demonstrations. What more could we ask? That the Bishop go so far as to approve the decree of the Privy Council! That he try to instil in the minds of the people that this sentence did justice to the rights of the Catholic Church! The newspapers in Toronto, especially the *Globe*, the *Mail*, and the *Leader* are quite acrimonious about this subject. The *Leader* goes so far as to say in mentioning this letter: "In the style of a martyr, loyal only to the lips which pronounce words of peace, this man of the Church is only repeating in another way, the same feelings of rebellion that the populace was expressing in its own way the week before. The significance of the surprise that came about on the occasion of carrying out the Privy Council decree was that if it was the will of the Church of Rome, as interpreted by M. Rousselot and his Bishop, and not the authority of civil law, which must prevail in this part of the British Empire. . . .

The Bishop's proposal to send a petition to the Queen is simply an insult to Her Majesty. The signature of Victoria is at the bottom of the decree that the Bishop wishes to petition, and this decree was not issued until after complete proof was brought before the high court."

We are surprised that fanaticism is pushing the newspapers to such insolence. If the Catholic religion does not have the right to exist in Canada; very well. All kinds of persecution could be organized against us, and all we could do is bow our heads. If however, in the free province of Quebec, the Catholic religion has certain rights guaranteed by treaties which carry the *signature* of the ancestors of Her Majesty Queen Victoria, it seems to us impossible to carry further the spirit of conciliation than to accept a decree which appears to us to be violating these treaties, and then to respectfully raise our voices to Her Majesty, to ask for a more rational state of affairs in the future, allowing the Catholic Church the freedom to handle its own internal difficulties and to define the cases where one ceases to be a part of this community. . . .

57 ARCHBISHOP LYNCH ON CENSORSHIP

The Globe, Toronto
September 14, 1875

(To the Editor of The Globe.)

Sir, – You will very kindly permit me to correct a few statements of your article on my second letter in the Guibord case. I presume you will pardon this liberty. It is not very humiliating for a non-professional adept in the canon law of the Catholic Church to know less about it than a prelate of that Church.

Hence I claim your indulgence. You say that I assumed, as proved, that Guibord died excommunicated. I certainly do, even against all the civil judges of the courts, from highest to lowest, and I continue to assert that the prelates of the Catholic Church should, and do, know more about the laws of their own Church than any lawyer. I would not affirm that Catholic prelates know more about civil law than the civil lawyers. We think, also, that surgeons and doctors know more about anatomy and medicine than the ordinary learned men of the day. Guibord knew that he was excommunicated and refused at death to be reconciled to his Church. He that refused the greater, that is, the Sacraments of the Church, whilst living, would refuse the less, that is the funeral rites. The State should rather protect the body of a man from Church rites after death which he refused during life.

The excommunication of Guibord is better known to the Bishop of Montreal and his priests than to the lawyers even of the Privy Council. But it is asserted that the Church cannot excommunicate Societies *in Globo*. This is precisely what the Church has done and continues to do; as, for instance, condemning all secret societies and those who belong to them.

There are excommunications major and minor, and excommunications for individuals and societies. There are interdicts for persons and things, but with many of those we have nothing to do. That Guibord died renouncing the Sacraments rather than give up a proscribed Society, put him also into the category of the contumacious sinner, for whose body Christian burial may also be denied.

But you say as Guibord thought himself right he should get the benefit of his own opinion.

This right, private judgment, we do not recognize in the Church, nor do Civil Courts either recognize it.

You remark also that we cannot excommunicate persons for reading. This is precisely what we have done and ought to do. Did not the Bishop of Montreal the other day forbid his Catholic people, under pain of excommunication, the reading of a certain journal that was vomiting all sorts of abuse against the Catholic Church and his mandate was obeyed.

If I found our young men here reading the works of Tom Paine, and Voltaire, etc., I would forbid them under pain of excommunication. I might permit the reading of such works to good and learned men, who carry in their own brains the antidote to these poisons, – but the giddy and unlearned ought no more to meddle with such works than the children with loaded revolvers and dangerous poisons. Prelates of the Catholic Church have authority from God – to govern, command, and guide – "Obey your prelates and be subject to them, for they watch as being to render an account of your souls." (Heb., xiii). This is for the true prelates – others can only entreat and beseech. The bad books that are inundating Germany and France are ruining the people with infidelity, especially the upper walks of society called learned. Is it not therefore our duty to warn and protect our people, especially our youth, against such a contamination, though this contamination be couched in masterpieces of English language? We know that the English language contains books of the highest culture, uncontaminated, too, with infidelity, and that it is the duty of the pastor of souls to denounce all evils against faith and morals. Though all our people may not listen to our injunctions, still the immense majority will; we shall always labour to do what is possible to prevent evil, to satisfy our own obligation of conscience for the sake of religion and the good of those committed to our care.

In conclusion, we will reassert emphatically (1) that Guibord died excommunicated, and had no right to Christian burial; (2) that bad books and bad reading can be prohibited under excommunication.

I have the honour to be Sir, with much consideration,

Your obd't. servant,

JOHN JOSEPH LYNCH
Archbishop of Toronto.

Toronto, Sept. 14, 1875.

58 THE GLOBE REPLIES

September 14, 1875

We publish this morning a further communication from Archbishop Lynch on the Guibord case, reasserting, although we venture to think it does not prove, that Joseph Guibord was an excommunicated person, and therefore subject, according to the laws of the Church, to a denial of burial in consecrated ground. . . .

. . . A Bishop may be a marvel of piety, he may be a professed theologian, he may be a deep student of the mysteries of revealed truth, and yet not be well qualified to act, especially *ex parte*, as a judge of even ecclesiastical law. He may have the right to excommunicate for reading a book; but he may make, as the Privy Council decided the Bishop of Montreal had made, a mistake in fulminating a wholesale excommunication against all and everybody who belonged to the Institut Canadien. . . .

. . . And that a merely sweeping decree directed against all the members of the *Institut* should not ruthlessly excommunicate every one of them, is only consistent with common sense. For what says the Archbishop himself? He does not allege that the prohibition against reading books objectionable to the Church should be universal and without limitation. "He might," he says, "permit the reading of such works to *good and learned* men, who carry in their own brains the antidote to these poisons." Now it is not denied that Joseph Guibord was a good man, and it is asserted that he was a very intelligent man. If he had applied to Archbishop Lynch for permission to read any one or all of the proscribed books in the Institute the Archbishop, who is, we believe, at heart very liberal, would doubtless have given him leave. But the Bishop of Montreal, without hearing Guibord, without summoning him before him, without discriminating – as Archbishop Lynch says he would discriminate – between the good and learned, and the giddy and thoughtless, condemned Guibord to be cut off from the Church on earth and the Church above, and sought to load his very name with the infamy of a dog's burial. Why there is surely not a member of the Roman Catholic Church, Bishop, Priest or Layman, that should not in the face of the assertion of such an authority thank Heaven for the Guibord judgment.

. . . We shall not attempt to enter into any argument with the Archbishop as to the propriety of ecclesiastical intervention in regard to the books or newspapers that members of his Church may or may not be permitted to read, either for intellectual amusement or, it may be, the better to be able to refute the principles therein set forth. Practically, such a system must fail, and in one instance referred to by the Archbishop it has, we don't doubt, most signally failed. A few books, a newspaper or two, may be prohibited, but they are still read. Hundreds meanwhile, just as objectionable, are circulated without the ban being placed upon them; and there are plenty of immoral or irreligious influences in the world that good men of all denominations labour to counteract, but which no penalties are ever inflicted for. No Church and no prelate pretends to say exactly where the line as to reading or any other action shall be drawn. And then, supposing the question as to what books shall or shall not be read be determined, who is to say just how *good and learned* a man must be to be trusted with them. All old men are not wise; all young men are not giddy; all deeply read scholars are not insensible to brilliant even if perverse reasoning. The Archbishop says – *The*

bad books that are inundating Germany and France are ruining the people with infidelity, especially the upper walks of society called learned. But the Archbishop told us that it is the *learned* he would allow to read them, *for they have the antidote to the poison in their own brains.* When the Archbishop speaks of *warning people against contamination,* and protests *it is the duty of a pastor of souls to denounce all evils against faith and morals,* we agree with him; and if he goes further, and prohibits any reading or other acts in which his own people may indulge, but which he as their pastor regards as objectionable, it is not for us to complain. Only he must excuse us if, in the assertion of such prerogatives, we see all the more reason for such a jealous anxiety to assert their just rights, even on the part of members of the Catholic faith, as has been exhibited by the friends of Joseph Guibord.

---

59 JOSEPH DOUTRE REPLIES TO ARCHBISHOP LYNCH

The Globe, Toronto
September 15, 1875

(To the Editor of The Globe.)

Sir, – From the high tone of some of the public utterances of His Grace the Archbishop of Toronto, I have conceived, in common with others, a deep feeling of respect for his talents and his sincerity of purpose. His letters on this Guibord case, notwithstanding, or I should say on account of, the errors of fact they contain, are not of a character to diminish that respect. His Grace, knowing evidently nothing of the main facts, and having to explain to himself and to the public a conflict which has put the whole American Continent in commotion, imagined everything which could make a plausible defence of his Montreal colleague's position. When he learns that his facts are fictitious and imaginary, it will hardly be necessary to discuss his conclusions.

1. WAS GUIBORD EXCOMMUNICATED. – The parallel attempted to be

found between the members of the Institut Canadien and the Fenians has no other merit than being a piece of diplomacy to prepare the ears of his audience. However, I have no objection to accept the parallel in its entire bearing, provided it be treated from a Lower Canada standpoint. The Catholic Church in Lower Canada partakes of the character of an established Church. The laity constitutes, in each parish, a corporate body as regards the properties of churches, cemeteries, and parsonages. The properties belong to the parishioners, and not to the Bishop or the *curé*. The *curés* have the right to recover, before the Courts, the tithes from the parishioners. The Church, composed of the *curé* and laity, has the right to collect through processes of law any amount of taxation for the building of churches, parsonages, and the purchase of burial grounds, and the repairs and maintenance of the whole. These things do not exist in Ontario. There everything is voluntary, and I am not prepared to express an opinion on the respective rights and duties of the clergy and laity. But the condition of things in Quebec has constituted clear and well defined rights and duties for the two bodies. Decisions from the highest Court in Quebec, a Court uniformly composed of a majority of Catholic Judges, have laid down as a rule formally approved of by the Church, until the recent changes in the Constitution of the Catholic Church, that the old ecclesiastical law of France was still the ecclesiastical law of Lower Canada. The *Manuel des Curés*, by Mgr. DeSantels, Curate of Varennes, one of the honorary attendants of the Pope, and honorary Canon of the Montreal Bishopric, published in 1864, contains as a preface a circular letter of the present Bishop of Montreal, commending the book to the clergy of his diocese. At page 17 it says: – "No one can doubt that the common ecclesiastical law which obtained in France, before the cession of Canada to England, is the ecclesiastical law of Canada."

Viewing the case of the refractory Fenian in the light of these laws, I would not question the right of a priest to refuse communion to him at his last moments; but I would unhesitatingly deny him the right to refuse ecclesiastical sepulture to his remains. From time immemorial, Catholic France, both at home and in the colonies, has maintained that the sepulture of the dead, even in the times when ecclesiastical courts were in full operation, was exclusively cognizable by civil courts. *Excommunication major* only could justify the refusal of ecclesiastical burial, by separating, in a measure, from the Church the object of that excommunication. I need not tell an Archbishop how such excommunication should be pronounced to be valid; but for his readers and mine I must say that the law never acknowledged excommunication unless it were publicly denounced and personal, after monitions. No secret or collective excommunication has ever been admitted as valid. In fact, no system of public laws could coexist with a collective or secret exclusion from an Established Church. The French ecclesiastical and public law, as left us at the time of the Treaty of Cession, goes further. It claims for the civil Courts the right to examine whether excommunication, when pronounced, is conformable in its causes with the canons or not. When the case was argued here, numberless decisions of the French Courts were cited, declaring null and void excommunications pronounced with all the external formalities of the law, in order to reach the consequences of excommunication. And let me remark, that not one single case could be cited contradicting the doctrine above mentioned, both as regards the absolute necessity of a public and personal excommunication, and as to the right of enquiring into the causes of excommunication.

Bringing these principles to bear on the Guibord case, I must tell Archbishop Lynch (1) the members of the Institut Canadien were never excommunicated, even collectively; (2) Guibord was never excommunicated, either collectively with others or personally. An Archbishop or one hundred bishops would lose their time and words in asserting the contrary. If facts of a past age may be distorted, and made convenient to support a system, contemporary history is beyond such manipulation.

Here is what existed in regard to the members of the Institut Canadien, at the time of Guibord's death, on the 18th November, 1869. The Bishop had published a pastoral on 30th April, 1858, in which he stated that the Council of Trent pronounced excommunication against those who read or kept bad books, and that if the members of the Institut Canadien should persist in the bad path they had entered into, they would incur terrible penalties. The path so mentioned is nowhere defined, – no other is indicated – what it meant always remained a mystery, until Guibord was told, four or five years before his death, that it meant withdrawing from the institution, which he refused to do. For this, communion was denied to him. Refusing communion is of daily occurrence, and does not in any way amount to excommunication. On the day of Guibord's death, the Administrator of the Diocese received from the Bishop, then at Rome, a letter in which it was contended that an appeal made to the Holy See, by the Catholic members of the Institut, in 1864, had been decided against them, because in 1868, four years after, an *annuaire* of the Institut contained matters derogatory to the rules of the Church, – a speech from Mr. Dessaules, and one from Horace Greely, on liberty of conscience. Guibord died before the latter document was made known, so that the pastoral above cited was the only dictum applicable to him. However it was on the last document that the administrator based his instructions to refuse burial to his remains.

The only excommunication which was ever pronounced in Canada, according to the rules of ecclesiastical law, was that of a newly married couple, who had gone to a Protestant minister to be married. This was some six or eight years ago at Rimouski. Guibord, not being excommunicated, any reasoning founded on that error falls to the ground.

2. THE INSTITUT CANADIEN. – After twenty years of uniformity in the calumnies heaped upon this Society, one feels refreshed in hearing something new in the shape of misrepresentation. I do not in any way impugn the sincerity of his Lordship. I am sure he believes what he says. "In the course of time, well-to-do Canadians revisited France, and brought back the seeds of irreligion and too much independence." The only French people with whom the Institute ever communicated, before incurring the displeasure of the Bishop of Montreal, were Abbé Charbonnel, who became Bishop of Toronto, and Father Martin, principal of the Jesuits in Montreal. The Guibord case brought some members over to France, but until then none of the members had any occasion to invest in French irreligion, unless it were through the teachings of Messrs. Charbonnel and Martin sometime about 1845 or 1846. The library of the institution was formed from donations. For ten years no one thought of enquiring about our books. In 1854 a crusade began all over the world. Laymen, who had not the password, did not understand much, what was going on amongst them. The beginning of this latent and subterranean work came about the *Witness* and the *Semeur Canadien*, two Protestant papers which were sent gratuitously, and were not then much read, if at all. A proposition was made to exclude them from the reading room and in order to conceal the end aimed at, it was asserted in broad terms that all religious newspapers were a nuisance and a plague. There was not probably more than one per cent of the members who had ever thought of the religious character of the papers. The first and predominating feeling was that it would be ungenerous and ungentleman-like to tell editors who sent their papers gratuitously not to send them any more. The Catholic editors, who were not in the secret of the movement, like the *Journal de Québec*, were scandalized at the intended proscription of religious papers in general, and fulminated against the proposal. This movement died of itself, and fast. Another was put on foot. An assertion was publicly made that the library of the Institute contained immoral books. On this, it was expected that both Protestants and Catholics would unite to condemn immorality. The plan had a partial success with the Protestants. They could not imagine a bishop making such an assertion without good grounds. For

several years the Protestants kept a cool and diffident attitude towards the Institut. The Catholics who did not belong to the association naturally believed everything the Bishop said. Something had to be done to right ourselves with all shades of opinion. A deputation was sent to the Bishop with a catalogue of the books contained in the library, and they requested his lordship to point out any book which he considered objectionable, and we would try to satisfy him. The catalogue remained over six months in his hands, and, his lordship being about to leave for Rome, the deputation went back for an answer. The catalogue was handed back to them without the indication of a single book. When asked what he thought of the library, the Bishop said he did not signalize any book, as it could not bring a practical result. "What result do you desire, and what do you suggest for the guidance of those who heard from you that our library contained bad books?" "They will consult their confessors," answered his Lordship. Ever since, the matter remained in the same condition. Four or five years ago the *Nouveau Monde*, the organ of the Bishop, said the same thing as Archbishop Lynch, that the library of the Institut Canadien was filled with books fetid with the most rampant infidelity, such as was destroying faith and morality in France – or something to that effect. The Bishop of Montreal had never gone to that excess; his assertions were diplomatically enveloped, and he could not be called to account. It was different with the *Nouveau Monde*. An action for libel was brought against it by the Institut Canadien, and after a protracted investigation the *Nouveau Monde* was condemned as a defamer. The case, if I mistake not, is reported in the Lower Canada Jurist, and may be perused. I hope that Archbishop Lynch ignored these facts when he repeated the calumny of the *Nouveau Monde*, which could have appealed from that judgment, but tamely submitted by paying principal and costs.

The Catholic members of the Institut Canadien never claimed the right to read a disapproved book. They claimed the right of being members of a literary society which might have condemned books in its library. If they are wrong no Catholic could become a member of Parliament, because the library of Parliament contained books condemned at Rome. The facts, as I state them have been established under oath, both in the Guibord case and in that of the Institut Canadien and the *Nouveau Monde*. There has not been an attempt made at contradicting them. I do not care how many bishops or archbishops would give their words to the contrary, – we have judicial records on our side, and it is useless to think that we live in times when minds are degraded enough to accept the *ipsi dixit* of any man against the judicial evidence on which the whole structure of our institutions exist.

3. CEMETERIES. – All shades of worship possess cemeteries for the burial of their deceased members, with very slight differences as regards consecration, which it is not necessary to mention here. Let us speak of the cemetery of Cote des Neiges, where it was ordered to bury Guibord. When this suit began, and long after, the cemetery was unconsecrated. This fact deprived the Fabrique, defendant in the case, of the benefit of all the flourish we now read in the Archbishop's letters about the desecration of holy ground. It was, I think, after the appeal to England that, in order to create to themselves a new weapon, the defendants caused the cemetery to be consecrated. They imagined, in their great strategical combinations, that after fighting us from one court to another they kept in reserve an unsuspected torpedo to upset us after our victory, and they consecrated the cemetery at the eleventh hour. The Courts, both here and in England, failed to see the distinction, whether the cemetery was consecrated or not. The Privy Council took it as a fact that Catholics dying with their rights unimpaired were buried in a certain part of the cemetery, and they ordered Guibord to be buried there. It was ordered that he be buried where the Catholics were buried, with ecclesiastical ceremonies. After the death of his wife the Institut Canadien, as representing her estate, bought a lot for the purpose of burying her and her family. This

implied her husband, and in that lot he will be buried! Having taken from the Archbishop's feet the solid platform of the excommunicated Guibord, I wish him to stand on something in his next letter.

4. CHURCH AND STATE. – "It appears to me," says his lordship, "that the State &c. is manifestly interfering in matters not of its competency and consequently need not be obeyed, for conscience's sake, but (thanks!) this interference is rather to be tolerated to avoid a greater evil." That means: rather obey than be hanged. Many people, more commonly known in police courts than in palaces, use the same reasoning. In his first letter His Grace, politely bowing to Orangemen, asks them if they would acquiesce in an unjust decree of a Catholic Sovereign, in a like case, where they would be the aggrieved? After the revocation of the Edict of Nantes, the Huguenots said, Rather go away than be flogged or decapitated, and they made the fortune of England, of the United States shortly after, of Switzerland, of Flanders; and Germany. These were, like the Plymouth Pilgrims, the flower of their native country.

The difference between their case and that of the champions of the Church at the Guibord funeral on the 2nd Sept., 1875, may be found in the utterances of the drunken rowdies who blocked up the gates of the Montreal cemetery. There are times when unholy words have to be repeated. The Montreal drunkards shouted – "No bloody . . . . . . will pass over this gate! God damn Guibord!" &c., &c. None of them could stand erect on his legs. These were the modern champions of *religious convictions*. They would rather be hanged than obey, not knowing at the time the difference between a rope and a glass of whiskey. Let us go up the ladder and come back to the venerable Archbishop. He evidently wants to convey the idea that Protestant Judges know nothing of Roman Catholic ecclesiastical law, and have no moral authority in the matter, and must have been guided by religious prejudice and enmity. That argument was propounded by one of our Superior Court Judges, who expressed the wise opinion that if the Judges of Lower Canada were called upon to grant damages for the refusal to bury Guibord, they would be obliged to inquire fully into the canonical causes of the refusal, and grant such damages if the refusal were not justifiable, but they had no competence and no adequate knowledge of ecclesiastical law to order the burial! This opinion did not carry conviction in all minds. Simple people asked themselves if the Catholic Church were constituted under the Egyptian and Chinese Systems of old times, when priests kept to themselves the whole knowledge and laws of their country, and so closely that none but themselves could understand anything in it. Even Catholic judges were not supposed to know anything of ecclesiastical law. What could be said, then, of Protestant English lords of the Privy Council? They could competently decide cases coming from India, governed by Indian legislation, cases coming from Gibraltar, under Spanish legislation; cases from former dependencies of France, Holland, Italy, Denmark, &c., governed by the legislation of these respective countries; but Catholic ecclesiastical laws were beyond their attainments. Roman Catholicity claims to be *semper eadem,* and no one but priests and bishops are competent to understand its laws. – If we had said no, we would be branded as the most impudent defamers. Where and how could human wisdom constitute a more impartial and enlightened tribunal or jury than the Privy Council? The ecclesiastical law of England is almost the same as it was before the Reformation. Ecclesiastical Courts are in constant operation, and lawyers are trained as actively as they were at Rome, until the unification of Italy, in Courts *ad hoc.* The contest was not between Protestants and Catholics, but between Catholics alone. Whether one way or the other, the decision could have no manner of influence on Protestant matters. If it be contended that the Lords might be tempted into an assumption of power over Catholic questions; it must be remembered that they were exactly the proper tribunal to dispose of such a question. The Fabrique invoked the treaty of cession from the Government of France to that of England. The Privy Council is the Queen herself, acting with her advisers. One of the parties to that Treaty was in effect called upon to interpret it. Was it possible to come nearer to the source from which the law emanated?

I feel it to be tiresome to explain that we owe light to the sun, and I must close. That light is shining brightly everywhere, except in the Guibord case. Since its opening, half a dozen members of the Institut Canadien have been buried with ecclesiastical honours; one of them, a Freemason besides, was buried (after) three days of hesitations and discussions, about these two qualities, under the chancel of the church of Pointe Claire, near Montreal. Another who died at St. Paul, Minnesota, another in Chicago, and three or four others in Montreal, were all buried here with the honours of the Church under the direction of our good and converted Bishop. These facts are as notorious as the Guibord case itself. A little effort at humility and submission to the law would have settled the Guibord burial in the same manner, and I do not despair to witness that result, though not under the auspices of good grace. The Guibord case will have this beneficial influence on the future of this country – it will teach those who invoke treaties and law, that these facts act both ways; that rights have their correlative duties; that no one has the privilege of using rights and repudiating duties; that there is only one Sovereign over these lands, the civil and political Government; that any attempt to defy that authority may have the support of a few, but will be frowned down by all men of any worth or standing, without distinction of creed or nationality.

Yours, &c.,
Joseph Doutre.

Montreal, Sept. 13th, 1875.

---

60 M. DOUTRE IN ONTARIO

Le Nouveau Monde, Montreal
September 20, 1875 [translation]

. . . His letter, whatever he may say about it, is nothing less than an incendiary epistle.

If it were not for the good sense of the public, and the moderation of sensible men, the letter would be enough to subvert and revolutionize the whole country. As the genuine protector of well-being, social tranquility, and good understanding among all, we feel ourselves more strictly obligated to bring to the attention of the public, the perilous action M. Doutre is pursuing to the death.

Nevertheless, truth can also make itself heard in Ontario, as well as here; and there are powerful advocates of the rights of this Church whose foundations he has foolishly tried to shake.

Already, His Grace the Archbishop of Toronto, through the two letters he published on this burial question, has shown the public the true side from which it should be considered.

We have no doubt that this wise prelate is in the proper position to do equal justice to the falsities contained in the letter written by the defender of the *Institut Canadien,* that he is especially competent to enlighten respectable moral families, Protestant as well as Catholic, as to the nature of the books possessed by this institution which has earned for it ecclesiastical censure.

M. Doutre thought he could oppose the judgment of the Church with that of a free-thinker and above all free-*reader* who confessed in open court to having reveled in the reading of works denounced as contrary to doctrine and morality.

It suffices to cite the abominable novels of Georges Sand, – of abbé ***, of Eugène Sue, Michelet, Paul de Kock, etc., without counting Voltaire, – which are enumerated in the Catalogue of the *Institut Canadien's* Library, to realize the character of the decision by which our newspaper was convicted for libel, in the amount of $20,000 for having said that this library contained evil books.

The right-thinking public will weigh the import of the two authorities – civil and religious, in this matter.

61 THE ERRORS OF THE PROTESTANT PRESS

La Minerve, Montreal
September 23, 1875 [translation]

The unfortunate matter that caused so much emotion in Montreal a short time ago is hardly a concern among us now. For the time being, calm has settled over the remains of Guibord. This is not the case in neighbouring provinces. The Protestant newspapers continue to find fault. The commentaries continue; and God knows how we are treated! The first pamphleteer has appeared, the last of the 'quill drivers' who, not being familiar with even one aspect of the problem, puts the Catholic Church on trial, and, it goes without saying, invariably condemns the Catholic Church in support of MM. Doutre and Laflamme.

To be sure, these gentlemen have reason to be happy. The war they have begun is well carried on. The attacks against the tyranny of the Church, against its views on authority, will not mar the pleas of our two great lawyers. If they wanted to stir up the whole Protestant press against the Canadian Clergy, they can congratulate themselves at their complete success.

What is most revolting in the diatribes directed against us, is that all those who make use of the work of MM. Doutre and Laflamme for the basis of their argument, invariably make the clergy appear as the destroyer of the acquired rights of Catholics. They represent the clergy as wanting to innovate and impose new laws. They make the clergy appear to be a tyrant, who wants to bend the will of the faithful under a dishonourable yoke. If the allies of M. Doutre had taken the trouble to study the question, as would be expected of them from the moment they wanted to become involved in a situation that was not their concern, they would have seen that they are switching roles, and ascribing to the Church the role that the *Institut Canadien* has played.

In this notorious trial, it is the Church that is defending itself; and the attack against her does not relate only to the principles of immediate concern, but also to the whole structure of its government, its doctrine, and the spirit of the Church. If the Protestants had witnessed the attacks of MM. Doutre and Laflamme, they would be ashamed of their protégés: they would have seen the spirit that animated the lawyers of the *Institut*. They would have understood that is was, for them, not so much a question of obtaining the honours of burial for Guibord, but rather an attack on the Church.

When we read the pleas of the lawyers of the *Institut*, we cannot help but acknowledge them as the aggressors, and that the Church was merely trying to defend itself. We can also see, in this notorious case, that M. Laflamme was placing himself above the clergy, above the bishops, and even above the Pope: lording it over all, treating both the Bishop of Montreal and the Holy Father as litigants whom one would not expect to be worth a cent. M. Doutre went much farther, he advocated the annihilation of the Jesuits, and praised the savages who had martyred the first missionaries in Canada. We will say to our Protestant brothers that these lawyers thus used language none of those raised on prejudice against Catholicism would want to use. As we are writing for their benefit at this moment, and as it is meant to enlighten them, we ask them frankly if they can find someone among themselves who would dare to sign his name to the words pronounced by M. Doutre during the course of his defence:

"There is a circle of men in the world (Jesuits) who are in a permanent conspiracy against all that brings material and moral happiness to humanity – a circle of men who call themselves Catholic and who have been outlawed thirty-seven times by the Pope and the princes of all Catholic countries. In the course of these exchanges, the spirit of evil passed from the serpent into this circle of mankind. You proscribe it, you parcel it out, you cut it up in a hundred pieces to deliver it up to the winds of destruction – and slowly, secretly, and silently, these pieces seek each other's company in the darkness; from Africa to Europe, from Asia to America – and the serpent recomposes itself with a recrudescence of venom and hatred against Christian society. And when you think it has completely disappeared forever, sunken beneath the time-honoured origin of men's curses, you see its HIDEOUS head reappear, you see it spread its tortuous and SLIMY coils around the trunk and limbs of society, to strangle the body and soul of its victim – the civilized world.

"The clients of our adversaries are the Jesuits, who with their infernal art, are pleading here under the name of the priests and churchwardens of Montreal. At this moment they are laughing in their sleeves at the trick they are playing on the entire population, to put it into such a flutter, without even their fingertips being seen.

"Already our society is tied up in the coils of the serpent, ready to take its last breath without sounding the alarm. It's the hand of a dead man that brought it back to life: it is Guibord, still outstretched on the ground who will tear off the disguise of the defence. *Let us honour the savages of this continent who began to rid the soil of Canada of the first seeds of the Sacred Society of Jesus!*"

How do our Protestant brothers find this language? Do they admire its moderation, its reason, and its high-mindedness?

Let them alter the situation a little change the roles – let them imagine a Protestant who says in an open Court of Justice: Honour to those men who massacred our clergymen, honour to those who killed the ministers sent into the wilderness to preach the Gospel to the infidels, – and they will be able to explain better the disturbance they witnessed in Montreal a few days ago. . . .

62 PRESBYTERIANS SUPPORT THE CATHOLIC POSITION

La Minerve, Montreal
September 25, 1875 [translation]

We bring to the attention of the public in general, and our fellow Protestants in particular, the attached article, which we translated from a Protestant newspaper in Toronto, the *British American Presbyterian*. It is the most intelligent and impartial evaluation of the Guibord case that we have yet encountered in the English press.

In this article, one can see what the calm, rational Protestants think of this whole case, which was distorted and poisoned by the bad faith of a few fanatical Protestants, aided by a few free-thinking apostles of the Catholic faith.

The newspaper which we quote begins by stating, first of all, that the Guibord case is an issue which has nothing to do with the Protestants, Presbyterians, or others. It is a simple problem of ecclesiastical discipline, in which the Church must have the right of final decision. It demonstrates that, as a result, the Privy Council violated the rights of Catholics in rendering its decree, and it brings to mind that this is not the first time that this court has committed a similar injustice against religious liberty. It cites the example of the Scottish Church, persecuted for so long by the English parliament and the Court of England.

We reproduce here in full, that part of the article written by our Protestant colleague:

"The case of Guibord versus the Catholic clergy is not, in itself, of great interest to the Presbyterians. Here is an honest, worthy fellow, Guibord, who claims right to the end, to be an excellent Catholic. After his death, his friends, trusting his word, demand that he be buried in sacred ground with the customary ceremonies of the Roman Catholic Church. The priests deny that he died a good Catholic, and thus refuse to grant him an ecclesiastical burial.

Such is the original basis of the case.

At present, for the Presbyterians, who regard with perfect indifference all these superstitions concerning sacred ground, prayers for the dead or the destination of the dead, this dispute over burial with or without these prayers has absolutely no significance.

If Guibord and his friends believed that he could lead a pious life while rebelling against the clergy of Montreal, and if they also believe that he could have died a good death without the help of that clergy, they should then logically have carried it right to the end. They should have been courageous enough to draw the only logical conclusion: *that a man who is willing to live without the help of a priest, and die without absolution, should be equally satisfied to be buried without sacerdotal consecration.* Nothing would have been better than for Guibord and his friends to have come to this conclusion. Guibord lived as a Protestant against ultramontanism, now the doctrine of the Church of Rome, and he died in the same frame of mind in which he had lived. This being the case, why should he cease to be a Protestant at the time of his burial?

His friends, however, did not see the issue that way, *but demanded the ceremonies and burial of a Church from which they had been altogether estranged.* The Church was, in all probability, justified in rejecting their demand; as were the members of the *Institut Canadien* in taking the decision of *their* Church (as they called it) to the civil authorities.

When the case is presented in this light, those outside of the Roman Catholic communion must excuse themselves for thinking, with respect to the burial, like Galius when the Jews wanted him to submit to their court matters which were outside their jurisdiction. He replied, *that it did not concern them.*

The appeal was taken before the Privy Council of England. The Presbyterians have not forgotten that judicial opinion in this country, based on the Erastian constitution and the status of the Established Church, is quite uncertain and obscure on the subject of the separation between ecclesiastical and civil issues.

The Presbyterians were familiar with how the English Parliaments and judges had treated the Scottish Church on various occasions: thus it would seem strange to them that the Privy Council should take a similar position in the Guibord case – ordering the Catholic Church of Canada to provide, not only a burial ground for Guibord, but also Catholic ceremonies on his grave.

This is how the Parliament and the Privy Council view the Established Church, and this is how they believed the Scottish Church should be treated, to the point where they held that "there are two kings in Scotland, King James and Jesus," or in other terms, that *Church and State are two co-ordinate powers,* in which each has supreme jurisdiction in its *own domain.*

If the Privy Council had ordered the priests to carry out ordinary services over Guibord's remains at the time of his burial, the Roman Catholic Church would have been justified in disobeying the injunction: and would have had the sympathy of all enlightened Presbyterians. *Religious acts do not fall under the jurisdiction of the state,* and it is nothing less than persecution on the part of the state to order these acts carried out against the conscience of the Church; whether the Church be established or not, Protestant or Papal. Fortunately, the Privy Council avoided this danger in its judgment, although its reasoning in the question of whether Guibord was or was not really excommunicated borders closely on it."

A Catholic newspaper could not have made a more honest and just evaluation of this issue than did this Protestant newspaper. There is only one point which the *British Presbyterian* did not understand – that of Guibord's supposed right to be buried in the plot which was purchased by his heirs. This point is nevertheless quite plain: and once he understood this better, our colleague could not help but think that, as in the other instances, the decision of the Privy Council violates the rights of the Church. It is not a simple matter of the sale of ordinary land. The Catholic Church of Montreal consecrates a cemetery, reserved exclusively for the burial of its followers. It grants to Catholic families the privilege of purchasing plots or private ground in the cemetery, in which these families have thereafter the exclusive right to bury their members. But it is understood that these members must be Catholic as well: this is obvious. If it were otherwise, the Church would refuse the families this privilege, and would retain the right to determine the location of each burial.

The *Presbyterian* could not claim that a Catholic who bought a consecrated plot in a Catholic cemetery, would then have the right to bury there whomever he wishes, without regard to the laws of the Church which owns the cemetery. The sale is always *conditional*. That being the case, it is as unjust to force the Church to allow the burial of a Protestant or excommunicated person in consecrated ground as to oblige it to grant them funeral ceremonies. The only difference between the two instances is that the consecration of the cemetery as a whole is a preceding ceremony, while the other takes place at the time of the funeral. Anyone who is buried in consecrated ground, whether he does or does not receive the funeral ceremonies, is a participant in the previous consecration of that ground.

We will now conclude the citation on the question of the excommunication of Guibord!

As for the stand taken by the Privy Council, says the *Presbyterian* when it discusses the ecclesiastical question as to whether Guibord was excommunicated or not, one must concede that *this position is absolutely untenable....* If the Roman Catholic authorities are agreed among themselves on this point, that is sufficient: and it is an established fact that Guibord died excommunicated, whatever interpretation you may wish to put on that word.

It is useless to comment on this article. Originating from such a source, it has unquestionable authority and importance. We will content ourselves with recommending that it be read by the Protestant newspapers, such as the *Witness*, the *Herald*, the *Globe*, and the *Leader*. These people put reason and justice aside for the pleasure of criticizing Catholicism; by supporting freethinkers, so-called Catholics who wish to violate the rights of the Church. It costs these newspapers nothing to trample underfoot the great principle of religious liberty, which they demand for themselves, in order to better criticize the Catholic Church. This is, nevertheless, the common tactic of fanatical Protestants and liberals throughout the world. Freedom for them, and for those who think like them, slavery for others: liberty is allowed only for delusion, truth is enslaved. We would like to point out that the *Presbyterian* is the organ of the Presbyterian clergy of Toronto. We know that the Presbyterians form the largest sect in Canada, after the Catholics.

---

63 TORONTO PROTESTANTS MORE VICIOUS THAN MONTREAL CATHOLICS

La Minerve, Montreal
September 28, 1875 [translation]

Strange news comes to us from Toronto. The Catholics of this city celebrated on Sunday the opening of the first provincial assembly of Ontario, which is presently in session. On this occasion, our co-religionists wanted to stage a religious demonstration in the form of a procession. They had already traversed a few streets and were arriving at the end of their route, when they were suddenly attacked and furiously charged by a horde of fanatical Protestants, Presbyterian grits and Orangemen. This crowd was armed. Many pistol shots were fired, without the counting of cudgellings. The Catholics fought back as best they could. There were a number of wounded, and the procession was violently dispersed. One can judge the consequence of the disturbance by the fact that more than 5,000 people took part. The police were powerless to prevent the riot, and a corps of sixty policemen who tried to force back the rioters were tumbled by them in a twinkling. Most of the policemen cudgelled by the loyalists are now in the hospital. The gang thus remained mistress of the battle field. According to the despatches, it is "the most shameful riot that has taken place in the last 30 years." . . .

What do the *Witness,* the *Globe,* the *Leader* think of such events? Are these newspapers now going to denounce the rioters in Toronto as they denounced those in Montreal? If they were sincere, they would have to do so. With regard to respect for law and for the liberty of others, they should now be convinced that their fellow citizens do not have the right to accuse the French Canadians: on the contrary. The men at the cemetery were illegally pleading their own case against a *legal* violation of their rights. The rioters in Toronto attacked peaceful citizens who were exercising a right that neither concerned them, nor did them any harm. These are the men who come to preach charity to the Catholics, and who denounce *our intolerance.* Good God, what would become of us and of religious liberty, if these fanatics were the rulers of this country! How tolerant and loyal are these smooth talkers!

---

64 THE QUESTIONABLE LOYALTY OF L'INSTITUT'S LEADERS

Le Nouveau Monde, Montreal
September 29, 1875 [translation]

Today, when there seems to be a little more calmness of spirit about the Guibord case, we can avail ourselves of the opportunity to show our English compatriots what sort of a man it really is, who can defile the word loyalty, as well as the British flag. He has abused their good faith, and shamefully betrayed their confidence.

The truth is that the cause of M. Doutre and the *Institut Canadien* is just as opposed to loyalty to the British Crown, in the realm of politics, as it is to respect for the Church in the realm of religion.

M. Doutre cannot be separated from the *Institut Canadien.* He was, along with M.

Dessaulles, its founder and high priest. His ideas dominated it completely. Moreover, what, in relation to loyalty, were the ideas professed and preached by this school? Democracy, in its most liberal form, the apotheosis of Papineau's extreme views. *L'Avenir* was, in the beginning, the newspaper which was the spokesman of this school. M. Doutre cannot be isolated from *L'Avenir,* for which he wrote constantly.

But, no other newspaper has despised England more, nor carried radical and revolutionary ideas further in Canada. Our English compatriots greatly deluded themselves about the intentions of these masters of demagogy: it is time to open their eyes to this fact.

To demonstrate to their readers the two sides of the coin in this issue, like the well-informed newspapers they pretend to be, our English colleagues could do no better than to publicize facts as edifying as the following which we have chosen from among a thousand others.

First of all, here is the list of names of writers for *l'Avenir*: MM. J. B. E. Dorion, Joseph Doutre, Rodolphe Laflamme (the next leader of the Liberal Party of Lower Canada), Pierre Blanchet, Papin, Labrèche-Viger, C. Laberge, C. Daoust, D. E. Papineau, J. Lenoir, G. Laflamme, C. Duranceau, C. F. Papineau, V. P. W. Dorion, Magloire Lanctot, C. H. Lamontagne, G. Papineau, and E. U. Piché (Tu quoque).

This list was published as correct by the *Défricheur* in 1864, the owner of which, J. B. E. Dorion, also owned *l'Avenir.*

We could give more citations, but for the sake of brevity, we will content ourselves with placing before the public eye the few lines which follow. These say just enough to make our impartial English compatriots appreciate the true merit of the philosophy of MM. Doutre, Laflamme, etc.

L'Avenir of the 31st of May, 1849, said:

"In politics, there is neither faith nor authority to bind men together." The *Institut Canadien* has always performed the function of a platform for those who preached disloyalty towards the British Crown, and annexation to the United States: and if Canada is still united with

England today, it is in spite of the efforts of this revolutionary school. In one of his lectures, M. Dessaulles said, to the great approval of all the adherents, in effect:

> Let us suppose for the moment, that in 1812 the country had been enlightened enough to free itself of its allegiance and of its prejudices against republican institutions. Let us suppose that we had not committed the deplorable mistake of fighting to maintain the glorious privilege of being English subjects. Suppose, finally, that we had been thrown into the great American confederacy. . . .

Another time he said, still to the approval of the school, which, in its entirety, encouraged him in his revolt against lawful authority:

> It is obvious that to claim that we in Canada are subjects of Her British Majesty, is to utter a myth and even a *falsehood* . . . in the absolute sense of the word. The Queen of England being sovereign only in name, we are not necessarily her subjects.
> Nothing therefore is more ridiculous or as pitiable as these exhortations of loyalty made to us every day; as these silly banalities with which our public bodies try to outdo one another in their inviolable loyalty, in their *supposed* duty toward *Her Most Gracious Majesty*. She should feel most honoured indeed by all these hypocritical protestations, of which she knows we DO NOT MEAN ONE WORD.

These are the so-called loyalists that a sector of the English press has taken under its protection against a clergy which, on two especially memorable occasions, has proven its loyalty. It preserved Canada for England by making the French Canadians understand that their duty as Christians bound them to remain loyal to the lawful authority.

If people cannot henceforth discern which side is good, the one which is loyal and sound; and which side is revolutionary, treacherous, and as dangerous as a viper, eh! – well, it is because to live in the blindness of a fatal prejudice. . . .

65 THE PATRIOTIC WORK OF L'INSTITUT CANADIEN

The Daily Witness, Montreal
October 1, 1875

The Canadian Institute holds the position of standard-bearer in the conflict going on in this province between the friends of intellectual and religious freedom on the one side, and ecclesiastical usurpation and priestly tyranny on the other. To those who look below the surface of events and regard the conflict of the principles which underlie them, the history of the Institut since its foundation in 1844 is one of absorbing interest. It was at first, as it is still, a purely literary society, organized by a few young French-Canadians of talent and enterprise. Their object was to cultivate a pure spirit of patriotism and obtain knowledge, and, by means of essays and public discussions, prepare themselves for the honorable activities of life. Full of the generous enthusiasm of youth, and inspired with a fine ambition to acquire distinction for themselves and their country, these young Canadians adopted as their motto the noble words, *Altius Tendimus*. The Institut soon became the centre of most of the activity and intelligence among the young men of the city, and at their weekly meetings they listened to the reading of essays by members, and discussed the public questions of the day. By these means large and liberal views were being developed among them on society, government, commerce and kindred subjects. The Institut increased so rapidly in numbers and influence that it began to excite the jealousy of the clergy. The latter could not bear to see so important an intellectual movement going on independently of themselves. As they beheld the growing power of these young Canadians, left to the unfettered exercise of their minds, they began to tremble lest the sceptre of intellectual authority they had so long wielded should depart from their hands. Moreover, this intellectual *renaissance* was spreading all over the country, and nearly every town and large village had its Institut, founded upon the model of the original one in Montreal.

The flower of the French-Canadian youth were making a common movement towards higher and better things. This spectacle, so cheering to the heart of the patriot, was witnessed by the clergy with dismay, and they resolved to extinguish the Montreal Institut and its numerous sisterhood throughout the province. The work they set themselves to do was to stifle one of the noblest impulses that ever arose among the Canadian people, and one which, had it been encouraged, would by this time have raised the French-Canadian race to a far higher plane among peoples than they now hold. Well may the Canadian patriot mourn when he sees how far the Romish Church was successful in arresting this movement, so bright with promise, and in folding once more about the people the mantle of intellectual servility and spiritual tyranny.

In 1857 the Institut had a membership of 700, and naturally exerted a wide political influence. Its members took an active part in the movements for the abolition of the Seigniorial Tenure, and for changing the character of the Legislative Council from nominative to elective. At the close of the Parliamentary election in 1854 no less than fourteen of the representatives returned were members of the Institut. Its members held for the most part Liberal and progressive principles, but principles which are abhorrent to the Church of Rome; therefore, the latter determined on effecting the overthrow of the Institut.

The first movement of the Bishop against the Institut was to raise the nationality cry, and he endeavored to persuade them to admit to membership no one but French-Canadian Roman Catholics; but in this he was unsuccessful. Next he attacked the Institut for keeping the *Witness* and the *Semeur Canadien,* (a French Protestant paper) in its reading room, and in this he also failed, though he succeeded in making the Institut unpopular in the eyes of the faithful. Finally he attacked the library for containing what he called immoral books which had been placed in the *Index Expurgatorious* at Rome, and he desired the Institut to purge its library of these books. A majority of the members, however, were in favor of maintaining their library intact, and though they gave the Bishop a catalogue of their books, asking him to point out those that were objectionable and promising to put them away, that prelate never deigned to condescend to these particulars. About this time the Bishop organized several rival institutions in the city, though under clerical control, and by this means and by the exercise of spiritual pressure upon the weak-minded, he succeeded in drawing off more than half of the membership of the Institut, so that in 1867 its membership only numbered about 300, of whom not more than 150 paid their subscriptions. Those who seceded were feeble and timid spirits who had not the courage to avow their convictions, while those who remained composed the most outspoken elements of the original society. Meanwhile all the other Institutes in the Province had either been suppressed or brought entirely under clerical control. The Montreal Institut alone held out, and bravely resisted the flood of ecclesiastical denunciation directed against it. In 1868 [*sic.*] the Bishop secured the condemnation of the Institut at Rome, and declared those excommunicated who should persist in remaining members of it. It was this excommunication, pronounced *en bloc,* which gave rise to the famous Guibord case, which case the Institut made its own and has followed up with admirable persistency ever since.

In the meantime the Institut became embarrassed pecuniarily. Owing to the widening of Notre Dame street, the building had to be demolished and rebuilt, and by this it incurred a debt from which it was never able to relieve itself. In 1867 an appeal was made to all who loved freedom of thought and speech to assist in keeping up its usefulness. On that occasion nearly $8,000 was subscribed, about one half coming from English Protestants. Since the beginning of the Guibord trouble the Bishop and the clergy have redoubled their efforts to crush the Institut, and in consequence of their denunciations the masses of the people not only in Montreal, but throughout the province, have come to regard it with a sort of superstitious horror, and its members as infidels, atheists and even worse. Under these circumstances it is not surprising that the membership should be reduced at present to 163, of whom about one half are English. It is, however, still doing immense good. It has a library of 9,000 volumes and a reading-room well stocked with French and English newspapers of all shades of opinion. It is the only free reading-room of the kind in Montreal, and is visited by over one hundred persons in summer and by a much larger number in winter, most of whom are poor laboring men and artisans. The usefulness of the Institut is, however, greatly lessened by the heavy debt of $15,000 resting upon it, of which $1,000 was incurred in carrying the Guibord case to the Privy Council. It is a question deserving the serious attention of the Protestants of Canada whether they should not come to the aid of the Institut in its present hour of greatest need. Protestants would do well to remember that the principle of religious toleration which the Institut proclaimed in 1857, was one of the grounds specially mentioned by the Bishop, upon which he declared its members excommunicated. For years it has been engaged in a life and death struggle with Ultramontanism, until it has been deserted by all but a few brave men who still stand as a bulwark against the alarming and intolerable enroachments of the Romish Church. The Institut is contending for those very principles for which our Protestant ancestors fought and died, and why should not the wealthy and powerful Protestants of this Dominion hold out a helping hand? These men are true Canadians, though Catholics, the only true Canadians among the French Catholics seeing they have not shut out their countrymen from their societies, and the principles they are contending for are those which must prevail if the different races and creeds in this Dominion are to live together in peace. Therefore true patriotism as well as the self interest of Protestants would indicate that they should come to the assistance of the Institut and not allow it to be overwhelmed by the tide of Ultramontanism. At a moment of excitement English-Canadians would be lavish of men and means to face Ultramontanism. We know

no way in which this could be so wisely done as by giving sympathy and aid to the few brave men who are struggling against fearful odds for all that their Protestant fellow-citizens hold most dear.

The way for the Protestants of Canada to prevent the recurrence of any more Guibord cases, and to put some limits to Ultramontanism, which is their deadly foe, is to contribute one hundred thousand dollars to L'Institut Canadien. This will lift the Institut out of debt, give it a library, reading-room, and premises which will restore it to its former prestige, and immensely extend the circle of its influence. It will also enable Mr. Doutre and his coadjutors to fight Ultramontanism in the Courts, and secure the equal and impartial administration of British justice to men of all races and creeds.

---

66 LAW AND ORDER

The Globe, Toronto
October 6, 1875

La Minerve and other French papers try to make a distinction between the rioters over the Guibord matter and the rioters in Toronto on the last two Sundays. It seems the rioters in Montreal "illegally defended themselves against the legal violation of their rights," but the Toronto rioters "attacked persons in the exercise of a recognized right, and who had done them no wrong." Who told the Montreal rioters that their rights were "violated", when the highest Court in the Empire said they were not? Individual opinion or whim. Who told the rioters of Toronto that Roman Catholics had no right to walk the streets in procession as a religious body? Individual opinion or whim also. Why has the whole civil and military force of Toronto, backed by the universal support of public opinion, turned out to put down these rioters regardless of consequences? Because it was felt that law had to be vindicated, and mob rule and individual caprice resolutely put down. Why ought the whole civil and military force of Montreal, backed by the same overwhelming power of public opinion, to have been turned out to put down and keep down the rioters there? For exactly the same reason.

It is very possible that some of the young ruffians who made the disturbance in this city may have had some vague idea that they ought to do something as a counterpart to the proceedings of their fellow *canaille* in Montreal, but the citizens of Toronto did not put them down because they believed the disturbance in Toronto was indefensible while that in Montreal had a good excuse. We believe that even a wrong is to be rectified in a legal way, and that mob rule, whether over Guibord's grave or in the streets of Toronto, must have no place where British law has rule, but must be unsparingly put down, if necessary, by *a whiff of grape* or rifle shot. The difference between Montreal and Toronto in this matter has been that in the former a larger or smaller number of the citizens sympathized with and apologized for the rioters; in the latter, not a solitary individual possessed of one shred of character has even uttered one word of apology for the rioters, or expressed any wish but that they should be punished to the utmost rigour of the law.

67 A BRITISH VIEW

Times of London
September 21, 1875
[in The Globe, Toronto, October 7, 1875]

The City of Montreal has been cast into a state of something like civil war by the question whether a man who died five years ago shall be buried in consecrated ground. The story, which our Canadian Correspondent told yesterday, and which our Philadelphia correspondent recounts to-day, is scarcely freed from an element of comedy, even by the solemnity of the grave; but in truth it is seriously important to this country, as well as to Canada. Lower Canada, the scene of the quarrel, is noted for the tenacity with which it has clung to the Catholicism of its early settlers. The Jesuit missionaries who were among the first leaders of the French Colonists left imperishable memories of their energy, and some of the worse elements of their zeal seem still to live in the Canadian priests. Nor have the descendants of the early settlers fallen away from Catholicism like the French of the present day. The cynical criticisms of Voltaire never reached Lower Canada, and the faith of the Colonists is pretty much what it was when Louis XIV. dipped deep into his privy purse to pay for the missions by which he helped to soothe the memory of his sins. As the religious fervour of the people has been quickened by the influx of Irish, the Pope has good reason to be pleased with the devotion of Lower Canada.

But in these days even the best guarded haunts of religious peace cannot be kept free from the spirit of criticism; and it appeared in a peculiarly unwelcome form in a literary institute at Montreal, called the Canadian Institute. The members of it placed on their shelves several books which Rome had put in the Index. In a Pastoral issued in 1858 the Roman Catholic Bishop ordered the guilty works to be removed, but the members would not obey their spiritual chief, and after years of wrangling there was an appeal to the Vatican. That was in 1865, and four years afterwards the Pope declared that the penalties of the Church should fall on any Catholic who belonged to the Institute while it kept the wicked volumes. Still the members would not yield, and, accordingly, the Bishop formally laid them under the ban of the Church by proclaiming that, unless they should surrender, they would be denied the Sacraments in the hour of death. One of them, named Joseph Guibord, did die under these circumstances in 1869, and the trustees of a Roman Catholic burying-place would not allow his body to be laid in the consecrated part of the ground, although a piece of it belonged to his heirs. His widow was told that, as he had died excommunicate, he could be buried only with criminals and suicides. She appealed to the Civil Courts for the restoration of her rights, and, after the Canadian tribunals had given conflicting decisions, the case came before the Judicial Committee of the Privy Council. The arguments on both sides were highly technical. The counsel for the Catholic authorities contended that Guibord has been unworthy of Christian burial because he had been a "public sinner," but as he in reality had been of blameless moral character, that phrase signified nothing worse than his defiance of the bishop. The counsel for the representatives of his widow did not deny that the bishop might have cut him off from the right of Christian burial if he had excommunicated him by name; but they argued that he could not be branded as a "public sinner" merely because he had been included in a general excommunication. This distinction was based on the law of the Gallican Church, which the Canadian Catholics had inherited, and it met with the approval of the Privy Council. Guibord's body had, meanwhile, been lying in the vault of a Protestant cemetery, and an order of the Crown was sent for its removal to the consecrated ground of the burying place. But the Catholic authorities defy the Crown. M. Rousselot, the Curé of the parish in which the graveyard is situated, declares that he will obey his bishop rather than the law, and the Catholic mob of Montreal is of the same mind. The attempt to bury the body was resisted by an excited crowd, who drove back the mourners and filled up the grave. An armed force had to be called out to restore order; every regiment of troops in Ontario had to be kept in readiness for a fresh outburst of passion; and as neither of the parties would give way it seemed highly probable, at the date of the latest intelligence, that the ceremony of Christian burial would be stained by bloodshed.

It would be difficult to find a more instructive example of the inevitable collision between the civil authority and the Roman Catholic Church wherever that Church feels itself powerful. What happened in Canada might easily occur in Ireland, or even in England. The authorities of the Catholic Church claim supreme jurisdiction over their flocks in all matters spiritual, and the merely abstract demand may be readily granted. In the eye of the law their Church is merely a corporation, with no greater and no less rights than any other. It is in pre- cisely the same position as the London and Northwestern Railway or the Carlton Club, and it is allowed to exercise powers of discipline, not because it has a sacred character, but simply because its members have the same civil rights as other citizens. If they agree to obey a particular man and to be bound by a particular set of rules, they may be held to their bargain so long as it contains nothing essentially illegal. Within these wide limits the authorities of the Catholic Church are certainly the supreme spiritual judges of their flock, and they may deny any member of their communion the Sacraments on precisely the same ground as a Committee of a Club may expel any member who has broken its rules. Nay, the Bishop of Montreal would have had a right to prevent the body of Guibord from being buried in consecrated ground if the man had really forfeited his spiritual privileges. But here comes the collision between the law and the Church. Did he forfeit these privileges? The Catholic priests reply that they alone are entitled to answer a question which is purely spiritual. But, in reality, it is civil as well, because the denial of Christian burial has inflicted a stigma on his memory and the reputation of his family. When his representatives claim redress the Courts must treat the matter simply as a dispute between certain members of a Corporation, and decide it as if it were an action brought by some shareholders of a Railway Company against the directors. All a Court of Law asks is whether a particular contract has been kept, and if the bargain has been broken it is bound to give relief. But, as it must retain the power of determining whether a contract has been fulfilled, really it becomes in the last resort the supreme judge of spiritual as well as temporal affairs. Roman Catholics, Methodists, Baptists, may all be free from any formal connection with the State, and they enjoy a large amount of liberty; but they can no more escape from the dominion of the law than the Church of England herself. All the declamation of the Montreal priests against Guibord's right to his grave being negatived by their spiritual jurisdiction comes from a confusion of ideas. They have merely such spiritual authority as they draw from explicit or implied contract with their flocks, and the Courts of Law must determine whether they have broken the bargain. Now, the Judicial Committee of the Privy Council has declared that, according to the law of the Canadian Church, Guibord did not forfeit his rights to Christian burial merely because the Bishop included him in a wholesale excommunication. Sir Robert Phillimore and the other judges of the cause did not pretend to decide whether the law is good or bad. That is a matter which the Vatican and the Canadians must settle for themselves. If the Pope and the Bishop do not like the law, they can endeavour to obtain a change in it; but, so long as it exists, they are as much bound to obey it as if they were the most secular of traders. Any attempt to resist the decree of the Judicial Committee must, therefore, be punished just as severely as the most vulgar breaches of the public peace.

68 LAWBREAKERS AT MONTREAL AND TORONTO

The Globe, Toronto
October 8, 1875

A letter we publish this morning from *A Catholic* only proves how difficult it is for the most temperate and impartial of observers to divest themselves entirely of prejudice in matters appealing closely to their religious opinions and sympathies. But for this the writer could hardly have put a wrong construction on the article to which he refers as, in his view, doing an injustice to the more respectable of the Roman Catholic population of Quebec. In the first place we said nothing to show that rowdyism in Toronto, in the name of Protestantism, was in the smallest degree justified or palliated by rowdyism in the name of religion at Montreal; in the next we only stated what is patent to the whole world when referring to the tacit approval the riotous proceedings at Montreal had received at the hands of some of those whose influence ought to have rendered such outrages impossible. In both cases the actual law-breakers are in a

very small minority; in both, those who should have known better, and who had the power more or less to control the spirit of mischief or rebellion against the law, were wanting in their duty to the law. In Toronto some amends for this has been made; in Montreal we have yet to see whether the same results will follow upon the second attempt to carry out the mandate of the Crown acting under the advice of the Privy Council.

In Toronto, however, the rioters have had no open apologists or defenders; at most a clumsy attempt has been made by one uninfluential paper to gloss over their offence or misrepresent what actually occurred. There has been an all but universal condemnation throughout Ontario of the scoundrels who protested against *the desecration of the Sabbath* by pelting the police and attempting to sack a tavern on the Sabbath day, while, unhappily, in Quebec there has been a good deal of apologetic writing in behalf of the brutal crowd that *defended the sanctity of consecrated ground*, ready to proceed to any extremity in order to accomplish their lawless designs. Our correspondent lays great stress on the fact that Bishop Bourget warned the municipal authorities of Montreal that there would probably be a breach of the peace if the attempt to inter Guibord's remains took place. That may saddle the said authorities with a share of the responsibility for what afterwards occurred. But it does not relieve the Bishop or the Fabrique of the blame that attaches, at all events, to passive complicity in the resistance offered. Has the Bishop, have the Fabrique, to this day publicly announced their submission to the law? Does it not stand on record that, when notified some time since by M. Doutre of the decree of the Privy Council, the curé replied with a letter of open defiance, alleging the authority of his Bishop for his contumacious refusal to obey the decree? When and where has this open defiance been revoked? Supposing the crowd of ignorant men who barred the access to the ground were not actually instigated – a thing very hard to believe – to act as they did, how were they to know that Bishop and Fabrique had submitted? If they really were the good Catholics the clerical organs would have us believe, docile submission to the clergy – who again are, we are told, absolutely bound to obey their ecclesiastical superiors – should have been their very first principle of action. Did Bishop or Fabrique – knowing, as they admitted, disturbances would take place – impose their commands on the people who were said to be excited by the intended funeral? The publication of any pastoral advice or injunction given in anticipation of the riot would be to the point, and show that an injustice had been done in supposing the clerical authorities to have been *particeps criminis* in a matter so discreditable to every one who engaged in or defended it.

However, these disagreeable occurrences both at Montreal and Toronto will probably in the end do good, if they only provoke – as they doubtless have provoked – the indignation of the more respectable portion of the community, of all in fact who regard a loyal submission to the law of the land as their first duty. Protestants in Ontario have nothing but regret for the odious conduct of the rioters on the last two Sundays; Catholics, all the world over, will, we expect, to a very large extent feel that the course taken from first to last in the Guibord controversy has been a mistake and a blunder, and that to allow the violence of a mob resisting the law to take the place of at least passive submission to the law was the greatest blunder of all. Let us hope that, with these disagreeable experiences before us, we may all be the more zealous in promoting, without regard to any sectarian differences, the administration of even-handed justice, and the maintenance of the law which is the foundation of every right and all our liberties.

69 A PASTORAL LETTER FROM THE BISHOPS OF QUEBEC

The True Witness, and Catholic Chronicle, Montreal
October 15, 1875

Our Dearly Beloved Brethren, – We deem it our duty as Your Pastors, to address you on many most important subjects to which divers circumstances have given rise.

I

AUTHORITY OF THE CHURCH

. . . Not only is the Church independent of the civil body, but is superior to it by its origin, by its extent, and by its end. . . .

A civil body embraces but one people; the Church has received dominion over all the earth; Jesus Christ himself has given the mission *to teach all nations, docete omnes gentes* (Matt. xxviii. 20); the State, then, is in the Church, and not the Church in the State. . . .

This submission does not stop at those bodies that may be distinct for the sake of their aims and independent each in its proper sphere. But the moment a question touches on faith, morals or the divine constitution of the Church, on its independence or on that which is necessary to fulfil its spiritual mission, it is for the Church alone to judge. . . .

But in thus vindicating the rights of the Catholic Church over its children, by no means do we intend to usurp or fetter the civil rights of our brothers who differ from us, with whom we will always be happy to be on the best of terms in the future as we have been in the past. The principles we announce are not new; they are as old as the Church itself. If we repeat them to-day, it is because certain Catholics appear to have forgotten them. . . .

III

CATHOLIC LIBERALISM

The Catholic doctrine founded on Liberal principles, says Pius IX, is the most troublesome and dangerous enemy to the divine constitution of the Church. Like a serpent that glides through the terrestrial paradise to entice and destroy the human race, it presents to the children of Adam the deceptive allurement of a certain liberty, and knowledge of good and evil; a liberty and knowledge which leads to death. It endeavours to crawl imperceptibly into the most holy places; it fascinates the eyes of the clearest sighted; it poisons the hearts of the simplest, if one wavers ever so little in faith in the authority of the Sovereign Pontiff.

The followers of this subtle error concentrate all their strength to burst the bonds which unite the people to the Bishops and the Bishops to the Vicar of Jesus Christ. They applaud civil authority every time it invades the sanctuary; they seek by every means to induce the faithful to tolerate, if not approve, of iniquitous laws. – Enemies so much the more dangerous that often, without even being conscious of it, they favor the most pernicious doctrines, which Pius IX has so well described in calling them *a visionary reconciliation of truth with error.*

The Liberal Catholic reassures himself, because he still has some Catholic principles, certain pious practices, a certain ground of faith and attachment to the Church; but he carefully shuts his eyes to the rent made in his heart by the errors which silently devour it. He still boasts to all about his religious convictions, and is angry when warned that he has dangerous principles; he is perhaps sincere in his pride; God alone knows it! But, beside all these fine appearances, there is a great depth of pride which lets him believe he has more prudence and wisdom than those to whom the Holy Spirit gives authority and grace to teach and govern the faithful people. He will censure without scruple the acts and writings of the highest religious authority. Under pretence of removing the cause for dissensions and of reconciling with the Gospel the progress of the present society, he puts himself in the service of Caesar and of those who invent pretended laws in favor of a false liberty; as if darkness could exist with light, and as if truth did not cease to be the truth when one violated it, therein turning it aside from its true meaning and despoiling it of that inherent immortality of its nature.

In presence of five Apostolic Briefs denouncing "Catholic Liberalism" as absolutely incompatible with Church doctrine, although it may not be yet formally condemned as heretical, it can no longer be permitted in conscience to be *a Liberal Catholic.*

IV
CATHOLIC POLITICS

. . . "Law is a rule dictated by reason for the common good, and promulgated by he who has the care of society." The Catholic Church recognizes in this short definition all the features of Christian Politics.

The common good is the only and supreme end.

Reason ought to be the source of law. Reason, that is to say, the conformity of means to employ, not only with the end to attain, but also with justice and morals; reason, and not the mind of party, not the intention of remaining in power, not the wish to any of the party opposed. . . .

Far be it from us to forget the advantages of a constitutional government, respected in itself, and consequently the usefulness of its distinctions of party, who hold one another in check, in order to signal and stop the errors of power. That which we deplore, that which we condemn, is the abuse of it; it is the pretension that politics, reduced to the mean and ridiculous proportions of party interests, becomes the *supreme rule* of every public administration, that *everything* may be *for party* and nothing for the *common good*; nothing for *that society of which one has the charge.* What we still condemn is that one allows himself to say and to dare all that can tend to the triumph of a party. . . .

V
THE PART OF THE CLERGY IN POLITICS

Men, who would lead you astray, Our Dearly Beloved Brethren, tell you repeatedly that the clergy have nothing whatever to do in politics; that no religious principles should be observed in the discussion of public affairs; and that the clergy have no duties to perform but towards the Church and sacristy; and that the people should in politics, practise moral independence.

Monstrous errors, Our Dearly Beloved Brethren; and woe to the country in which they take root. In excluding the clergy, the Church is excluded; and in putting aside the Church, we deprive ourselves of all the Church contains, both salutary and unchangeable. – God, morality, justice, truth; and when we have laid violent hands upon these, we can then only count upon force!

. . . The greatest enemies of the people are, therefore, they who wish to banish religion from politics; for, under pretext of freeing the people from what they call *the tyranny, the undue influence of the priest,* they are preparing at the same time for the people heavier chains, and ones which will be more difficult to throw off; they place might above right, and take from the civil power the only moral check which can prevent it from degenerating into despotism and tyranny! . . .

Up to the present we have considered the priest as a citizen, and as speaking of politics in his own name, as any other member of society.

Are there questions in which the Bishop and the priest may and sometimes should, interfere in the name of religion?

We answer without hesitation: Yes, there are questions in which the clergy can, and even should, interfere in the name of religion. . . . There are, indeed, political questions which affect the spiritual interests of souls, either because they have relation to faith and morals, or because they affect the liberty, independence or existence of the Church from a temporal point of view.

A candidate may present himself who may be hostile to the Church, or whose antecedents may be such as to cause his candidature to be considered dangerous to the interests of the Church.

Thus, a political party may be judged dangerous not only by its programme and antecedents, but also by the programme and antecedents of its chiefs, of its principal members, and of the press which represents it, unless the party disavow them in case they persist in their error after having been notified of the fact. . . .

Thus, the priest and the bishop can in all justice, and should in all conscience, raise their voices, signalize the danger, declare that voting in such a manner would be sinful, and that to be guilty of such an action would expose the guilty parties to the censure of the Church. They can and should speak, not only to the electors and candidates, but also to the constituted authorities. . . .

It will probably be contended that the priest would, like every man be liable to transcend the limits assigned to him, and that then it would become the duty of the State to make him return to his duties.

To this we would reply, firstly, that it is a gratuitous injury to the entire Church to suppose that there is not in the hierarchy a remedy for the injustice or error of one of its ministers. In fact, the Church has its regularly constituted tribunals; and if any one has reason to complain of a minister of the Church, he should not cite him before the civil tribunal but before the ecclesiastical tribunal, alone which is competent to judge of doctrine or of the conduct of the priest. For this reason Pius IX, in his bull *Apostolicae Sedis,* in October, 1869, declares major excommunication against those who, either directly or indirectly, oblige lay judges to cite before them, ecclesiastical personages against the provision of the canonical law.

Secondly, when the State invades the rights of the Church, and tramples under feet its most sacred privileges, as to-day happens in Italy, France and Switzerland, would it not be the height of derision to give to the same State the right to gag its victim?

Thirdly, if we would establish a principle that a power does not exist because it may happen that somebody abuses it, it would be necessary to ignore all civil powers, because all persons in whom these powers are vested are fallible. . . .

VIII

ON ECCLESIASTICAL BURIAL

Ecclesiastical burial has not, doubtless, the same degree of sanctity as the sacraments, but it nevertheless belongs entirely and solely to the judgment of the Church. . . .

It may be said that the privation of the honours of ecclesiastical burial brings with it disgrace and infamy, and that it thus becomes the province of the civil authorities to protect the honor of the citizens.

We answer that disgrace and infamy are found rather in the revolt of a child against its mother, and that nothing can wipe out a grievous disobedience persevered in at the hour of death. All the trials, appeals and sentences of the world will only serve to make the crime more known, and render the degradation and infamy more notorious and more deplorable in the eyes of all true Catholics. . . .

Now, Our Dearly Beloved Brethren, we must say with sorrow that a celebrated occurrence has proved to us that the Catholic Church in Canada is threatened in its liberty and most precious rights, and what makes our affliction more keen is that we can say with the Prophet, "I have nourished my children and loaded them with benefits, and they have despised me;" . . . (Isaiah i 2). The first authors of this attempt were brought up on the knees of a Christian mother; in their youth they knelt at the holy table; they received the ineffaceable mark of confirmation, and to-day, notwithstanding their revolt, they style themselves Catholics, in order to have the right to cause the forcible opening of the gates of a cemetery consecrated by the prayers of the Church, and destined for the burial of the faithful children of the Church.

In order to disguise that usurpation, the *Gallican Liberties* were invoked, as if Catholic unity, founded by Jesus Christ on the supreme authority of St. Peter and his successors, were but a vain and empty title. . . . What prince, what republic, would recognize a like principle invoked by a province, notwithstanding the express declaration a hundred times repeated, of the constitution and of the supreme tribunals of the state?

Let those who are outside the Church consider these principles good and admirable if they will, because they do not believe in the authority which makes the foundation of the Catholic Church. But that those men still dare to call themselves children of the Church, while ignoring the teachings and the hierarchy, is an incomprehensible error.

Those who by their subscriptions have commenced, sustained and encouraged this unqualified attempt against the just rights of the Church, we hold guilty of an overt act of revolt against the Church, and a grievous injustice, for which they will not obtain pardon unless they try to repair the injury by all means in their power. . . .

CONCLUSIONS

Such Our Dearly Beloved Brethren, are the important advices we deem it our duty to give you under the present circumstances.

Beware, above all, of this *liberalism* which hides itself under the beautiful name of *Catholic,* the more surely to accomplish its criminal work. You will easily recognize it from the picture the Sovereign Pontiff has so often drawn of it. 1st. Efforts to subjugate the Church to the State. 2nd. Incessant attempts to divide the bonds which unite the children of the Church to the clergy. 3rd. Monstrous alliance of the truth with error under pretence of making all things to agree and to avoid conflicts. Lastly, illusion and sometimes hypocrisy, which, under a religious exterior and fine protestations of submission to the Church, hide a pride beyond measure. . . .

Given under our signatures, the seal of the archdiocese and the countersignature of the secretary of the archepiscopal palace of Quebec the twenty-second of September, one thousand eight hundred and seventy-five.

+ E. A. Arch. of Quebec.
+ IG. Bish. of Montreal.
+ L. F. Bish. of Three Rivers.
+ Jean, Bish. of S. G., of Rimouski.
+ E. C. Bish. of Gratianopolis.
+ Antoine, Bish. of Sherbrooke.
+ J. Thomas, Bish. of Ottawa.

+ L. Z. Moreau, Pst. Adm.
  of St. Hyacinthe.

By Messeigneurs,
  C. O. Collet, Priest,
  Secretary.

---

70 GUIBORD BURIED AT LAST

The Gazette, Montreal
November 17, 1875

The long-deferred burial of the remains of Joseph Guibord took place yesterday, as was announced would be the case. The morning, very fittingly as some may have thought, opened dark and gloomy – weather mild and footing uncomfortable. A considerable portion of the city was at an early hour on the *qui vive*; volunteers were on the alert, and many seemed really apprehensive of such serious trouble as to warrant very serious faces, while in one or two instances it is understood men were warned to appear on parade by a couple of visitors in uniform and furnished with rifles. At 7.15 o'clock a number of volunteers had collected about the Drill Shed ruins, but the number was not worthy of any particular mention until towards 8.30. At this hour some seventy policemen, armed with Sniders, under command of Deputy-Chief Naegely, marched from the Central Station, and defiling into Notre Dame street, proceeded to the Protestant Cemetery via Bleury Street, when the coffin containing the dust of the late Joseph Guibord, in his life-time printer, was taken from the vault and placed in the hearse, a very plain vehicle indeed. The Trustees of the Cemetery present were as the former occasion, Messrs. Galt and Macrae and the Secretary, Mr. Turner. A coffin being produced after some search, Mr. Boisseau inquired whether this was the coffin deposited in the vault almost six years ago, removed on the 2nd of September last, and returned on the same day. Mr. Spriggins, the superintendent, replied that it was, and Mr. Boisseau thanked the trustees for their kindness in permitting the coffin to remain in the

vault for such a length of time.

The hearse, surrounded by policemen, was driven to the road leading around the mountain, and had gone but a short distance when it was joined by the military detachment.

. . . The muster, we are informed, comprised 950 men, who fairly merit a compliment as to their personal appearance. In this order the troops under the command of Lieut.-Colonel Fletcher, Deputy Adjutant General, Lieut.-Col. Bacon, acting as Brigade Major, and Lt.-Col. Lovelace, Cavalry Drill Instructor, being present, left the Champ de Mars, followed by several carriages and took the following route: – St. Gabriel street, Craig and St. Lawrence, joining the funeral a short distance above the road leading to the Mount Royal Cemetery. St. Lawrence street was of course lined with citizens, who either leisurely inspected the volunteers or followed them as far as Mile End, numbers rapidly thinning as the distance from the city grew greater. The windows of the houses facing the street were monopolized by women, girls and babies, who manifested an equally profound curiosity with reference to this very extraordinary occurrence. Nothing passed worthy of the slightest comment, however, until the troops reached Prendergast's hotel, where they halted and were gratified with luncheon – the most interesting item on the programme, in their regard. The hearse, escorted in front, on the sides and in rear by the armed blue coats, under command of Chief Penton, proceeded onward to the cemetery, and here the duties of the military escort terminated happily, as their services were no longer required. The gates of the Cemetery were open as usual – they had been removed from the hinges by the employees of the Fabrique, as they had been closed in the morning by a few mischievous youngsters – and the strange *cortège* passed these aforetime barriers to such progress, wound up the hill, on which stands the monument erected to the French-Canadians who fell in the skirmishes in 1837, and without the slightest interruption wended its solemn way to the opening in the ground, in which all that is perishable of the now somewhat famous printer, was to be laid: – a noticeable peculiarity in all this proceeding, in Roman Catholic eyes, was the passing of the little Chapel situated in the Cemetery grounds, in which last offices are piously performed in memory of the lamented deceased. The grave reached, it was noticed, that near by were placed several barrels of Portland cement; the lower portion of the grave was already covered with this material, and a large box was filled with the mixture, ready for instant use. The policemen formed around the *fosse*, in a circle, into which few persons were admitted; these few included, of course, Chief Penton, Sub-Chief Naegely, Sub-Chief Paradis and sergeants, also Mr. Boisseau, Secretary of the *Institut Canadien*, who, astonishing to relate, was the only well-known member of this body present; Mr. Henry Lyman and others. The coffin, which was very wide in make, being lowered, several English-speaking laborers, who had been waiting, shovel in hand, began filling the grave with cement, stones, and scraps of iron and tin; with an occasional opening of a fresh barrel of cement to furnish new material, this work continued, while one of the most cheerless of miserable drizzles steadily fell, until the grave was filled within a few inches of the surface of the ground; earth formed the final layer, and the last shovelful being thrown, the interment of Guibord, in accordance with the terms of the decree of the Privy Council in the consecrated part of the Cemetery, became *un fait accompli*. Spectators were not present in great numbers; when the cortege entered the grounds, people were standing in groups about the "Patriot's" monument and the chapel, and were scattered over the ground. No feeling was exhibited either in favor or against the deceased or the men who have been considered his friends, either in the cemetery or along the line of route. Several hundred persons, perhaps, witnessed or attempted to witness the performance of the last possible civil rites, with no other sentiment apparent than a mere feeling of the most ordinary curiosity, and it is surmised that if the volunteers, with their bands, had not attracted the attention of the public, in the most public manner, to the event, the attendance would have been remarkably less than it was. An incident which created a good deal of comment at the time, was the arrival of Rev. Mr. Rousselot, cure of Notre Dame, in company of a detective, Mr. Cinqmars, detailed probably to see to his protection. When, to the surprise of all present, this clergyman alighted from his carriage and made his way through the policemen and spectators surrounding the grave, the belief was hazarded in various quarters that the Church authorities had relented, and rather than permit a civil burial – the first that ever took place, by the way, in any Roman Catholic cemetery in this country – had decided to perform the customary religious services, so great a solace to the friends of deceased persons; but it was soon known, at least by inquisitive journalists, on the tip-toe of expectation in consequence of this unexpected arrival, that the Rev. Father merely came to be a witness of the fact that the coffin was placed in the grave, in order that the proper register might be made, as exigency requires. He asked of Mr. Boisseau if he had identified the coffin containing the remains of Joseph Guibord; a reply being given in the affirmative, he asked if the grave had been dug to a depth of four feet, as the rules of the Fabrique require; a similar reply was made, and the curé turned away, remarking to a journalist that he was merely present in his civil capacity; he immediately left the cemetery. The absence of Mr. Joseph Doutre, Q.C., and of the other prominent members of the Institut, who paraded on the 2nd of September, gave rise to divers conjectures, and in certain instances, to severe comments; when asked why Mr. Doutre was absent, Mr. Boisseau simply shrugged his shoulders, and added, his absence was possibly due to his having other transactions on his hands. The grave filled, the police returned to the city, arriving at the Central Station early in the afternoon; one hundred men were on duty, a portion having been detached to guard the grave, prior to the arrival of the hearse. The volunteers left the Champ de Mars at 9.45;

the cortege arrived at the cemetery at 11.30 o'clock, and the grave was filled at 12.30 o'clock.

THE MAYOR

His Worship, the Mayor, who had the exclusive supervision of the entire proceedings, managed matters in their every detail in a most admirable manner; he rode to the Champ de Mars at 9 o'clock, and going from thence to the Cemetery in company with Judge Coursol, both on horseback, superintended the removal of the remains. . . . Shortly after noon he received the following note from Mr. Boisseau: –

> Côte des Neiges Cemetery,
> Half-past twelve.

To His Worship the Mayor:

Thankful to your Worship for the protection so far granted to the burial of Guibord, I would now ask you to extend it further by ordering a squad of police to remain on the spot all night if possible, or otherwise it is most certain, that the body will be snatched. The *Institut Canadien* will cheerfully stand all expenses.

> Yours most respectfully,
> A. Boisseau,
> Superintendent of the Institut Canadien.

His Worship at once granted the request; and Sergeant Burke with five policemen has been detailed to perform this by no means cheerful or pleasant duty. It may also be mentioned that the cemetery authorities previously intimated to His Worship, that such a guard would be advisable – showing their good faith in the matter. . . .

JOTTINGS.

Each volunteer received twenty rounds of ammunition, and guards were placed during Monday night on the places where it was stored for the different regiments. The men will be paid ninety cents per day: – The officers in proportion – by the Government, and not by the *Institut Canadien,* as many citizens imagine.

It is related, that when French Canadian women quarrel, and wish to enrich their ordinary billingsgate, in the most extreme possible manner – one reviles the other as a Guibord. The cursing of the ground, – or cement, in which the remains lie, will be awaited by some with anxiety – by others with interest.

The detectives were on duty on the line of the march, and also in the Cemetery. An incident, somewhat touching in its character, occurred as the grave was being filled. A French Canadian printer stepped forward, and spoke briefly to this effect – If there is nobody to speak a word for him, I would like to do so; he taught me my trade, and I would like to make the sign of the cross for him. He did so and retired.

---

71 BURIAL OF GUIBORD

The Mail, Toronto
November 17, 1875

The Dominion at large will hear with a feeling of relief that Guibord's body was interred yesterday without the slightest attempt at disturbance or opposition. The order of the Privy Council, which is our most supreme law, has been asserted and respected, and an end put to one of the most unhappy difficulties that ever threatened to disturb this country. The civil and military authorities, who adopted every conceivable means to prevent an outbreak, and the ecclesiastical superiors, who restrained not alone the anti-Institut population in the city, but the fierce pro-Church *habitans* in the neighbouring districts, are to be congratulated on the complete success that has happily attended their efforts. All that remains is for both to be equally vigilant and earnest in preserving the grave from desecration by fanatics, who obeyed the law only because they dreaded the exercise of its power and submitted to the request of their spiritual advisers for the same reason.

Let us hope that with the settlement of the Guibord case we have got rid of the last of a vexing series of questions which at any moment might have become internecine.

The Manitoba troubles, the New Brunswick school question, "better terms" to the minor Provinces, the legality of Roman Catholic pilgrimages, and, lastly, the Guibord case, which involved the supremacy of the civil law over the rights of the subject, have practically all been settled. Our new Constitution has been tried and found to possess the elements of solidity and elasticity necessary for the amalgamation of men of different creeds and races into a law-abiding commonwealth. Confederation was a political dogma enforced without a *plebiscite* on Provinces having conflicting interests, nationalities with traditional jealousies, and creeds mutually antagonistic, and difficulties were to be expected at first. The Guibord one was by no means the least of these; and its happy termination is a fair augury of future freedom and exemption from others at least of a similar nature. The result of our experience in the settlement of the troubles we have named may be summed up in the old saws, "Live, and let live," and "Give and take." The utmost liberality, national, political, and religious, is the only preventive against the growth of a second crop of tares in our wheat. It is a virtue easy of cultivation, and one which we cannot plant too soon, if we hope for the growth, development, and greatness of the country.

---

72 BURIAL OF GUIBORD

The Globe, Toronto
November 17, 1875

The authority of the law has triumphed, the mandate of the Sovereign has been obeyed, and the body of Joseph Guibord reposes in peace in his own plot in the Catholic Cemetery of Côte des Neiges. The contumacious Fabrique has succumbed, Bishop Bourget and his clergy have counselled non-resistance, the civil magistrates have been equal to the occasion, and that was done yesterday which the exercise of a little wisdom would have allowed to be done six years ago. Guibord died on the 28th of November, 1869, and within twelve days of the sixth anniversary of that event he has been buried with honours little anticipated by the quiet and unobtrusive printer when pursuing his peaceful avocation in the city that yesterday thronged to view the ceremony of his interment. Horse, foot, and artillery, mayors, judges, and police, to say nothing of the thousands of people, made an imposing demonstration as the corpse of Joseph Guibord was conveyed from its temporary to its final resting-place.

There was good reason to believe that from the advice given to their flocks by the Catholic clergy no attempt would be made to interfere with the burial in the terms of the Privy Council's decree, but it was necessary, after what had already occurred, to provide against the possibility of disturbance, and it was an act of merciful consideration towards any who might be tempted to create disorder to show that any successful interference was altogether out of the question. At the last moment the use of the stone sarcophagus in which it was intended to place the coffin in order to prevent any evil-disposed person from disinterring the body was dispensed with, out of deference, if we understand the report correctly, to the wish of the Mayor, who, possibly, may have had reason to suppose that the conveyance of the cumbrous casket and the preparations that would be required for placing it in position would protract the proceedings and increase the risk of disturbance. A bed of Portland cement, mixed with iron-filings, was substituted, which would answer the purpose nearly as effectively as stone. It may be hoped, however, that even this precaution was unnecessary.

A painful and irritating quarrel is thus happily terminated. Probably those who originated it are now of the opinion that a mistake was committed when they raised, in the first instance, the plea of Guibord's excommunication. Many who have no sympathy with the Institut or with those who have taken Guibord's case in hand have regretted that the question of his right to burial in consecrated ground was ever put forward at all. It has been abundantly demonstrated that the law even of their own Church was against them, and no Church can, in the end, be the gainer by compelling its members to set the law in motion to compel or coerce those who act in its behalf. But, on the other hand, there need be no humiliation involved in the event of yesterday to the Bishop or the Fabrique. They took one view of their duties, and the exponents of the law have taken another. By co-operating at the last with those whose duty it was to provide for the due fulfillment of the law's requirements, they have done themselves more honour than could have accrued to them from further resistance.

We hope, too, that the determination shown by all on whom the responsibility of keeping the peace officially rested to allow no excuse for its infraction, will be a sufficient answer to those wonderful homilies addressed to the people of Canada by some British journalists on the occasion of the former attempt to bury Guibord. The turnout of troops, police, and officials of all ranks, was quite irrespective of creed or nationality, and showed that Canadians are quite as ready to support lawful authority as any people on the face of the globe. The only effect, in fact, of the opposition offered in the first instance has been to call forth an emphatic protest against the notion that in any part of the Dominion the law can be long defied. That the worthy printer's bones may rest undisturbed in the place prepared for them – that the legal and ecclesiastical controversies over the disposal of them may now cease and the whole affair become simply a matter of history, must be the desire of every one who has watched and pondered over the events that culminated yesterday in the burial of Joseph Guibord.

---

73 THE TRIUMPH OF PERSECUTION

La Minerve, Montreal
November 18, 1875 [translation]

Today, from one end of our province to the other, liberalism is leaping with impious joy. It has finally attained the goal it has been pursuing for so long. Guibord is buried in consecrated ground, the Church is humiliated, insulted, handed over to the outrages of its enemies. What joy was felt among the nationalists of the *Institut*! Tuesday was such a fine day for the gentlemen of *les rouges*, Doutre, Laflamme, Thibeaudeau, Duhamel and the rest of the gang! Yet, what a pity that M. Dessaulles was not here to sing the hymn of triumph!

While liberalism triumphs, the Catholics of our province lower their heads and own that an unprecedented outrage has just been committed against the name *Canadien*, and that this blot has been imparted by men who have made it their business to debase it. Is it not a national disgrace to see *Canadiens* dare to do what the English never attempted, even on the day of their triumph and moment of our weakness! There was a time in our history, after the conquest, when our conquerors thought of getting Catholicism out of the way, but they never laid a hand on the forbidden territory of our rights. They drew back from the responsibility for this odious profanation which the *rouges* took unto themselves. In the fury of their impiety, they must have felt, like Voltaire, the thrill of *stamping out infamy*. To see *Canadiens* mount the assault against the Citadel, which contains everything dear to us; to see *Canadiens*, so-called Catholics giving themselves up to profanities which would appall the Protestants . . . this is truly a humiliating spectacle for us.

The public spirit, fatigued by this long battle, is not perhaps aware of the gravity of the act on Tuesday. It does not at all realize that a liberalism which is a disgrace to the name has committed an offence against freedom of religion, has opened the door to the most despicable infringements on our rights and privileges as Catholics. The treaties guarantee us the free exercise of our religion, and consequently grant us the rights which the Church exercises over those who consent to form a part of the communion of the faithful. Well, one can be Catholic, but on certain conditions. Whosoever does not want to comply with the obligations imposed by the Church, has full liberty to depart from its bosom. It is absurd to maintain that a member of this communion should have the right to shake off certain duties, to disobey authority, and remain within the Church. But with our dissident brothers, for whom the principle of authority has lost all significance, and who owe their existence as Protestants to the violation of this principle, such a claim would appear absurd – monstrous. Have we not just recently seen an English court decide that an individual who refused to believe in certain dogmas of the Episcopalian Church, did not have the right to his privileges as long as he would not renounce his errors? How is it, that in the same country where such a judgement is rendered, there should be judges who will impose obligations on the Catholic Church, which appear to shock the English public spirit. That is, to us, a very strange system. How can these judges presume to be familiar with a case which has so little to do with their line of thinking! We can only conjecture, on their part, a profound ignorance of the organization of the Catholic Church.

We have spoken of the atmosphere of prejudice in which they move, of the prejudices that a powerful biblical society has installed in them, of the weakness of the hands entrusted with our defence: but all this does not explain the strange verdict of the Privy Council.

Brute force, backed up by the judges' decision – judges who were either perverse or ignorant of the organization of our Church, attempted on Tuesday to put into practice the abominable claim that one may demand privileges for an individual who did nothing during his lifetime for the procuring, after his death, of the prayers and honours reserved by the Church for those who depart this life in her bosom! If someone should make up his mind to demand the same privileges for a pagan, we would not be surprised.

One must understand that the Guibord case was only a pretext for this battle which liberalism has been planning for a long time against the Catholic Church. . . .

Up to now the fortunes of war have been in favour of liberalism. M. Laflamme merited the congratulations of the fanatical Protestant press; M. Doutre found material if not spiritual advantages there. All this nice anti-Catholic zeal procured for him a useful clientele, recruited from among the Protestants, who were as blind as they were fanatical. They do not realize that, in attacking Catholicism, they are attacking the greatest moral force in the world; and that if the Church lost its influence, Protestantism would find itself in the hands of godlessness. But, patience; the Church has not uttered its last word. Let them all hasten to enjoy their triumph, for it will not last long. The Church has had to suffer the assaults of enemies beside whom MM. Doutre and Laflamme are mere dwarfs. For nineteen centuries it has fought against kings, emperors, and has watched them fall one after the other. It has overcome the strongest; the German emperors, Napoleon I. After all that, the Church can well look forward to getting the better of MM. Doutre, Laflamme, and company.

---

74 BISHOP BOURGET'S REMARKABLE RHETORIC

The Globe, Toronto
November 24, 1875

The Roman Catholic Bishop of Montreal has issued a pastoral in reference to the interment of Guibord. This document was read last Sunday in all the churches of the diocese, and will be found elsewhere.

The Bishop has still not one word of condemnation for the rioters who resisted the carrying out of the law, and did all in their power to provoke a collision and cause the effusion of blood. He says it was their zeal that led them to make such a display, and that it was a zeal not according to knowledge. This is certainly a very gentle way of putting it. How would Bishop Bourget have relished the idea of any Protestant clergyman, or any number of such, very tenderly saying that the rioters in the Toronto pilgrimage trouble were *moved by spontaneous zeal,* but that their *zeal was not according to knowledge*! The Bishop also tells all the faithful that he has de-consecrated (we suppose we must say) the ground in which the body of Guibord has been placed. In his own words, we read that "in virtue of the Divine Power which we exercise in the name of the Pastors, we have truly declared that the place in which has been laid the body of this rebellious child of the Church is actually separated from the consecrated cemetery, as to be henceforth only a common or profane place." We fear that the Bishop, in his zeal, has overstepped discretion in this matter, and might even be called to account in a civil court for seeking to depreciate, contrary to law, the value of the property owned in the cemetery by the representatives of the late Joseph Guibord. The law has declared that Guibord has done nothing which could legally prevent his being buried in consecrated ground, and the Bishop has as little right to single out the burying-place of the defunct printer, and put what was intended to be a brand of dishonour upon it, as he had to close the gates of the cemetery and prevent the funeral procession from entering. In the one case he is resisting the law as much as he would have been in the other. As far as lies in his power he has depreciated the value of that property, and may any day, therefore, be sued for damages by those who now own it. The proceeding is, besides, an invitation to violence and law-breaking. Nay, it is not only an invitation to law-breaking, it is law-breaking itself, for it is making all the representatives of Joseph Guibord suffer in their material affairs on account of his doings, though the highest Court of the realm had said that he had done no wrong. There is no difference that we can see in principle between refusing sepulture to those now celebrated remains and cursing the place after the body has been placed there.

True, the denunciation of any man can do the dead no harm, and the *blessings of heaven* will, in spite of the Bishop's malediction, rest upon the place quite as much as ever. But the legal aspect of the affair is quite another matter. We don't know that any one will push the case further. We rather hope not, though we are pretty sure that any one who did would be tolerably certain of a verdict. In noticing this tedious and painful matter for, we hope, the last

time, we cannot help giving a few sentences of this Episcopal pastoral in which Bishop Bourget thinks it decent to talk in the following wild, and we must think scarcely Episcopal, style: –

Everyone who visits this cemetery, upon sorrowfully looking at this tomb, which is not covered with the blessings of Heaven, because it has been separated from the holy ground which the Church has blessed, will surrender himself to emotions more or less painful. 'Here lies,' he will cry in the depth of his soul, 'the body of the too famous Joseph Guibord, who died in rebellion against the common faith of the Church and under ecclesiastical anathema; who could not pass through the gates of this consecrated place except escorted by a troop of armed men as for battle against the enemies of his country; who, had it not been for the good disposition of his fellow-citizens, would have caused the shedding of a great deal of blood; who was conducted to this grave not under the protection of the cross, but under that of the bayonets of the military; who was laid in this ditch two feet from the surface, not with the chanted prayers which the Church is in the habit of presenting for her children when they die in the peace of the Lord, but in the midst of the curses of those who were present at the interment. A man this, for whom the priest, forced to be present, could perform no religious ceremonial, nor offer up any prayer for the repose of his soul, nor say even a single *requiescat in pace*; over whom he could not sprinkle one drop of holy water, whose virtue it is to moderate and quench the flames of the terrible fire which purifies the soul in another life.'

This is strong language, but the following is stronger still: –

There will day and night issue from this tomb, which holds the remains of this deluded man, who persevered even unto death in his revolt against the Church, a sorrowful and lugubrious voice, which will cry sufficiently loud in the following terms: – 'O, all ye who pass through the field of the dead, stop for a moment near this tomb and seriously reflect on my unhappy lot. Let my example teach you that no one can with impunity mock God and His Church. Alas! The more stir they have made over my dry and withered bones, the more they have affixed to my name a mark of infamy and dishonour. Would that I had been hidden in an obscure spot and in ground forgotten! I should have been today as if I had never been born. My memory would not have been accursed from age to age as it must now be, and my name would have been forgotten instead of being in the mouths of all to be cursed from generation to generation. Alas! They pretended to make me triumph, and they have only succeeded in perpetuating my shame and my dishonour!'

It may be all a matter of taste, but we cannot admire this style of Episcopal composition.

75 EPILOGUE: LAURIER DEFENDS LIBERALISM

June 26, 1877

[Editor's Note: The excerpts printed below are from Ulrich Barthe, ed., *Wilfrid Laurier on the Platform*. Quebec, 1890, pp. 51-80. It is perhaps a measure of the extent of Bourget's victory over liberalism that Laurier's 1877 address, which now occupies a prominent place in the history of Canadian political thought, was ignored by the contemporary press. One or two journals, for example the *Courier de St.-Hyacinthe*, carried a very brief précis of his remarks, but otherwise failed to comment on them.]

. . .

All the charges made against us, all the objectives to our doctrines, may be crystallized into the following propositions: 1° Liberalism is a new form of error, a heresy already virtually condemned by the head of the Church: 2° A Catholic cannot be a Liberal.

This is what our adversaries proclaim. . . .

. . .

. . . Those who condemn Liberalism as a new idea have not reflected upon what is transpiring every day under their eyes. Those who condemn Liberalism as an error have not reflected that, in so doing, they condemn an attribute of human nature.

Now, it should not be overlooked that our form of government is a representative monarchy. This is the instrument which throws into relief and brings into action the two principles, Liberal and Conservative. . . .

. . .

Now I ask: between these two ideas which constitute the basis of parties, can there be a moral difference? Is the one radically good and the other radically bad? Is it not evident that both are what are termed in moral philosophy *indifferents*, that is to say, that both are susceptible of being appreciated, pondered and chosen? Would it not be as unfair as it would be absurd to condemn or to approve either the one or the other as absolutely bad or good?

Both are susceptible of much good, as they are also of much evil. . . .

Certainly, I am far from blaming my adversaries for their convictions, but for my part, I have already said, I am a Liberal. I am one of those who think that everywhere, in human things, there are abuses to be reformed, new horizons to be opened up, and new forces to be developed.

Moreover Liberalism seems to me in all respects superior to the other principle. The principle of Liberalism is inherent to the very essence of our nature, to that desire of happiness with which we are all born into the world, which pursues us throughout life and which is never completely gratified on this side of the grave. Our souls are immortal, but our means are limited. We constantly gravitate towards an ideal which we never attain. We dream of good, but we never realize the best. We only reach the goal we have proposed to ourselves to discover new horizons opening up, which we had not before even suspected. We rush on towards them and those horizons, explored in their turn, reveal to us others which lead us on ever further and further. . . .

This condition of our nature is precisely what makes the greatness of man, for it condemns him irrevocably to movement, to progress: our means are limited, but our nature is perfectible and we have the infinite for our arena. Thus, there is always room for improvement of our condition, for the perfecting of our nature, and for the attainment by a larger number of an easier life. Here again is what, in my eyes, constitutes the superiority of Liberalism. . . .

. . .

I have too much respect for the opinion of my adversaries to ever insult them; but I reproach them with understanding neither their time nor their country. I accuse them of judging the political situation of the country, not according to what is happening in it, but according to what is happening in France. I accuse them of wanting to introduce here ideas, which are impossible of application in our state of society. I accuse them of laboriously and, by misfortune, too efficaciously working to degrade religion to the simple proportions of a political party.

In our adversaries' party, it is the habit to accuse us, Liberals, of irreligion. I am not here to parade my religious sentiments, but I declare that I have too much respect for the faith in which I was born to ever use it as the basis of a political organization.

You wish to organize a Catholic party. But have you not considered that, if you have the misfortune to succeed, you will draw down upon your country calamities of which it is impossible to foresee the consequences?

You wish to organize all the Catholics into one party, without other bond, without other basis, than a common religion; but have you not reflected that, by the very fact, you will organize the Protestant population as a single party and that then, instead of the peace and harmony now prevailing between the different elements of the Canadian population, you throw open the door to war, a religious war, the most terrible of all wars? . . .

* * *

. . . While reproaching us with being friends of liberty our adversaries further reproach us, with an inconsistency which would be serious, if the charge were well founded, with denying to the Church the freedom to which it is entitled. They reproach us with seeking to silence the administrative body of the Church and to prevent it from teaching the people their duties as citizens and electors. They reproach us with wanting to hinder the clergy from meddling in politics and to relegate them to the sacristy. . . .

In the name of what principle, should the friends of liberty seek to deny to the priest the right to take part in political affairs? In the name of what principle should the friends of liberty seek to deny to the priest the right to have and express political opinions, the right to approve or disapprove public men and their acts and to instruct the people in what he believes to be their duty? In the name of what principle, should he not have the right to say that, if I am elected, religion will be endangered, when I have the right to say that if my adversary is elected, the State will be endangered? Why should the priest not have the right to say that, if I am elected, religion will be inevitably destroyed, when I have the right to say that, if my adversary is elected, the State will go into bankruptcy? No, let the priest speak and preach, as he thinks best; such is his right and no Canadian Liberal will dispute that right.

Our constitution invites all citizens to take part in the direction of the affairs of the State; it makes no exception of any person. Each one has the right not only to express his opinion, but to influence, if he can, by the expression of his opinion, the opinion of his fellow citizens. This right exists for all and there can be no reason why the priest should be deprived of it. I am here to speak my whole mind and I may add that I am far from finding opportune the intervention of the clergy in the domain of politics, as it has been exercised for some years. I believe on the contrary that, from the standpoint of the respect due to his character, the priest has every thing to lose by meddling in the ordinary questions of politics: still his right to do so is indisputable and, if he thinks proper to use it, our duty, as Liberals, is to guarantee it to him against all denial.

This right, however, is not unlimited. We have no absolute rights amongst us. The rights of each man, in our state of society, end precisely at the point where they encroach upon the rights of others. . . .

. . .

I am not one of those who parade themselves as friends and champions of the clergy. However, I say this: like the most of my young fellow countrymen, I have been reared among priests and among young men who have become priests. I flatter myself that I have among them some sincere friends and to them at least, I can and I do say: see, if there is under the sun a country happier than ours; see, if there is under the sun a country where the Catholic church is freer or more privileged than it is here. Why, then, should you, by claiming rights incompatible with our state of society, expose this country to agitations, of which it is impossible to foresee the consequences?

Guide to Journals

For additional information, consult: André Beaulieu et Jean Hamelin, *Les Journaux du Québec de 1764 à 1964.* Québec: Les Presses de l'Université Laval, 1965.

Le Bien Public, Montreal.

Founded by L.-O. David and Cléophas Beausoleil, both prominent Liberals. Attacked by the ultramontanes and banished from parish to parish. Published from 1874 to 1876.

The Daily Witness, Montreal.

Founded by John Dougall, owner and editor, who gave place in 1870 to his son, John Redpath Dougall, militantly Protestant, annexationist on occasion (notably in 1849-50), and opposed to Confederation. Generally supported the Reform (or Liberal) cause. Published from 1846 to 1938.

The Gazette, Montreal.

Founded in 1778. Traditionally associated with the large business interests (finance, transportation, manufacturing). Thomas and Richard White bought the journal from Brown Chamberlin towards the end of 1870. Thomas White (Minister of the Interior, 1885-1888) was the editor during the 1870s. Staunch supporter of the Liberal-Conservative Party of Macdonald and Cartier.

The Globe, Toronto.

Founded in 1844. Under the editorship of George Brown became the most influential journal in Canada West. Supported the Confederation Coalition, of which Brown was a member from 1864-65, but was otherwise strongly identified with the Grit or Reform (Liberal) cause.

The Montreal Herald.

During the period 1840-1880 was largely the organ of the mercantile interests of Montreal. Was annexationist during 1849-50. During the period of this study generally supported the Liberals. Its editor in the late 1860s and 1870s was

Edward Goff Penny, who was considered the best Canadian journalist after George Brown. Published from 1811 to 1959.

The Mail, Toronto.

Founded in 1872 as the official organ of the Liberal-Conservative Party in Ontario. Merged with *The Empire* in 1895 to become *The Mail and Empire.*

La Minerve, Montreal.

Founded by A. N. Morin, and in its early years supported the cause of Papineau and the Patriotes. Later, Ludger Duvernay, D.-B. Viger, and E. R. Fabre were associated with it. After the death of Ludger Duvernay in 1858 it became the property of Napoléon and Denis Duvernay and C. A. Dansereau, the latter eventually acquiring control. It became closely identified with the Liberal-Conservative Party and particularly with Sir George Cartier. Moderate, right-of-centre. Published from 1826 to 1899.

Le Nouveau Monde, Montreal.

Founded by Chanoine Lamarche. Among its editors were Lamarche, Alphonse Desjardins, Joseph Royal, G.-A. Nantel, and F.-X. Dionne. Until 1880 voiced the views of Bishop Bourget and the ultramontanes. After 1884, was under the control of Sir Hector Langevin, Macdonald's chief Quebec lieutenant. Published from 1867 to 1900.

L'Ordre, Montreal.

Founded by Cyrille Boucher and Joseph Royal. Extreme right-wing Catholic journal. Anti-Confederation during 1864 to 1867, but then returned to its Liberal-Conservative allegiance. Its editor during the closing years was Alphonse Desjardins who, with Chanoine Lamarche, was one of the authors of the *Programme Catholique.* Published from 1858 to 1871.

Le Pays, Montreal.	Founded by J.-A. Plinquet and Edouard-Raymond Fabre. Took the place of the defunct *L'Avenir* as the organ of *le Parti rouge.* Among its editors were Charles Daoust, Emile Chevalier, L.-A. Dessaulles, Labreche-Viger, Arthur Buies, and N. Aubin. Opposed to Confederation, and in 1870 favoured annexation to the United States. Closely identified with the *Institut Canadien,* of which a number of its editors were officers. Published from 1852 to the close of 1871.
The True Witness And Catholic Chronicle, Montreal.	Founded by Edward Clerk, a convert to Roman Catholicism, who remained its editor until his death in 1875. The Roman Catholic Bishops of Canada had evidently agreed to subsidize it. A weekly paper, its objects were to explain and espouse Roman Catholic doctrines. In the words of Clerk: "Catholicity is of no nation, of no particular shade of politics. *The True Witness* therefore will not be a political paper." (Beaulieu et Hamelin, *op. cit.,* p. 161.) Published from 1850 to 1910.

For Further Reading

Boisseau, A.

Catalogue des Livres de la Bibliothèque de l'Institut-Canadien. Montreal: Alphonse Doutre, 1870.

Cook, Ramsay.

Canada and the French Canadian Question. Toronto: Macmillan, 1966.

————.

French-Canadian Nationalism: An Anthology. Toronto: Macmillan, 1969.

Dessaulles, L.-A.

"La Grande Guerre Ecclésiastique": "La Comédie Infernale et les Noces d'Or": "La Suprématie Ecclésiastique sur l'Ordre Temporel." Montreal: Alphonse Doutre, 1873.

————.

"L'Index." Montreal: L. Perrault, 1870.

————.

"Réponse Honnête à une Circulaire assez peu Chrétienne: Suite à la Grande Guerre Ecclésiastique." Montreal: Alphonse Doutre, 1873.

Dougall, John.

History of the Guibord Case: Ultramontanism versus Law and Human Rights. Montreal: *Witness* Printing House, 1875.

Fremantle, Anne.

The Papal Encyclicals. New York: Mentor Books, 1956.

Hudon, Theophile, Père.

L'Institut Canadien de Montréal et l'Affaire Guibord: Une page d'Histoire. Montreal: Librairie Beauchemin, 1938.

Institut Canadien.

Annuaire. Montreal: Imprimerie du Journal Le Pays, etc. 1866-1870 incl.

Pouliot, Léon.

"L'Institut Canadien de Montréal et l'Institut National." *Revue d'Histoire de l'Amérique Française*, Vol. 14 (No. 4, mars, 1961), 481-486.

Roman Catholic Church.

Diocese of Montreal. *Mandements, Lettres Pastorales, Circulaires et Autres Documents Publié dans le Diocèse de Montréal.* Montreal: J. A. Plinquet, 1887, tomes II à VI incl.

Rumilly, Robert.

Histoire de la Province de Québec. 34 Vols. Montreal: Editions Valiquettes, 1940-1963.

————.

"Monseigneur Laflèche et les ultra-montains," *Revue d'Histoire de l'Amérique Française,* Vol. 16 (No. 1, juin, 1962), 95-101.

Schull, Joseph.

Laurier: The First Canadian. Toronto: The Macmillan Co. of Canada, 1965.

Skelton, O. D.

The Life and Times of Sir Alexander Tilloch Galt. Toronto: Oxford University Press, 1920.

————.

The Life and Letters of Sir Wilfred Laurier. Toronto: Oxford University Press, 1921. 2 vols.

Sylvain, Philippe.

"Libéralisme et ultramontainisme au Canada français: affrontement idéologique et doctrinal (1840-1865)," in *The Shield of Achilles,* W. L. Morton, ed., Toronto: McClelland & Stewart, 1968, pp. 111-138; pp. 220-255.

Theriault, Adrien.

"L'Affaire Guibord," par Adrien Therio. *La Presse.* 1er avril, 1967.

————.

"Mgr. Ignace Bourget: Novateur audacieux et lutteur intrepide," par Adrien Therio. *Perspectives,* No. 19, 13 mai, 1967.

————.

"Les Grandes Batailles de Mgr. Bourget: L'Institut Canadien, l'Affaire Guibord et l'Université de Montréal," par Adrien Therio. *Perspectives,* No. 20, 20 mai, 1967.

Trudel, F. X. A.

"Affaire Guibord: Discours de
F. X. A. Trudel, Ecr. Prononce les 28
et 29 mars et le 1er avril, 1870."
Montreal: La Minerve, 1870.

————.

"Réflexions d'un Catholique à
l'occasion de l'affaire Guibord."
Montreal: La Minerve, 1870.

Wade, Mason.

The French Canadians, 1760-1945.
Toronto: The Macmillan Co. of
Canada, 1955.